critique
influence
change

critique confronts the world
without new princip...
instead de...
be ruthles
powers it n
the world, o
develop new

influence is ...critique towards the
future, when eff... ...s begin to be felt, when the
ground becomes unstable, when a movement
ignites. These critiques of the state of our world
have influenced a generation. They are crucial
guides to change.

change is when the structures shift. The books
in this series take critique as their starting point
and as such have influenced both their respective
disciplines and thought the world over. This series
is born out of our conviction that change lies not
in the novelty of the future but in the realization of
the thoughts of the past.

These texts are not mere interpretations or reflections,
but scientific, critical and impassioned analyses of
our world. After all, the point is to change it.

TITLES IN THE CRITIQUE INFLUENCE CHANGE SERIES

Reclaiming Development
An Alternative Policy Manual
by Ha-Joon Chang and Ilene Grabel

Realizing Hope
Life Beyond Capitalism
by Michael Albert

Global Governance and the New Wars
The Merging of Development and Security
by Mark Duffield

Capitalism in the Age of Globalization
The Management of Contemporary Society
by Samir Amin

Ecofeminism
by Maria Mies and Vandana Shiva

Patriarchy and Accumulation on a World Scale
Women in the International Division of Labour
by Maria Mies

Grassroots Post-modernism
Remaking the Soil of Cultures
by Gustavo Esteva and Madhu Suri Prakash

Male Daughters, Female Husbands
Gender and Sex in an African Society
by Ifi Amadiume

A Fundamental Fear
Eurocentrism and the Emergence of Islamism
by Bobby S. Sayyid

Debating Cultural Hybridity
Multicultural Identities and the Politics of Anti-Racism
edited by Pnina Werbner and Tariq Modood

'Esteva and Prakash courageously and clear-sightedly take on some of the most entrenched of modern certainties, such as the universality of human rights, the individual self, and global thinking. In their efforts to remove the lenses of modernity that education has bequeathed them, they dig deep into their own encounters with what they call the "social majorities" in their native Mexico and India. There they see not an enthralment with the seductions of modernity but evidence of a will to live in their own worlds according to their own lights. Esteva's and Prakash's reflections on the imperialism of the universality of human rights avoids the twin pitfalls of relativism and romanticism. Their alternative is demanding and novel, and deserves our most serious consideration. *Grassroots Post-modernism* is a much-needed and most welcome counterpoint both to the nihilism of much post-modern thinking as well as to those who view the spread of the global market and of global thinking too triumphantly.'

Frédérique Apffel-Marglin, professor emeritus, Smith College

'Quite simply, a book which will transform how one sees the world.'

North and South

ABOUT THE AUTHORS

Gustavo Esteva is one of Latin America's leading
critics of the development paradigm. An author
of more than thirty books, he was advisor to the
Zapatistas for their negotiations with the government
in 1996 and is the founder of Universidad de la
Tierra in the Mexican city of Oaxaca.

Madhu Suri Prakash is a philosopher of education
at Penn State University. Her labors of love include:
the proliferation of Friendship Gardens through
organic contagion; honoring wild diversity in teaching
and learning, along the lines of such learning
centers for radical marginals as Bija Vidyapeeth,
Bhoomi College, Unitierra, and the Via Campesina
universities; and healing damaged multicultural
rainbow coalitions on earth. She celebrates
as contributing editor to *Yes! Powerful Ideas,
Practical Actions*.

GRASSROOTS POST- MODERNISM

REMAKING THE SOIL OF CULTURES

GUSTAVO ESTEVA AND MADHU SURI PRAKASH

WITH A FOREWORD BY

VANDANA SHIVA

Zed Books
London

Grassroots Post-modernism: Remaking the Soil of Cultures
was first published in 1998 by Zed Books Ltd,
7 Cynthia Street, London N1 9JF, UK.

This edition was published in 2014

www.zedbooks.co.uk

Typeset in Monotype Bembo by illuminati, Grosmont
Cover designed by www.alice-marwick.co.uk
Printed and bound by TJ International Ltd

A catalogue record for this book is available from the British Library
Library of Congress Cataloging in Publication Data available

ISBN   978-1-78360-182-0 paperback
ISBN   978-1-78360-183-7 PDF
ISBN   978-1-78360-184-4 EPUB
ISBN   978-1-78360-185-1 Kindle

CONTENTS

Foreword *Vandana Shiva*   ix

Preface to the critique influence change edition   xiv

1 Grassroots Post-modernism: Beyond the Individual Self,
   Human Rights and Development   1

2 From Global to Local: Beyond Neoliberalism to the
   International of Hope   19

3 Beyond the Individual Self: Regenerating Ourselves   50

4 Human Rights: The Trojan Horse of Recolonization?   110

5 People's Power: Radical Democracy for the Autonomy
   of their Commons   152

6 Epilogue: The Grassroots Post-modern Epic   192

   Bibliography   208

   Index   217

THE ENCLOSURE AND RECOVERY
OF THE COMMONS

VANDANA SHIVA

I join Gustavo Esteva and Madhu Suri Prakash in celebrating and growing the commons in a period when an attempt is being made to enclose them in every aspect of life – seed, food, land, water, air, culture. And in every sphere, everywhere, people are rising to recover the commons.

The entire edifice of dominant science, technology and economics is based on transforming the commons into commodities, presenting commodification as creation, when in fact it is destruction – of ecosystems, of local economies, of cultures.

Four decades ago I joined the Chipko movement as a volunteer and learnt from women in the village community that commercial forestry that focused on forests as timber mines was an enclosure of the forest commons – the forest as our mother, the source of water, fodder, fuel, food, biodiversity, medicinal plants. It was the women of the Himalayas who defended the forest commons, saying they would embrace (Chipko) the trees to protect them from being logged. They showed the world that forests are not timber mines but communities of diverse species. They showed how heterogeneous living forests produce soil, water and pure air, not just timber and profits.

Today there is a new attempt at the enclosure of forests through the financialization of the "ecological services" of the forests, in particular the capacity of forests to absorb carbon dioxide for mitigating climate change. And, again, indigenous communities are rising to defend the commons, and the lifeworld that the commons support.

Three decades ago, when I realized that our biological and intellectual commons were being enclosed through genetic engineering and patents, I started Navdanya to recover the commons of biodiversity and people's knowledge, the knowledge of both peasants and our ancestors, brought to us by our grandmothers.

Seed is the ultimate commons. It holds millennia of the Earth's evolution. It holds centuries of cultural memory. It holds the nourishment that came from millions of soil organisms. It holds the gifts of the butterflies and bees that have pollinated and fertilized the seed. It holds the sun's rays that contributed to the photosynthesis of the plant's green leaves. It holds the future in terms of its capacity to multiply and regenerate.

Yet corporate arrogance and greed allow the enclosure of seed as commons through genetic engineering and patenting. A patent is an exclusive right granted to an inventor. But seed is not an invention. A patent on seed is theft from nature and from the cultures that co-evolved the seed with nature. And all this is done just for profit, just to allow corporations to collect trillions of dollars in royalties from seeds that were the commons of the farmers. As we have witnessed in India, royalty collection from poor cotton farmers has pushed nearly a quarter of a million farmers into a debt trap and to suicide.

Our commoning of the seed includes creating the commons of the seed and cultivating seed freedom through seed saving, seed exchange, and participatory breeding.

"Freedom" has become a contested term. We use it to refer to the freedom of nature and people; corporations use it to refer to their freedom to enclose our commons. We refer to people's freedom to live and have a livelihood, to access to the commons – seed, food, water, land. And we refer to the freedom of the Earth and all her beings, based on recognition of the rights of Mother Earth, Pachamama, Bhoomi, Gaia...

"Free trade" rules are written by corporations to enlarge their freedom to commodify and privatize the last inch of land, the last drop of water, the last seed, the last morsel of food. In the process they must destroy the freedom of the Earth and the Earth Family, and destroy the freedom of people to their lives and livelihoods, their cultures and democracies, by enclosing the commons, commodifying and privatizing every aspect of life.

For example, the Trade Related Aspects of Intellectual Property Rights (TRIPS) agreement of the World Trade Organization imposes patents on seeds. Patents allow corporations like Monsanto to prevent farmers from saving seeds. Worse, as in the case of *Monsanto* v. *Bowman*, farmers cannot buy grain in the market and grow a crop from it. And, worse still, as in the case of Percy Schmeiser, a Canadian farmer whose canola crop was genetically contaminated with Monsanto's Roundup Ready Canola, Monsanto can use patents to sue farmers whose crops it has contaminated with its GMOs.

Monsanto acknowledges having drafted the TRIPS agreement. In doing so, a representative stated, the corporation was the "patient, diagnostician, physician" all in one. And the "disease" they diagnosed and sought to cure was that farmers saved seeds. The cure was that farmers should be prevented from saving and exchanging seeds by defining these fundamental freedoms as a crime.

For me, saving and protecting life on Earth, specially biodiversity and seeds, is the highest duty, the highest dharma. That is why I started Navdanya in 1987, when I heard the corporations spell out their vision of total control over life through genetic engineering and patents on life and seeds, along with a "free trade" agreement.

Navdanya is dedicated to creating Earth Democracy based on *bija swaraj* (seed freedom/sovereignty), *anna swaraj* (food freedom/sovereignty), *bhu swaraj* (land and forest freedom/sovereignty), *jal swaraj* (water democracy), *van swaraj* (forest sovereignty), and *gyan swaraj* (knowledge sovereignty). *Swaraj* was used by Gandhi to describe self-rule and self-organization by people and communities committed to governing themselves. It is the highest expression of people's sovereignty. Since 1987 we have used *swaraj*, "freedom" and "sovereignty" as interchangeable terms.

Bija swaraj = seed freedom = seed sovereignty. Commons are spheres of life self-governed by local communities. They are not governed by the market or the state. The state, at best, can recognize the rights of local communities, but it cannot prohibit the freedom of communities to self-govern the commons. For us seed freedom includes farmers' rights to save, exchange, breed, and sell farmers varieties – varieties that have evolved over millennia without the interference of the state or corporations.

Today the seed freedom movement has spread worldwide. We use the term "seed freedom" to mean the right of the seed as a living, self-organized system to evolve freely into the future, without the threat of extinction, genetic contamination from GMOs, and the threat of termination through mechanisms such as the "terminator technology" designed to make seed sterile. "Seed freedom" is the freedom of bees to pollinate freely, without threat of extinction due to poisons. "Seed freedom" is the freedom of the web of life to weave itself, in integrity and resilience, in interconnectness and well-being for all.

We refer to "seed freedom" as the freedom of farmers to save and exchange farmers' varieties freely among themselves. Seed and biodiversity are the ultimate commons, and commons are governed by local communities through local self-rule and self-governance, not by markets through privatization, nor through centralized authority and its bureaucratic apparatus. We refer to "seed freedom" as the freedom of access to food grown from seeds propagated for diversity, taste, flavour, quality and nutrition. "Seed freedom" is also the duty to save and exchange the native seeds developed by farmers: that is, seed sovereignty. The conservation, use, and development of seeds as a commons involve self-organization and self-rule at the level of local communities. At national and international levels, it includes the obligation of governments to protect the freedoms of biodiversity and people by regulating corporations to prevent them from undermining people's sovereignty through biopiracy, on the one hand, and threats to biosafety from genetically engineered seeds and crops, on the other. Freedom and sovereignty mean the freedom to self-govern at the level of the community in order to take care of the commons, and to share sustainably and equitably in their fruits. This also involves freedom from harm by way of national and international regulation on biosafety and the prevention of biopiracy.

Corporations have unprecedented capacity to harm the Earth and its people with new technologies like genetic engineering and new monopoly power involving intellectual property rights on seeds enshrined within so-called "free trade" treaties – which are based on freedom of action for corporation at the expense of unfreedom for people.

Defending people's freedoms in times of "free trade" means challenging the laws that create and expand corporate rule to every dimension of our lives. That is why we created the International Forum on Globalization, stopped the WTO Ministerial in Seattle, and declared that our world is not for sale. That is why we started the Indian People's campaign against the WTO under the inspiring chairmanship of the late Shri V.P. Singh, a former prime minister, and the convenorship of S.P. Shukla, India's ambassador to the GATT during the Uruguay Round.

However, even though the WTO has been in intensive care since the Seattle Ministerial, the ideology of free trade as corporate rule continues to be imposed undemocratically on people across the world.

To push free trade as corporate freedom, state or interstate bodies write laws on behalf of corporations to privatize the commons of seed through intellectual property rights and seed laws. Thus patents on seeds were imposed through genetic engineering. This is the privatization of seeds and life as a commons. It is the enclosure of the biological and intellectual commons. Genetic engineering has failed to increase yields, or to control pests and weeds (Navdanya report, *The GMO Emperor has No Clothes*). And growth in Monsanto's profits through collection of royalties goes hand in hand with farmers going into debt to pay for royalties and committing suicide. When the failure of GMOs and the high economic and social costs borne by farmers are taken into account, there is no justification for privatizing seeds through patents. Intellectual property rights on seed lead to the policing and regulating of citizens by the state to increase corporate control. Instead of being a defender of people's sovereignty by regulating corporations, the state becomes an instrument of corporate sovereignty and producer of people's slavery.

Seed laws for compulsory registration, which are being pushed everywhere, are based on the illegitimate restriction of people's freedom in order to enhance corporate freedom to establish seed monopolies. Examples of the expansion of corporate freedom by extinguishing people's freedom to save and exchange farmers' seed varieties are the proposed EU seed law and the push for harmonization of seed-related laws in Africa.

Other examples are the 2004 Seed Law of India, which could not be enacted due to our resistance through a Seed Satyagraha, and the laws passed to implement the US–Colombia Free Trade agreement, which include "Controls on the production, use and marketing of all seeds in the country" (Resolution 970 of 2010). The law has been put on hold on account of an uprising.

Across the world people are commoning their everyday lives, and their relationship with the Earth. This is the story told in Gustavo Esteva and Madhu Suri Prakash's classic *Grassroots Post-modernism*. This takes us beyond the market and the state, and beyond the corporate state founded on the enclosure of the commons – which will collapse as we reclaim, recover, and grow the commons.

PREFACE TO THE CIC EDITION

PATHWAYS TO COMMONING

"An epic is unfolding at the grassroots."

In 1996, our book opened with this first sentence: an epic announcing itself.

As we carefully held our ears close to the ground, we heard in fresh voices and contemporary harmonies epics sung through centuries. We heard old silences – filled with pain – breaking free; seeding with new words soils in which common people plant, water and grow their hopes; bringing common-sense self-governance into their lives.

An epic is unfolding at the grassroots. Walked, marched, danced by common women and men whose lives depend on the strength and creativity of their feet, hands and noses.

An epic is unfolding at the grassroots. Commoners are affirming themselves; resisting the domination of the corporations that rule the world; freeing their hopes and dreams from global blueprints concocted in anesthetized labs or elite think-tanks. Their beautiful tapestry is being painted and spoken in diverse hues and tongues: moving stories of how peoples of all races, cultures, and traditions are creatively re-generating their places, their cultures, and their traditions; reclaiming hope as a social force.

Close to where we lived, twenty years ago, we heard the resounding roar of silenced, indigenous peoples declaring to the global powers that suppress and destroy humanity: *¡Ya basta!* Enough!

Echoing from village to village, from nation to nation through the vast ocean of the web, *¡Ya Basta!* catalyzed *Grassroots Post-modernism: Remaking the Soil of Cultures.*

Today, in 2014, the power of that *¡Ya Basta!* echo continues to delight and amaze us. The genius we could only paint with rough brush strokes in 1996 today makes murals stretching the human imagination, in dimensions clearly surpassing even our wildest dreams.

They are coming. No! They are here! Everywhere! Common folks, ordinary men and women, the salt of the Earth! They know that their beloved Mother Earth is very sick; out of balance. They need to heal her. Here. Now. Today. In reclaiming their lives, land, places, traditions – their commons – they are also communing with and healing Mother Earth: from Cochabamba to the Himalayas.

How have these so-called illiterate peasants created the biggest organization in the history of humankind, with hundreds of millions of committed members? How have they organically grown solidarities and consensus about food sovereignty? How is the first truly global grass-roots organization already changing the way we eat and undermining the pillars on which the food giants rest?

Via Campesina had a very modest beginning in Belgium, in 1993. It is today one of the main actors in all matters related to food, and the millions of hectares cared for by its members are healing our bodies, our seeds, soils, and waters. In more than a hundred countries, Via Campesina is daily nourished by the vitality, legitimacy, and autonomy of their countless local organizations. An ever-increasing number of people are today applying the notion of food sovereignty launched by Via Campesina at the World Food Summit in 1996. Pure peasant wisdom: we must determine by ourselves what to eat; and we must produce it. That is all! No governments. No corporations. No media. We don't want their toxic harvest. We know how to sow, harvest, and prepare what nurtures our body and our Mother Earth. Via Campesina and its uncountable allies and conspirators are increasingly recognized as the most powerful response to the current food, poverty, and climate crises.

One of its founding members offers a quick illustration of Via Campesina's organic ascent. Born in 1985, the Brazilian Movimento dos Trabalhadores Sem Terra (MST, Landless Workers' Movement), with 1.5 million affiliates, is the biggest peasant movement in Latin America today. Over thirty years of struggle it liberated 6 million hectares of land from profiteering, thieving landlords, and rerooted in it 350,000 families; meanwhile 100,000 more families are still reclaiming their lands in encampments, on roadsides, or on occupied land. Wherever they are, MST organizes assemblies and schools. MST also operates fifty establishments of higher and technical education and an alternative university. Some 16,000 delegates and hundreds of international allies attended its 6th Congress, on February 10-14, 2014, and rendered naked the reality lurking behind the mask of the so-called Brazilian "miracle". Both Lula da Silva and Dilma Roussef have supported the advance of transnational agribusiness, displacing indigenous peoples and peasants from their lands; producing immense deforestation to establish monocultures of transgenic soya and corn; massively using agrotoxics that devastate soil, water, and biodiversity. The MST Congress acknowledged the value of government subsidies for half the people of Brazil, alleviating their hunger, but denouncing the policies of those "progressive" governments which are the root cause of such hunger. The MST Congress announced a campaign to radically change the political system. It will continue its struggle against landowners, agrotoxics, transgenics and those policies, while embracing agro-ecological production, local agro-industrial co-operatives, defense of natural and cultural diversity, and control and protection of seeds.

"Freedom starts with a seed ... Seeds are life itself and the embodiment of culture" (Shiva, 2013). Seed sovereignty struggles, Vandana Shiva underscores, reflect the contemporary genius of Gandhi's March for Salt sovereignty. Seed, soil, and water sovereignty gather millions of "dirty" commoners across the Earth in their daily struggles for freedom. They radically resist the mindlessness of becoming atomistic individuals stuffing and starving their sickened bellies on fast-food assembly lines.

In the gut of *Grassroots Post-modernism* is sacred cultural food: *comida, bhojan,* communal eating. Our inspiration came from the grassroots movements that did not succumb to the violent destruction of agri-*culture* by agri-*business.*

The Uruguayan poet Eduardo Galeano, musing on global fear, recognizes that "whoever doesn't fear hunger is afraid of eating". One billion people will go to bed tonight famished; hunger, our ancient plague, rules the Earth again. Yes, millions today fear hunger while further millions are afraid of eating, increasingly aware of the toxins and carcinogens industrial agribusiness is stuffing into our medicalized bodies.

Commoning commoners' common sense liberates us from the illusion that governments, the FAO and other international institutions will fix the mess they continue engineering and promoting; or that the CEOs of Monsanto or Walmart will suffer a moral epiphany. We need to take into our own hands all matters related to food. And that is exactly what more and more people are currently doing.

Women produce 70 percent of the food grown on the Earth today. They are leading social change everywhere, as a matter of life or death. By refusing to mimic or submit themselves to what men do for power and profits, they are reassuming their ancient historical role of birthing while nurturing Mother Earth.

In the cities, where 60 percent of the world's population lives today, people are increasingly assuming serious responsibilities for food and healing. From Havana to Detroit, they are literally derailing Fast Food Nation's assembly lines for atomized individuals. They are transforming their manicured lawns into vegetable gardens, and reclaiming the sensual, healing pleasures of "slow food" enjoyed with family and community. Protesting against the first McDonald's in Rome's central square in 1986, Carlo Petrini threw a big pasta feast in Piazza di Spagna. Today, Slow Food includes more than 100,000 people in 150 countries. Transition Townships in Great Britain have their own stories of growing "slow food" commons.

Cultivating food in the cities and processing it at home is now epidemic, spreading health, wealth, and happiness everywhere. In Detroit, epitomizing the failures of industrial capitalism, 900 community gardens are thriving. In 1996, we failed to notice the revolution being launched by starving *Cubanos,* once they lost all foreign subsidies after the collapse of the Soviet Union. With amazing courage and ingenuity, they started to produce food everywhere, in backyards, on street corners, within the interstices of buildings. Today, their cities produce more than half of the food they consume, demonstrating the potential of urban agriculture.

COMMONING:
MARGINALIZING THE MARGINALIZERS

"Commonism" was a term coined in 2007 by Nick Dyer-Witheford to celebrate the spread of commons and common sense. If the commodity is the cellular form of capitalism, he mused, the cellular form of a society beyond capital is the "commons." Commonism celebrates the multiplication of the commons in three domains – ecological, social, and networked. The word draws a clear line to abandon what was called communism… and all other modern "isms."

In 1992, *The Ecologist* team had already discovered a new social trend. "Reclaiming the Commons" is the subtitle of the book (1993) describing the failure of the Earth Summit, while rigorously documenting what common people were accomplishing at the grassroots during that time. They identified the enclosure of the commons as the mechanism through which all forms of predatory colonialism have been practiced to create industrial society; and how current economic forces still follow this pattern. The team also revealed why people's initiatives are resisting the new enclosures, reclaiming and regenerating their commons; creating new ones; ingeniously enclosing the enclosers.

Today the commons movement is in full swing; increasingly acknowledged for offering the elements needed for conceptualizing the new society emerging in the womb of the old. In *The Wealth of the Commons: A World Beyond Market and State* (2013), David Bollier and Silke Helfrich boldly recognize that

It has become increasingly clear that we are poised between an old world that no longer works and a new one struggling to be born. Surrounded by an archaic order of centralized hierarchies on the one hand and predatory markets on the other, presided over by a state committed to planet-destroying economic growth, people around the world are searching for alternatives.

In this context, the Nobel Prize for Economics awarded to Elinor Ostrom is an ambiguous blessing. While drawing attention to the commons, it is also generating confusion. In her effort to introduce some refinements to the theory of collective action (Ostrom, 1990; Poteete et al., 2010), Ostrom remains trapped within "economic efficiency" and other assumptions of economics for resource management.

Vandana Shiva clarified twenty years ago that "resource" is the opposite of commons (Shiva, 2010: p. 233). The transformation of commons into resources dissolves the former. To treat commons as "common-pool resources" à la Ostrom poses a very serious threat to commons. As Peter Linebaugh explains,

> To speak of the commons as if it were a natural resource is misleading at best and dangerous at worst; the commons is an activity and, if anything, it expresses relationships in society that are inseparable from relations to nature. It might be better to keep the word as a verb, rather than as a noun, a substantive. (Linebaugh, 2008: p. 279)

Commoning, the commons movement, is not an alternative economy, but an alternative to the economic society. With *Home Economics* (1987) Wendell Berry rescued the original meaning of the word "economy" (*oikos* and *nomos*): the administration of the household. What passes today for economics has strayed far from home. *Commonomics* may thus emerge as a pertinent substitute for the dismal science.

We need to be fully aware of the limitations of the word "commons" to characterize the current transformation. It does not have a proper equivalent in Spanish and other languages. It clearly belongs to an Anglo-Saxon tradition but is no longer included in common parlance by English-speakers. For many people, it refers to a historical form of social organization, which has already vanished forever, a dinosaur. In spite of the fact that the term "commons" is currently regaining currency, it is still unable to capture the diversity of community forms existing and emerging across the Earth. We need to identify the families of words that can grasp the meaning of the very diverse initiatives peoples are taking around the world and the social experiments in which they are engaged. We are abandoning forever Margaret Thatcher's apothegm TINA (there is no alternative), which she applied to neoliberal globalization. TATA (there are a thousand alternatives) is a rigorous description of what happens in the real world, honoring all the riches of cultural diversity.

¡YA BASTA! ENOUGH!

Did you listen? It is the sound of your world falling apart. It is the sound of our world re-emerging. The day that was the day was night. And night will be the day that will be the day.

On December 21, 2012, 40,000 Zapatistas marched in silence, unarmed, in the same towns they occupied during their armed uprising on 1 January 1994. They left that brief communiqué.

Grassroots Post-modernism drew extensively on the Zapatista movement that awakened us with the songs, poems, and dances of the epic with which we open and close our book. For us, they were neither a "case" nor a "curiosity," and even less a "model." Their words and deeds were already, two decades ago, a source of inspiration for millions of people. In 2005, Immanuel Wallerstein acknowledged that the Zapatista rebellion "has been the most important social movement in the world, the barometer and alarm clock for other anti-systemic movements around the world" (*La Jornada*, 19 July 2005).

In August and December 2013/January 2014 almost 6,000 people, from more than forty countries, came to learn in the Zapatista communities what they have constructed in thirty years of struggle: a world without exploitation or social classes; without oppression or hierarchies; without domestic or structural violence; a world in which the patriarchal and sexist mentality of the last 5,000 years has been finally broken. Against all odds, with no funds, works or social services from the government, they are birthing a new, peaceful social order from scratch. All the norms of self-governance are conceived and enforced by the people themselves, at the grassroots.

The Zapatistas work hard, for many hours a day, for the sustenance of their families and for communal endeavors. They produce most of their own food. They have achieved a very high level of self-sufficiency. They learn all the time, from each other and from their visitors. The children learn in freedom, without a formal system of education, in disciplined, well-organized activities. The Zapatistas can be described as a very effective learning community.

They live a healthy life, exposed to a very solid system of preventive medicine, and cared for by their own healers and modern clinics. (People from non-Zapatista communities often come to the Zapatista clinics: they get better attention there than in the government hospitals.)

They have freed themselves from private ownership of the land or means of production. The land recuperated by the uprising has been allocated to the communities as communal land, where all families enjoy their own specific spaces.

The Zapatistas are unique but at the same time typical. Their social construction clearly illustrates the epic celebrated in our book. In Chiapas, ordinary men and women transformed one of the most unjust and miserable conditions of the world into a clear materialization of ancient dreams of emancipation. These are the winds now blowing across the world.

NO EPILOGUE

The epic unfolding at the grassroots has no epilogue. No predictive ending makes sense. Not knowing, we continue joining millions in their amazing capacities to cultivate hope.

Fifteen years after we conceived our book, millions across our Mother Earth are no longer merely murmuring quietly. Full of surprises, ingenuity, and imaginations escaping all confinements, they have finally marched together into squares; occupied Wall Street and other citadels of propriety; rendered naked the improprieties of the 1 percent against the 99 percent. True, the growing horrors of what we called the Global Project still loom over us. The idea that even our survival as a species is at stake has already entered into mainstream discourse, often expressing a realistic, concerned acknowledgement of the current situation and the urgent need to do something. Now. Today.

As the new millennium started, the image of eternal prosperity shaping the early 1990s had already vanished. Fukuyama's "end of history" was clearly losing relevance. In the years that followed, the word "crisis" lost any precision; it became merely a standardized label for very diverse diagnoses. The Washington Consensus, the package of policies towards Latin America that became the universal catechism for neoliberal globalization, discreetly slithered off the podium. What emerged, instead, was a growing awareness that the time had finally dawned to study the "archeology of the development idea" (Sachs, 1990, 2010).

Our book was birthed as we joined other conspirators in imagining what lies beyond the post-World War II "development era." Today, most thinking on development can be categorized by one of the three Sachses. Goldman Sachs' savage capitalism represents the dominant attitude in the economic elite and in governments and international institutions. Jeffrey Sachs's philanthropic capitalism represents attempts to take care directly of modernized misery, malaria, aids, civil war victims and other evils of capitalism and democratic despotism; to protect them and the development enterprise. Wolfgang Sachs takes us "beyond development": opening escape routes from the development prison, symbolizing the hopes and dreams of increasing millions all over the world resisting all forms of development, defending their own ways of life and self-governance while revealing postdevelopment initiatives (Esteva et al., 2013, pp. 22–3).

¡Basta! Enough! Our book celebrates how common folk are escaping apocalyptic or fantastical scenarios, birthing new societies. Their radical transformations do not operate through cataclysmic episodes; they emerge from the stuff of daily life's innovations. They materialize, for example, through the silent revolution of indigenous peasants in Peru who reclaimed a million hectares, one by one, and today produce half of the food in that country based on their traditional agricultural wisdom. They are living, dancing proof that the marginalizers can be marginalized; that people know how to become the creative centers of their own commons. It is happening every minute in offices like that of Sarah van Gelder's *Yes!* magazine team: patiently and joyfully collecting, since 1996 (the year we were writing this book), the stories of grassroots initiatives which are the very "stuff" of the epic celebrated in it; the stories, as she said, of "those who are reclaiming the well-being and exuberance" that are part of healthy practices (Van Gelder, 2013: 1; see also Van Gelder, 2011). Howard Zinn described this with poetry and precision:

> It happens in the little corners which cannot be reached by the powerful but clumsy hands of the state. It is not centralized or isolated: it cannot be destroyed by the powerful, the rich, the police.
>
> It happens in a million places at the same time, in the families, in the streets, in the neighborhoods, in the work places.
>
> Suppressed in one place, it reappears in another until it is everywhere. Such revolution is an art. That is: it requires the courage not only of resistance but of imagination. (Zinn, 1954)

It is a revolution. It is not the old kind of revolution, whose design started in the twelfth century, when Pope Gregory VII attempted the first total reform of the world; or the Leninist revolution which dominated the twentieth century, defining social engineering for both the left and the right. Three areas of this revolution illustrate its fascinating, hope-nurturing character: democracy, the social subject, the daily life.

DEMOCRACY IS DEAD. LONG LIVE DEMOCRACY

> Our dreams don't fit into your ballot box. (Indignados, Spain)

The current crises have left democracy in complete disarray. It is increasingly evident that the modern nation-state is just a conglomerate of economic and political corporations at the service of their own interests.

Periodically, the political parties convene their stakeholders to elect the board of directors. Occupy Wall Street rendered transparent its nature. They remain at the service of the 1 percent. It is increasingly difficult to believe that the people freely elect their representatives; that they really represent them; that the monopoly of legitimate violence protects them. To submit to the horrors of engineered and bought ballot boxes is not democracy. Today's so-called democracies are now being given their real, descriptive, honest name: democratic despotism.

Grassroots Post-modernism celebrates and honors all the movements close to the soil, of people who are not trying to seize power "upstairs," in boardrooms or oval offices. They are not looking for a leader or another authoritarian design. Their creativity, attention, and energy are reorganizing society from the bottom up and locating democracy where democracy should be, where people are. Regenerating ancient traditions of assemblies, they organize the oxymoron of self-government at the level of communities, neighborhoods and small towns, and reclaim the best of liberal thinking and practice, the parliament, an institution found in the most diverse cultural traditions.

Yes, democracy is dead. That is why we are celebrating the birth of radically new political regimes also called democracy. These are finally catching up with the original meaning of the word, people's power; people's governance at the grassroots.

A NEW, VERY OLD, SOCIAL SUBJECT

People are escaping from the conservative mood of both the wage workers and the political classes; transcending the limitations of their mental, political, and practical frameworks. Their initiatives are essential for the creation of a new social subject, on old grounds. Its ranks include, first of all, those who ignore what a job is and have no hope of getting one in their lives. They don't have any option but to live without a job. Many of them are oxymoronically called self-employed, freed from bosses. They have some means or skills that allow them to work independently. Among these, we find millions of migrants, temporarily leaving their places of birth to support their families and communal positions with their remittances; returning to their communities as soon as possible. This immensely heterogeneous sector is the biggest in the global South. It includes the peasants and those still called "urban marginals." Far from being in the margins, they increasingly constitute the center of social life in their communities and commons.

Many people constituting this "new" social subject are not suffering as much as the workers who are being fired and losing employment forever. Urban marginals know how to survive by themselves. Both crises and struggle have always defined their vitality and resilience. To struggle is a daily affair – with the police, the inspector, all the legal agents seeing them as pathologies. Struggling, for marginals, is like breathing, the "stuff" of being alive. However better off they may be than the unemployed, neither is well. Modern crises affect everyone.

Those defending their fields and forests and their ancient ways of life are not neo-Luddites. Nor are they attempting to go back in history or to stop it. They oppose firmly the war against subsistence; against autonomy; against life itself. They are not just trying to conserve what they have. They know that the only effective way to resist is to create something new; new ways of thinking about how to live joyously and interdependently within communities. And that is what they are trying to do.

EVERY DAY, EVERYWHERE

Amartya Sen received his Nobel Prize for demonstrating that during all the great famines of the twentieth century food exports to Europe and the USA continued while the people producing the food were dying of hunger. We now know the dynamics of hunger, including the counter-intuitive fact that food aid produces it. We also know that we have today the technical means to prevent hunger forever, across the whole world. The time has come to eliminate it. Nobody will die of hunger when nobody dies of indigestion.

If one expression could capture the main meaning of the social movements currently surging across Latin America, it would be *sumak kawsay* (Quechua), *suma qamaña* (Aymara), *boa vida* (Portuguese), or *buen vivir* (Spanish). *Buen vivir* is "the state of living well." Defining what it is to live well was traditionally in the hands of the people themselves. This responsibility was transferred to the governments of modern nation-states. In time, it was turned over to or overtaken by the corporations. Traditional societies, however, have held it in the hands of the people, at the face-to-face level; in every urban *barrio* or every rural community.

Over the past sixty years, development ideologies have tried to destroy the rich diversity of these notions of "the good life": substituting for them the living conditions as experienced by the American middle classes. Spreading the American Dream as the new gospel of "the good life" became a daytime nightmare for all life on Earth.

Millions, indeed billions, of people today resist development in all its forms. That is how they affirm themselves in their own paths: culturally and locally defined. It is no longer acceptable (if it ever was) to continue to impose on them a foreign definition of what it means to live well.

More and more people are today reclaiming their own agency in communal settings. Sometimes these are their own original commons: the ones they were able to preserve or reclaim. At other times they create new commons: in urban contexts, after losing their original communities. For them, *buen vivir* is an idea based on a verb; living life well; in dignity; their guiding principles realized in actions. *Buen vivir* puts the emphasis on doing, in radical contrast to consuming or owning. Consumption (the original name for tuberculosis) was a disease that caused the body or part of the body to waste away. It applied particularly to tuberculosis of the lungs. This plague of the Middle Ages has returned with a vengeance with the disease of modern consumers hell-bent on buying. It is not a body or part of a body but a whole civilization wasting away in increasing private ownership and buying power.

The time has come to put consumption behind us forever; we need an end to being bloated and burdened by the stuff that we think we own. Who can deny that consumption keeps us permanently enslaved to "more"? Ivan Illich has won renown for his observation that "In a consumer society, there are inevitably two kinds of slaves: the prisoners of addiction and the prisoners of envy" (1999: p. 398).

For Howard Zinn, we need to rescue the innumerable small actions of unknown people that produce the greatest social changes. Even marginal gestures can become the invisible roots of social change. Revolutionary change, Zinn insists, is something immediate. Something we need to do today. Right now. Wherever we are. Where we live. Where we work or study (Zinn, 1954).

The time has come for commoners to guide themselves with their common sense; marginalizing the great expert planners of history; imposing the will of the 1 percent on the 99 percent.

¡Ya basta!

Among the Zapatistas, common folk of the communities serve temporarily as authorities in different bodies of self-governance. We embrace today, for our *commonist manifesto*, the seven principles that guide their behavior in such positions:

> To serve, not to serve yourself;
> To represent, and not to supplant;
> To construct, and not to destroy;
> To obey, and not to command;
> To propose, and not to impose;
> To convince, and not to win;
> To go down, and not to go up.

ONE

GRASSROOTS POST-MODERNISM:
BEYOND THE INDIVIDUAL SELF,
HUMAN RIGHTS AND DEVELOPMENT

An epic is unfolding at the grassroots. Pioneering social movements are groping for their liberation from the "Global Project"[1] being imposed upon them. Seeking to go beyond the premises and promises of modernity, people at the grassroots are reinventing or creating afresh intellectual and institutional frameworks without necessarily getting locked into power disputes. Ordinary men and women are learning from each other how to challenge the very nature and foundations of modern power, both its intellectual underpinnings and its apparatuses. Explicitly liberating themselves from the dominant ideologies, fully immersed in their local struggles, these movements and initiatives reveal the diverse content and scope of grassroots endeavours, resisting or escaping the clutches of the "Global Project."

This book is an attempt at sketching the first rough outlines of the unfolding post-modern epic at the grassroots.

GRASSROOTS POST-MODERNISM:
AN OXYMORON?

The fallen Soviet giant lies broken, scattered. The Berlin Wall no longer divides the capitalists from the socialists. The champions of the "Global Project" seize the opportunity provided by the end of the Cold War to announce the creation of One World. Five billion present, and the 10 billion waiting around the corner of the new century can all live together in the "global village." Finally, every individual (man, woman and child) can begin to claim human rights – *the* moral discovery of the modern era.

The modern era, however, is also ending. From their think tanks and ivory towers, deconstructing the castle of modern certainties, post-modern thinkers are slaying the modern dragons: science and technology;

objectivity and rationality; global subjugation by the One Culture – the "culture of progress" spread across the world through the white man's weapons of domination and subjugation.

While classified under the single banner of "post-modernism," slayers of the modern hydra emerge from ideologically incommensurable academic camps of the modern academy. Feminist post-modernists speak in a voice alien to the ears of post-modern pragmatists. American post-modernists underscore their departures from European post-modernism. Post-modern poetry does not draw its inspiration from post-modern architecture. Post-modern professional philosophers do not attend the same conferences as the theorists of post-modern art.

Yet, located within the same modern academy, these different ideological camps share an often unspoken consensus – not only of dissent, but also of assent. Regarding the latter, there are some "sacred cows" of the modern era that continue to be revered; cows that are neither touched nor deconstructed; modern "certainties" that retain their hold within the academy, even as all else that is solid begins to melt into thin air. These certainties constitute the remaining unfallen pillars for the world's "social minorities," the "One-third World," now living in fear that their familiar reality of jobs, markets and welfare threatens to collapse around them.

They do not share this reality with the "Two-thirds World." For the "social majorities" still alive or waiting to be born on this planet, all these familiar elements of the "social minorities"'[2] modern world remain alien to their daily lives. Equally alien is the word "post-modern," coined in the academies of the "social minorities." It remains totally outside their vocabularies. Both the word and the intellectual fashions that have launched post-modernism might as well be occurring on another planet.

At the same time, the promise and the search for a new era beyond modernity are a matter of life and death, of sheer survival, for these struggling billions – whom social planners call "the masses," "the people" or "common" men and women. Daily, they are compelled to invent post-modern social realities to escape the "scientific" or even the "lay" clutches of modernity. Modernization has always been for them, and will continue to be, a gulag that means certain destruction for their cultures.

The language as well as the conceptual framework of academic post-modernism are clearly of no use to the "social majorities" for escaping the modern holocaust looming over their lives. It is as ill equipped as that of modernism to describe the experiences of these "down under" billions, struggling to survive the horrors, destruction and threats that the "social minorities" present to their selves and soils, their communities and cultures.

For many years, observing or participating in some of these grass-roots struggles, we were unable to speak about them. Caught and severely constrained within the traps created by modern words and concepts, we suffered an incredible impotence, a peculiar inability to articulate what we were seeing and experiencing with people at the grassroots. The modern categories in which we were "educated" would not permit us to understand and celebrate today's grassroots post-modern pioneers. Rather than a solution to this predicament, academic post-modernism imposed additional inhibiting barriers for us. For their part, while trapped within neither the modern language net nor the "reality" of "educated" modern persons, the "social majorities" creating that post-modern epic seem to share our difficulties in articulating their experiences of modernity.

The birth of this book is an attempt to overcome that predicament.

"Grassroots post-modernism" appears at first glance like a contradiction in terms; an impossible marriage of the academic and the illiterate; a fancy academic concoction to give a new lease to life, however ephemeral, to the fast fading fashion of academic post-modernism, its swan song turned rancorous after tedious intellectual battles.

Yet, we dare to stand by our peculiar juxtaposition of "grassroots" and "post-modernism." For all its oddities in bringing together two incommensurable worlds, we find it useful for presenting radical insights, which include exploding the meaning of the two elements of the expression.

Through the marriage of "grassroots post-modernism," we are not trying to give birth to another school of post-modern thought. Instead, bringing these terms out of the confines of the academy to far removed and totally different social and political spaces, we hope to identify and give a name to a wide collection of culturally diverse initiatives and struggles of the so-called illiterate and uneducated non-modern "masses," pioneering radical post-modern paths out of the morass of modern life.

The epic to which we are alluding does not include all grassroots movements or initiatives. The Shining Path, the American or German Nazis or Neo-Nazis, the Ku Klux Klan, the Anandamargis and others of the same ilk are in our view fully immersed in modernity or pre-modernity. "Grassroots" is an ambiguous word, which we still dare to use because its political connotation identifies it with initiatives and movements coming from "the people": ordinary men and women, who autonomously organize themselves to cope with their predicaments. We want to write about "common" people without reducing them to "the masses."

PEOPLES BEYOND MODERNITY:
SAGAS OF RESISTANCE AND LIBERATION

Dramatically exacerbating five centuries of modernization during the past four "Development Decades" (Sachs, 1992), the "social minorities" are *consuming*[3] the natural and cultural spaces of the world's "social majorities" – with the stated intentions of developing them for "progress," economic growth and humanization.

For their part, with sheer guts and a creativity born out of their desperation, the "social majorities" continue resisting the inroads of that modern world into their lives, in their efforts to save their families and communities, their villages, ghettoes and *barrios*, from the next fleet of bulldozers sent to make them orderly or clean. Daily, the blueprints of modernization, conceived by conventional or alternative planners for their betterment, leave "the people" less and less human. Forced out of their centuries-old traditional communal spaces into the modern world, they suffer every imaginable indignity and dehumanization by the minorities who inhabit it. The only hope of a human existence, of survival and flourishing for the "social majorities," therefore, lies in the creation and regeneration of post-modern spaces.

So-called "neoliberal" policies, the free trade catechisms, the proliferation of "transnational" investments and communication networks, and all the other elements that are used to describe the new era of "globalization," are pushing the "social majorities" even further into the wastelands of the modern world. Relegated to its margins, they are "human surpluses": making too many babies – an "overpopulation"; increasingly disposable and redundant for the dominant actors on the "global" scene. They cannot be "competitive" in the world of the "social minorities," where "competitiveness" is the key to survival and domination. The dismantlement of the welfare state designed and conceived to protect the "benefits," dignity, income and personal security of the world's "social minorities" means little to the "social majorities." As "marginals," they have never had any real access to the "benefits" enjoyed by the non-marginals, the ones occupying the centers of the modern world. While some "marginals" are still striving to join the ranks of those minorities struggling to retain their jobs, their social security or their education, many more are not entering the trap of modern expectations: to count upon the market or the state.

Allotted the ghettoes, the dregs, the toxins, the reservations or the other wastelands of modern societies, the collapse of the market or the state is creating, in fact, new opportunities for them to stand on their own feet; to stop waiting for handouts or the fulfilment of all the false promises of equality, justice and democracy. Reaffirming themselves in their own spaces, they are daily creating the social frontiers of post-modernity; finding and making new paths with wit and ingenuity. The inevitable breakdown of modernity that terrorizes modern minorities is being transformed by the non-modern majorities into opportunities for regenerating their own traditions, their cultures, their unique indigenous and other non-modern arts of living and dying.

This book is an attempt to tell some of their post-modern stories. In this telling, we seek to learn from them their communal ingenuity and cultural arts for escaping or going beyond the monoculturalism of the modern world. In exploring their brands of post-modernism, we explicitly resist the urge of all modern experts: "helping" or "educating" the masses to join the mainstream minority march, headed onward and forward, towards global progress and development.[4]

Instead, we are inspired to join them in weaving the fabric of their evolving epic – all too human and yet so grand, revealing courage as much as it does the follies and foibles of those "down below" to be themselves; to retain and regenerate their cultures, despite the odds that threaten their lives and spaces.

Following them and their stories, we are drawing upon our own cultural roots and upon our own experiences with ordinary people's initiatives in Mexico and India. In telling their stories, we seek to offer images that spark the hope and imagination of others. In writing this book, we hope to engage in dialogues with modern men and women, inside or outside the academic post-modern fashion, who find themselves increasingly discouraged or pessimistic with the modern prospect; those who find the prison of the modern self to be an unbearable restriction. We hope to discover among them the allies inside the modern world which grassroots post-modernists badly need for realizing their endeavors more successfully.

Our book is addressed to all those struggling for a multiplicity of voices and cultures currently threatened by the monoculture of modernity, with its monolithic institutions: the nation-state, multinational corporations as well as national or international institutions. With intellectuals and grassroots activists who share our perplexities and predicaments, we are learning to identify and challenge the pillars and certainties that hold up these oppressive monoliths. These intellectuals and grassroots activists are the living links, our flexible swinging rope bridges with the "social majorities." Our book shares and expresses their hopes for intercultural dialogues, creating new pluralistic discourses: modes of conversation that can appropriately express the *conditio humana* in a pluriverse. For scholars and activists engaged in understanding and supporting indigenous knowledge systems, our book tries to open doors to escape the study of the world's "social majorities" as primitive or "underdeveloped" anthropological curiosities. Abandoning projects to help or develop peoples at the grassroots, we invite others to join us in learning from them the knowledge and skills required to survive and flourish beyond modernity.

DAVID AND GOLIATH

According to the myth of modern power, global forces can only be resisted and overcome by counterforces that must also be designed on the global scale. Succumbing to that myth of modern power, our outline of a grassroots epic should have discovered *the* super-grassroots movement that is a match for the global forces from which the oppressed seek their liberation.

The stories included in our book, however, are not about Promethean heroes; giants who "Think Big." Instead, they draw upon the experiences of common men and women in villages and *barrios*. Furthermore, through the entire course of this book we keep returning to stories of the Zapatista movement, which we continue to know and learn from "up close." This movement "made the news" on January 1, 1994, initiated by a small group of oppressed Indians, living in the poorest province of Mexico – a country that, according to the story told by the Harvard-educated economist, former President Salinas, and candidly believed by all the financial centers of power, stood then on the brink of joining the First World. Both Salinas and some of the billions of dollars he attracted rapidly flew outside the country, once its real condition took revenge over that fantasy world, even as Mexico collapsed into the shambles of monetary devaluation and economic recession.

What relevance can these grassroots stories have for others across the world, interested in their liberation from global forces? What can others learn from a provincial movement of desperately impoverished and oppressed Third World peasants struggling for their cultures, shamed and silenced for five centuries? Is it possible that such a small movement, militarily insignificant, can be of help to other oppressed peoples? Its relevance to other Indian movements or marginals in the Third World needs, perhaps, no explanation. However, how are we to explain the fact that people in more than a hundred countries reacted to the Zapatistas' liberation initiatives with meetings, encounters, mobilizations and thousands of specific proposals? How do we explain the fact that two Italian villages declared themselves Zapatistas, while stating that the questions and ventures of the latter are also their own? How are we to explain the independent initiatives that started disseminating daily news and comments about the Zapatistas through three electronic networks only a few weeks after January 1, 1994? Or that, a few months later, were publishing books in at least five languages and ten countries? How are we to explain the reaction in five continents to their invitation to animate the "international" of hope, overcoming the oppression of global neoliberalism?

By studying the impact of this movement, we cannot but recognize that it is not just a "case," a curiosity or a "model" for sociologists, anthropologists, political philosophers or critical cultural theorists interested in multicultural education. In drawing different lessons from the Zapatistas, we are not constructing an ideal type or the "best" representation of what is happening at the grassroots. We do hope, however, that our book will contribute towards explaining why such culturally diverse groups of peoples continue to find this movement to be particularly relevant for their own struggles. They identify themselves with the suggestion that "the actions of the Mayan Indians in Chiapas and the way they have circulated in Mexico, to North America and around the world, have some vital lessons for all of us" (Cleaver, 1994) – *us* being peoples interested in finding ways to react against the evils plaguing the lives of both the "social minorities" and the "social majorities" all over the world.

INTERLOCUTOR AND AUDIENCE

We can no longer write or speak from nowhere to abstract audiences. We can only address real men and women, with whom we share the same social and intellectual concerns. Since we cannot know in advance the readers of what we write, we imagine that some specific friends are sitting around our desk, playing the role of interlocutors. Our sense is that if our elaborations and ideas are of interest to them, there will also be others similarly drawn to this dialogue.

For this particular book, amongst those whom we have invited are first and foremost some ordinary men and women we know personally; who share both our daily predicaments and experiences at the grassroots; who refuse to uncritically believe what is manufactured for the consumption of TV-set owners, or of what is considered "publishable" by the editorial boards, constituted by "experts," of the "top journals"; who are increasingly sceptical about what is presented by pomp and circumstance, by hyper-text and hyper-sell. We have also invited some colleagues, acquaintances and friends, inside and outside the academic world, who have associated their lives and focused their interests as more than mere armchair intellectuals; who have been social activists in their own niches, personal and professional, participating in a multiplicity of ways in the daily dramas affecting the livelihood of the "social majorities" or the threats posed to them by the current trends. We have only invited those whose sympathies and understanding extend themselves to the imaginative struggles of people at the grassroots as their own.

To be our interlocutors, we have included some friends who resist being narrowly bracketed within the confines of specialized professional discourses that deliberately exclude and speak down to non-specialists; to educators, philosophers, feminists and environmentalists, who are puzzled by broad questions: What constitutes a good life? How do modern institutions like the educational/economic/political/medical establishments destroy the diversity of forms of thinking and being; bring in centralization of power and destroy the possibilities of the democratization, diversification and decentralization of power and politics? What does the genuine feminization of power and politics mean for creating cultural and other modes of diversification? What are the types of green movements or politics that do not become co-opted by the existing systems and structures of power and politics?

For those interested in narrow, specialized, professional discourses, our book offers little or nothing. We realize that in the age where even the debunking of specialized discourses becomes an elite "sub-speciality," our broad brush strokes with the major social issues of our time will be deprecated as a shallow skimming over the surface of questions that must be chopped and dissected, using research and writing techniques that define the dominant discourses of inquiry. Any specialist will reject our attempts to weave together the major issues we are bringing into this one small book. For even the post-modernists who, during the past decade, have been deconstructing their narrow disciplines continue writing principally for audiences confined by well-identified disciplinary interests and boundaries.

Learning from the paths being created by people at the grassroots, we have chosen to disregard those disciplinary boundaries, in order to be able to explore issues that do not adjust to them and cannot be grasped except by breaking the prison of academic disciplines. At the same time, we are fully aware that those issues have profound implications for the radical transformation of political structures, cultural transmission or initiation, post-modern theory and many other facets of social life. We have also chosen not to spell out those implications. For we are not trying to elaborate a blueprint for the future, another utopian dream, a trend or even a prospect. Rather, we seek to sketch an evolving epic that, by its very nature, will have many different futures, dreams and prospects, following very different impulses and trends.

BEYOND THE THREE SACRED COWS

The emerging epic of grassroots initiatives for resisting the oppressive-ness of modern minorities represents a clear rupture with some of the most fundamental premises of the modern era. In doing so, it leads the way in radically confronting some modern "sacred cows" (with apologies to the Hindus). Even academic post-modernism has still not dared to dissect or deconstruct them. As evident facts, certainties or moral ideals, they cannot be questioned by modern minds. The post-modern topology of the minds of people at the grassroots liberates them from those "certainties," seen as a horizon of intelligibility that is unsustainable and unbearable; one that they do not share.

As the workers of France recently demonstrated in their power disputes with the state, everywhere people are seeking ways to protect themselves against the threats posed by the current "global wave" to their jobs and security, their natural and social environments, their beliefs and expectations. Strikes and struggles like those of the French workers, however, are only brakes designed to slow down the pace of the transformation or to reduce the damage of the "Global Project." They are not challenging the project itself, or its foundations, but, instead, the way in which it is being implemented or its unequal benefits and impacts.

In contrast, however, peoples genuinely tired of marching the Great March of Progress have started to doubt the certainties which post-modern thinkers have left intact, and the meaning of struggles which involve getting locked into power disputes inside the nation-state. They are thus finding clear inspiration in the new people's struggles (no matter how distant or alien these seem to them at first sight) to conceive and implement their own initiatives for transformation. In France, during the recent strikes, many workers found that for the first time in years they actually had the opportunity to talk to each other about their predicaments, for a change free from the frantic pace of their daily industrial lives. Something radically new started to emerge in those informal talks spontaneously initiated in the paralyzed halls of the metro or the railways system. This was "the importance of the conversation," as a *Le Monde* editorial declared. Among rumors and shared puzzlements, new debates posing new questions started opening in marginal *quartiers* or villages. Our accounts, we hope, will be useful to peoples in diverse contexts as they articulate and implement their own initiatives for cultural and communal regeneration or transformation.

Gazing at the grassroots epic unfolding before us, we focus upon three modern sacred cows that still remain unchallenged.

The first of these is the myth of *global thinking*, the intellectu-al counterpart of the global economy. The promoters of economic globalization worship the economic system that has raised the "standard of living" of the "social minorities" over the centuries. During the last four Development Decades, they have made every kind of unfulfillable promise to bring this benefit to the rest of humanity, now and for eternity. Economic globalization, they now affirm, will do what the four Development Decades failed to provide. It will bring manna to all the peoples of the world; that is, the "goods" and "social services" currently enjoyed by the modern minorities: ballot boxes, health care, schools, paved roads, telephones, superhighways, flush toilets, toilet paper, among others. Many of these "goods" and "services" are classified by the world's "social minorities" under the modern moral umbrella of "human rights." To enjoy the shelter offered by this umbrella, people all over the world must abandon their own culturally specific local ways of living and dying, of thinking and working, of suffering or healing, of eating and defecating in order to become a part of the global economy. The latter is being forged by those who actually believe that it is both possible and necessary to "think global." Modernizers and post-modernizers alike assert that global thinking is superior to local thinking. Equally clear, for them, local thinking is limited, parochial and backward.

While academic post-modernists have taken scientific rationality by the horns, grassroots post-modernists are going beyond them in proceeding to do the same to the modern "certainty" of economic rationality. Grassroots struggles to resist the destruction of their local spaces by modernizers and developers (sustainable or other, including the proponents of green or eco-development) go far beyond academic post-modernism, turning on its head the modern myth regarding the rationality of *Homo oeconomicus*. By regenerating the different forms of rooted local thinking which inspire local actions, grassroots groups are learning how to keep economic thinking at the margins of their social lives, regenerating the traditions of the "social majorities," as they have thought and acted for centuries. Now in its global phase, the plague of economic thinking and living, like AIDS, is contaminating the non-economic cultures, defined by local, communal, thinking. The modern world can spread its economic tentacles only by destroying local cultures that keep the former outside their social margins. Criticizing the resistance of the latter as the ignorance of the uneducated, globalizers warn and threaten that without the global economy, human rights cannot be universally enforced.

The *universality of human rights* is the second modern sacred cow. It constitutes the moral justification behind "think global." Equally sacrosanct for academic post-modernists and modernizers, it is no surprise that they do not touch the Universal Declaration of Human Rights with their knives of dissection and "deconstruction."[5] These rights, in fact, continue to be salvaged from the junk-heap of deconstructed modernity as a (if not the) significant moral contribution. They constitute for many the gift of the modern era to the post-modern age that follows it, while improving upon it. Academic post-modernists engaged in race, class and gender studies, seeking to liberate multiculturalism from patriarchal western hegemony, dream of a world in which all those women and children, those classes and races deprived of their human rights in the modern era, will finally be "saved," a salvation supposedly secular and culturally neutral or transcultural. In the morally progressive, egalitarian and just global economy of the post-modern era, every individual will enjoy exercising his or her human rights. The western recolonization inherent in the global declaration of these human rights remains as imperceptible to post-modernists as to the modernists they accuse of cultural imperialism.

At the very core of this recolonization by human rights, claiming their universality despite differences in traditions, faith and moral outlook, stands the modern individual self. In the *myth of the individual self,* we discern the third sacred cow of modernity. Finally liberated from his or her pre-modern strings, the modern self can be fully incorporated into the "global economy," a member with full rights and privileges of the club, joining the society and culture of *Homo oeconomicus.* Neither modernists nor their post-modern academic critics dare to recognize the transmogrification of the human condition operated through the individualization of "the people." Neither seem capable of even conceiving "the good life" other than that being defined or sought by the individual self, more and more suffering within the unbearable straitjacket of loneliness, the dis-ease of homelessness. All that contemporary communitarians seem to be conceiving or offering are devices and techniques for plugging the contemporary individual self into social constructs which create the illusion of "interpersonal connectedness."

WHO ARE "THE PEOPLE"?

This book was born out of a two-fold "discovery": an opening to new ways of seeing, perceiving and living our experiences at the grassroots; and the increasing awareness that what we are perceiving and experiencing at the grassroots are not isolated or "unique" cases but conditions or situations that are generalized across the world. If the first amounts to an "epistemological rupture" (which we are still trying to digest), the second poses a very clear socio-political challenge: What kind of worlds are being created in front of our eyes at the grassroots? Are "the people" transforming the dominant institutions to improve them, or rather to replace them? And, if the latter is the case, what types of new institutions are they struggling to create? This last question, surfacing and resurfacing right till the end of the book, demonstrates how far we still are from the completion of our "epistemological rupture."

To tell our stories of the grassroots as being "typical" rather than "unique," we use a very imprecise Weberian model[6] for separating two different worlds: those of the "social minorities" and the "social majorities." While using these loose "formal" categories, we hope to maintain the diversity of their content: not reducing the diversified worlds of both "classes" of people, but still alluding to them through simple expressions.[7]

Many times, we also use "the people" as a substitute for the "social majorities." In doing so, we are referring to groups of persons composing the new commons. "The people," we realize, has all kinds of social and political uses, including certain pejorative connotations: basically opposing the rulers and the ruled, the powerful and the powerless, the strong and the weak. In its more technical sense, it differentiates the governing elites from the governed of the "civil society" – another imprecise term.

In its current incarnation, the notion of "civil society" is traced by Douglas Lummis to the

> struggles of the peoples of Eastern Europe against the communist bureaucratic states, to the struggles to bring about a "transition to democracy" in the Latin American dictatorships, to the autonomous self-help organizations that grew up in Mexico City after the September 1985 earthquake, to the writings of Antonio Gramsci, and more generally to the search for a theory and praxis for people's movements in the post-Marxist era. (Lummis, 1996, p. 30)

In our allusions to "civil society," we seek to draw attention to that sphere of social life which organizes itself autonomously, as opposed to the sphere that is established and/or directly controlled by the state.

> [U]nlike a class or a party, civil society does not rise up and seize the power of the state; rather, in rising up, it empowers itself. It does not take over the state or replace it, but rather stands against it, marginalizes it, controls it. Unlike mass society, civil society is not a herd but a multiplicity of diverse groups and organizations, formal and informal, of people acting together for a variety of purposes.... Because of its small-group organization, civil society is unlikely to fall prey to the danger of the "tyranny of the majority"; in fact the idea closely resembles, and is in part based on, the model of society which Alexis de Tocqueville, who invented the expression "tyranny of the majority," believed was the best protection against it. (Lummis, 1996, p. 31)

There is a need, however, to establish a clear distinction between the current use of the expression in popular movements and its meaning in the old model of liberal pluralism, which not only includes competition and private corporations within the civil society, but also affirms that "the United States has been the complete *civil society* ... perhaps the only one in political history."[8]

The expression "civil society" also alludes to a new semantic of social transformation, including new concepts and commitments.[9] "The people," in such a context, is the autonomous, democratic civil society, as it expresses itself in organizations independent of the state and its formal or corporative structures.

The epic now unfolding at the grassroots has its smattering of well-known actors. Some of them have even received the Nobel Prize: for example, Rigoberta Menchú. Others have either been nominated or selected for the alternative Nobel Prize: the Right Livelihood Award. Some have become well-known celebrities among sections of the "social minorities" after the successful international sale of books describing their dramas and successes: the Chipko movement or the Narmada struggle, for example. For the most part, however, the main actors of the unfolding epic remain unknown to the world created by modern media; thereby still protected or sheltered from the forces that co-opt, tempt or seduce those suddenly blinded by overnight fame and "front-page" limelight. In many cases, people's reactions to the "Global Project" have not yet taken the shape of "a movement": they have not a specific name or label with which they identify themselves or are identified by others. Their informal condition as the unnamed and the unidentified is an important aspect of their politics, often offering them the camouflage essential to their survival; as is their "failure" to adopt any "institutional structure."

To modern eyes, shaped by constant exposure to the so-called "precision" of formal categories, it may be useful to see that the historical experience of the modern era is not to be traced to a specific "group," a "movement," an "organization;" but, instead, to a wide variety of initiatives, taken by ordinary men and women, who reacted against the pre-modern structures that locked them in. Great thinkers and political movements were of course involved in that process, but none of them was "responsible" for it.

There is a similarity to this situation discerned by us in this unfolding era of grassroots post-modernism. The grassroots initiatives that we are alluding to and drawing upon are autonomously organized by "the people" themselves, for their own survival, flourishing and enduring; both independent from and antagonistic to the state and its formal and corporative structures; hospitable to "the Other" and thus open to diversity; mainly expressed in reclaimed or regenerated commons, in both urban and rural settings, and clearly concerned with the common good, both natural and social.

In addition to the burgeoning literature about such grassroots initiatives in journals like The Ecologist or Fourth World Review, there are new groups of independent institutions which are trying to systematically document and disseminate their experiences. Notable among them are the Intercultural Institute of Montreal (with a documentation center, the journal Interculture and the web called the International Network for Cultural Alternatives to Development); Opción, in Mexico (with a documentation center, as well as journals like *El Gallo Ilustrado, Opciones* and *El verdepinto* and the web *Red Intercultural de Acción Autónoma*); PDP, in Mexico (with a documentation center, the journal *La otra bolsa de valores* and active webs in Mexico and abroad); PRATEC in Peru, HISBOL in Bolivia, and REDES in Uruguay (each with a documentation center, a research group and a publishing program); Claude and Norma Alvares' The Other India Book Store (a documentation center and a publishing company), to mention only a smattering – far, far less than even the tiny tip of the proverbial iceberg. All these organizations, and the many thousands of others that constitute their ilk, are actively involved in their local/regional struggles at the grassroots. They tend to operate as "hinges," connecting the "inside" and the "outside" of the movements. The International Group for Grassroots Initiatives, founded ten years ago, reflects the interest and commitment of a group of activists and scholars from ten countries, interested in observing and supporting this process.

CONTENT AND STRUCTURE OF THIS BOOK

Chapter 2 of our book examines the grassroots epic as a challenge to global thinking. Chapter 3 presents explorations which open pathways beyond modern identity: that of the individual self. Chapter 4 views human rights through the different types of windows being created by this epic. Chapter 5 reveals the association between the "Global Project" and the death of democracy, while also examining the recovery and the regeneration of people's power at the grassroots. Chapter 6, bringing the book to a conclusion, describes the moral and other socio-political horizons now unfolding at the grassroots, along with the public virtues that are being nourished there.

Chapter 2 offers the entire book in a nutshell. All our arguments are contained there. Chapters 3 and 4 are elaborations – delving deeper into the same issues and themes of modern reality, probing the pathways of departure being made by the "social majorities" at the grassroots, even as they daily use their feet to walk away from it. Chapter 5, recollecting these lessons emerging out of the experiences of "the peoples," explores some of their ramifications for post-modern politics.

An epic, particularly one that has just started to unfold, cannot be reduced to empirical descriptions, abstract elaborations ("scientific" or philosophical), historical accounts or logical statements. Our book does not seek to present a systematic argument against the modern ideals of the "global village." Neither does it attempt to describe a global epic. Recognizing the nature of the recovery and regeneration that the people are engaged in at the grassroots, we know the folly of any mechanical addition; of summing everything up as one global movement. Remaining clear of such pretensions, our book also avoids its reduction into a technical report – the final conclusion of a research project.

We are articulating our experiences with people at the grassroots principally in Mexico, and secondarily in India – there where we have our roots. In sharing some of the stories we have heard or experienced there, we are making rough sketches which may appeal to the imagination of others – particularly those undergoing the epistemological rupture of abandoning modern certainties.

To escape from the crippling modern blindness that previously prevented us from "reading" our experiences at the grassroots, we continue to find guidance and help in the reflections of thinkers like Wendell Berry, Iván Illich or Raimón Panikkar, whose radical critiques of modernity emerge from plumbing the depths of their western tradition, unveiling forgotten truths that few contemporary minds even dare to imagine or probe. Their ideas continue to help us build bridges between modern "reality" and the far removed, the "other" worlds we experience at the grassroots. For that reason, we frequently start our reflections by pondering on some of their insights and ideas, using these to enter with humility and tentativeness the worlds of "the people," aware of the disrespect and damage we do to Others when we reduce them or assess them through modern categories.

Our "we," identified and articulated through the entire course of this book, is that of Gustavo Esteva and Madhu Suri Prakash, the authors. That "we" is in itself an exercise in intercultural dialogue. It is the "we" of a man and a woman, born and raised in two incommensurable living and vital cultures; belonging to radically different physical, cultural and intellectual worlds; attempting to weave the threads of our different perceptions, emotions and views into a common fabric. Ours is no statistical or abstract "we": that of a woman and man reduced to the common denominators offered by the modern ideals of equality (that of the homogenizing melting pot) and of scholarly objectivity (the pretensions of taking the view from nowhere). In this project, as elsewhere, we remain ourselves: a man and a woman in the flesh, our perceptions shaped by our senses, by the feelings that rise out of the very gut of our being a Zapoteco and a Punjabi, "educated" to be a de-professionalized grassroots activist and a scholar escaping the limits for studying the world imposed by the modern academy. While rooted and located in contexts that are worlds apart, we express and celebrate our first person plural, creating a harmony of distinctly different voices "speaking" in this book about "the otherness of the Others."

The epic which we can only but very roughly begin to outline here – the epic we have been experiencing at the grassroots – has not yet evolved to the point in which it is an *Iliad*, a *Mahabharata* or a *Popol Vuh*. Inspired as we are by its tentative beginnings, we hope that many others will be similarly moved to grope further, going beyond these early rough sketches into writing full sagas that celebrate "common" men and women. This book can be seen as an attempt to begin the telling and retelling of human stories, of struggles against forces inhuman or evil, which are woven into the fabric of all great epics, pre-modern as well as post-modern. They are stories in which the heroes are ordinary men and women (rather than extraordinary characters). To them we are dedicating this book, written with the stuff we are learning to learn with them.

NOTES

1. We use the expression the "Global Project" to allude to the current collection of policies and programs, principally promoted all over the world by the governments of the industrial countries with the help of their "friends": the international institutions and corporations equally committed to the economic integration of the world and the market credo (based on the modern doctrine of the self-regulating market, as described by Karl Polanyi in *The Great Transformation*, 1925). Other "friends" include most heads of state as well as the elites of "underdeveloped" states, aspiring to "catch up" with the "social minorities" of the "developed" nations, in the global race for "progress" and "development."

2. "Social majorities" and "social minorities" are two "ideal" types of groups of people – parts of the analytical devices we are employing to present our insights. In using these categories, we are not succumbing to the modern statistical reduction of people, qualifying or disqualifying them only by their numbers. At the same time, however, we are differentiating between groups of people by the "quality" of their living conditions, which usually determine their mode of thinking and their behavior. Our "ideal" types are constituted by a variety of groups of real people who share a common denominator. The "social minorities" are those groups in both the North and the South that share homogeneous ways of modern (western) life all over the world. Usually, they adopt as their own the basic paradigms of modernity. They are also usually classified as the upper classes of every society and are immersed in economic society: the so-called "formal sector." The "social majorities" have no regular access to most of the goods and services defining the average "standard of living" in the industrial countries. Their definitions of "a good life," shaped by

their local traditions, reflect their capacities to flourish outside the "help" offered by "global forces." Implicitly or explicitly, they neither "need" nor are dependent upon the bundle of "goods" promised by these forces. They, therefore, often share a common freedom in their rejection of "global forces." The previous classification of people and nations in North and South or First, Second and Third Worlds (and the Fourth and the Fifth) is clearly outdated. Our ideal types can be associated with the One-third World (the "social minorities" in both North and South) and the Two-thirds World (the "social majorities"). For our present purposes, there is no need to give more precision to these types. They can, of course, be empirically associated with economic and social indicators, if due consideration is given to the difference in the "common denominator" of both types: the "social minorities" share a "Yes," a way of life and the myths and paradigms of modernity; the "social majorities" share a "No," by not having access to most of the goods and services constituting that way of life, and by rejecting the forces encroaching upon their lives and destroying their traditions.

3. Following in the footsteps of the "social majorities," we will be articulating their critique of "consuming" as well as the degeneration of modern peoples into "consumers." From the former, we continue to learn what our elders also taught us: that there is no "good consumerism." "*Consum-ere*," the Latin root for consuming, means to take up completely, make away with, devour, waste, destroy, spend. The first meaning mentioned in the *Oxford English Dictionary* for "consume" is "to make away with, use up destructively." Said chiefly of fire, consume means: To burn up, reduce to invisible products, or to ashes; also of any similar destructive or "devouring agent." "Consume" is also "to destroy (a living being, or more usually a race or a tribe) by disease or any wasting process;" "to decompose"; "to spend wastefully," "to waste one's substance, ruin oneself"; "to wear out of use"; "to exhaust right of action"; "to waste away, decay, rot, perish." All those historical meanings of the active verb "consume" are now condensed in the daily modern practices of consumption. "Good consumerism" simply extends and legitimates our impulses to destroy, to ruin ourselves and our environments, to waste away our natural and social inheritance, to produce decay and rot.

All the consuming that is considered to be a "public benefit" today for keeping alive the modern global economy is either impossible or deemed to be expressions of undesirable "private vices" in the worlds of the "social majorities." For further reflections on the transmogrification of vices into virtues, see, for example, Mandeville's *The Fable of the Bees* (1755).

4. For analyses of "helping," "educating," "progress," "development," and other "toxic" modern words polluting the cultural and ecological, mental and physical landscapes of the world's "social majorities," see Wolfgang Sachs (1992) and Ivan Illich (1977).

5. In the eighteenth and nineteenth centuries, modern thinkers, like Burke, Hume and Bentham, deconstructed the idea of human rights as natural rights, which prevailed for several centuries. Supposedly, the origin of this idea can be traced back to the Greeks and the Romans. See the entry "Human Rights" in the *Encyclopedia Britannica*.

6. We are not, in fact, adopting a Weberian model: we are not assuming either the premises or the methodology of Weber's theory of social action; and, even less, his intention in the construction of ideal types. In alluding to two classes of

people in the world, the "social majorities" and the "social minorities," we are not trying to construct average or ideal types of social action. We use those classes as descriptive tools, similar to the "typical-ideal types" of Weber, in the sense that a type "does not describe an individual course of action, but a 'typical' one – it is a generalized rubric within which an indefinite number of particular cases may be classified" (Parsons, 1947, p. 13). But we do not use those types as a method to offer a "scientific" explanation of social action, or even less as normative types, but only to allude to the differences between two very generalized and complex patterns of behavior.

7. In this operation, we are carefully avoiding approaches which assume the reality of social classes. We are not rejecting the value of class analysis, or avoiding any reference to "class content" or "class struggle." To avoid throwing the baby out with the bathwater, we are keeping these categories in their place: as analytical tools. No matter how illuminating or useful the hypothesis of class struggle can be for explaining social conflicts, past or present, we realize that in the real world, classes do not struggle: people do. People cannot be reduced to a social class, defined through economic relations. Regardless of the successes of organizations to promote the interests of the members of their class, we cannot but recognize their limits and counterproductivity: they are inevitably trapped by the logic that defines their very constitution. Social "majorities" and "minorities" are of course two "classes" of people, but in a completely different sense. These two groupings of people are associated with distinct modes of living, of being on earth: those "globalized" in both North and South, fully immersed in a modern, homogeneous lifestyle; and those "marginalized" from it, living in a wide variety of richly diverse lifestyles in accordance with local or regional, non-modern cultural determinations – this, in spite of also being exposed to modern determinations, particularly those of capital.

8. Daniel Bell (1989), p. 48. For discussions of liberal ideals and civil society, see Robert A. Dahl (1961), Seymour Martin Lipset (1960) and Daniel Bell (1962). For a lengthy discussion on the origins of the concept of civil society, see Jean L. Cohen and Andrew Arato (1992). See also Adam Ferguson (1969) and "Civil Society?", in Lummis (1996), pp. 30–7.

9. For its evolution in Mexico, see Andrés Aubry (1994).

TWO

FROM GLOBAL TO LOCAL:
BEYOND NEOLIBERALISM TO THE
INTERNATIONAL OF HOPE

> ... the naming of the intolerable is itself the hope. When something is termed intolerable, actions must follow. These actions are subject to all the vicissitudes of life. But the pure hope resides first and mysteriously in the capacity to name the intolerable as such: and this capacity comes from afar – from the past and from the future. (John Berger, 1984, p. 18)

> The "global village" is not a village for the real villagers of the globe. Never before have there been so many "have-nots" in the world. If we were in a "global village," they would be visible to all. But they are hidden from the view of the defenders of the "global village." They are the under-pariahs, kept out of sight, hidden in three-quarters of the so-called Third World which, if it should be called anything, should be ·called the Two-thirds World. (Vachon, 1995b, p. 56)

The policies and political slogans which emerged at the end of the Cold War, usually associated with "free trade," "neoliberalism" and other key words, have rapidly become effective emblems for selling the promises of a new era. New political, economic and social paradigms are once again in the process of being imposed by a few upon the many. Some of those emblems and paradigms are being transformed into *presuppositions*,[1] as the constitutive elements of the myths of the "social minorities" of the world. These minorities are celebrating the opportunities being created by the Internet, World Wide Web or other global communications networks, as new forms of "global democracy." They are presuming that such "advances" will stimulate multicultural-ism, through human "communication" inconceivable only a few years ago. They are assuming that the "New World Order" being established by the World Trade Organization and other institutions will finally materialize the most cherished dreams of humankind, dreamed by the few for the many. The unprecedented global exchange of goods and services, maintain the makers of the global *mythos*, will give access to the best that modern technology and civilization can offer to every man and woman on Earth.

None of these policy and political approaches, emblems or presuppositions go completely unchallenged. Not everyone shares the spirit of celebration they seek to promote. Since the very beginning of these campaigns for globalization (of education, citizenship, language, currency, religion and all other aspects of social life) multiple voices have expressed alarm about the new marvels and paradigms being promoted through media-hype. Even the most enthusiastic fans of Bill Gates and his Windows '97 experience misgivings and doubts when they observe the peculiar behaviors of their children emerging for brief moments out of the "virtual reality" in which they are being raised. Even the most single-minded and ambitious free trade advocates cannot fail to recognize the social and human costs of the policies they are promoting. More and more voices are raising alarms about their growing sense of powerlessness, tugged and pulled by "global forces."

Until now, however, it appears as if most of the social movements or campaigns trying to resist the new "global" phenomena have proven to be highly ineffective. Some of them are even counterproductive, getting the opposite of what they are looking for; rooting and deepening in people and society the very evils against which they are struggling. True, many workers' strikes do succeed in protecting jobs or pension plans. At the same time, however, they also legitimize and consolidate the policies and orientations creating unemployment or dismantling the welfare state. Amongst the people struggling for some security in their lives, many assume that they have no more than one political option: that the best they can do is to protect their own situation; get some compensation for what they are losing; and hope that the promises offered in exchange for their sacrifices will one day be fulfilled. Such beliefs reinforce the "Global Project."

This chapter first explores the impossibility of regaining the experience of human agency and autonomy by supposedly "thinking" on the global scale to contend with the oppression of "global forces." No challenge to the proliferating experiences of people's powerlessness succeeds when conceived and implemented inside the institutional and intellectual framework which produced it. After closing the door to the fantasy of global thinking, we reflect on the multiplicity of local escape routes being invented or created daily to move out of the disabling global framework. These grassroots counterforces of liberation remain invisible to the mainstream world of media and scholarship.

The earliest alarm signals about the new global paradigms encroaching upon the minds and lives of ordinary people were expressed in the slogan "Think globally, act locally," supposedly formulated by René Dubos some decades ago. It is not only a popular bumper sticker today; it increasingly captures the moral imagination of millions of people across the globe. Our analysis for moving beyond the "global framework" to local autonomy exposes the successes and strengths of the social philosophy underlying the slogan, while going beyond it in exploring the measure to which it can also be counterproductive.

Often, those supporting this slogan embrace several "certainties": first, the modern age forces everyone to live today in a global village; second, therefore, across the globe, people face shared predicaments and common enemies, like Cargill, Coca Cola, the World Bank, Nestlé, and other transnational corporations, as well as oppressive nation-states; third, only a clear awareness of the global nature of such problems could help forge the coalitions of "human solidarity" and "global conscious-ness" needed for struggling successfully against these all-pervasive global enemies; fourth, this global consciousness includes the recognition that every decent human being must be morally committed to the active global defense of "basic needs" or universal human rights (to schooling, health, nutrition, housing, livelihood, etc.) and human freedoms (from torture, oppression, etc.).

The slogan reveals the illusion of engaging in global action. This is not mere realism: ordinary people lack the centralized power required for "global action." It is a warning against the arrogance, the far-fetched and dangerous fantasy of "acting globally." Urging respect for the limits of "local action," it resists the Promethean lust to be godlike: omni-present. By clearly defining the limits of intelligent, sensible action, it encourages decentralized, communal power. To make "a difference," actions should not be grandiosely global, but humbly local.

Extending the valuable insights contained in the second part of the slogan to the first part, we urge the replacement of "global thinking" with the "local thinking" practiced at the grassroots. We begin by presenting a synopsis of Wendell Berry's (Berry, 1972, 1991a, 1991b) well-elaborated argument, warning not only against the dangerous arrogance of "global thinkers," but also of the human impossibility of this form of thought.[2] Next, we debunk the other "certainties" that today pressure millions of modern, developed, "global citizens" into believing that they have the moral obligation to engage in global thinking. They disparage "think local"; for they suffer the modern illusion that local thinking must necessarily be not only ineffective in front of the global Goliath, but also parochial, taking humankind back to the dark ages when each was taught only to look after his/her own, letting "the devil take the hindmost." We reveal, instead, both the parochialism of "global thinking" and global action[3] as well as the open nature of "local thinking" and local action, practiced "down below," at "the margins" of modern society.

GLOBAL THINKING IS IMPOSSIBLE

The modern "gaze" (Illich, 1994b, p. 3) can distinguish less and less between reality and the image broadcast on the TV screen.[4] It has shrunk the earth into a little blue bauble, a mere Christmas tree ornament, all too often viewed on a TV set. Forgetting its mystery, immensity and grandeur, modern men and women succumb to the arrogance of "thinking globally" to manage planet Earth (Berry, 1991a, 1991b).

We can only think wisely about what we actually know well. And no person, however sophisticated, intelligent and overloaded with the information age state-of-the-art technologies, can ever "know" the Earth − except by reducing it statistically, as all modern institutions tend to do today, supported by reductionist scientists.[5] Since none of us can ever really know more than a minuscule part of the earth, "global thinking" is at its best only an illusion, and at its worst the grounds for the kinds of destructive and dangerous actions perpetrated by global "think tanks" like the World Bank, or their more benign counterparts − the watchdogs in the global environmental and human rights movements.

Bringing his contemporaries "down to earth" from out-of-space or spacy "thinking," teaching us to stand once again on our own feet (as did our ancestors), Wendell Berry helps us to rediscover human finiteness, and to debunk another "fact" of TV manufactured reality: the "global village." The transnational reach of *Dallas* and the sexual escapades of the British Royal Family or the Bosnian bloodbath, like the international proliferation of McDonald's, Benetton or Sheraton establishments, strengthen the modern prejudice that all people on Earth live in "One World."[6] McLuhan's (McLuhan and Powers, 1989) unfortunate metaphor of the "global village" now operates as a presupposition, completely depleting critical consciousness. Contemporary arrogance suggests that modern man and woman can know the globe, just as premoderns knew their village. Rebutting this nonsense, Berry confesses that he still has much to learn in order to "husband" with thought and wisdom the small family farm which he has tilled and harvested for the past forty years in his ancestral Kentucky. His honesty about his ignorance in caring for his minuscule piece of our earth renders naked the dangerousness of those who claim to "think globally" and aspire to monitor and manage the "global village."

Once environmental "problems"[7] are reduced to the ozone layer or to global warming, to planetary "sources" and "sinks," faith in the futility of local efforts is fed by global experts; while their conferences, campaigns and institutions present the fabulous apparition of solutions "scientifically" pulled out of the "global hat." Both a global conscious-ness and a global government (such as the Global Environmental Facil-ity "masterminded" at the Earth Summit) appear as badly needed to manage the planet's "scarce resources" and "the masses" irresponsibly chopping "green sinks" for their daily tortillas or chappatis, threaten-ing the "experts'" planetary designs for eco-development. The "ozone layer" or "global warming" are abstract hypotheses, offered by some scientists as an explanation of recent phenomena. Even in that condition, they could prove to be very useful for fostering critical awareness of the folly of the "social minorities." But they are promoted as "a fact," reality itself; and all the socio-political and ecological dangers inherent in the illusion of the "Global Management" of planet Earth are hidden from "the people." Excluded, for example, from critical scrutiny is the reflection that in order for "global thinking" to be feasible, we should be able to "think" from within every culture on Earth and come away from this excursion single-minded – clearly a logical and practical impossibility, once it is critically de-mythologized. For it requires the supra-cultural criteria of "thinking" – implying the dissolution of the subject who "thinks"; or assuming that it is possible to "think" outside of the culture in which every man and woman on Earth is immersed. The human condition does not allow such operations. We celebrate the hopefulness of common men and women, saved from the hubris of "scientific man," unchastened by all his failures at playing God.

THE WISDOM OF THINKING SMALL

With the traditional humility of Gandhi, Ivan Illich, Leopold Kohr, Fritz Schumacher, and others of their ilk, Berry warns of the many harmful consequences of "Thinking Big": pushing all human enterprises beyond the human scale. Appreciating the genuine limits of human intelligence and capacities, Berry celebrates the age-old wisdom of "thinking little" or small: on the proportion and scale that humans can really understand, know and assume responsibility for the consequences of their actions and decisions upon others.

Afraid that local thinking weakens and isolates people, localizing them into parochialism, the "alternative" global thinkers[8] forget that Goliath did in fact meet his match in David. Forgetting this biblical moral insight, they place their faith in the countervailing force of a competing or "alternative" Goliath of their own, whose global thinking encompasses the supra-morality of "planetary consciousness." Assuming that "Global Man" (the grown-ups' version of Superman) has more or less conquered every space on Earth (and is now moving beyond, into the extra-terrestrial), they think he is now advancing towards a collective conscience: one conscience, one transcultural consciousness, one humanity – the great human family. "It is the planetary conscience that takes us to a 'world society' with a 'planetary citizenship'," says Leonardo Boff, the Brazilian theologian, [9] describing a hope now shared by a wide variety of "globalists." Hunger in Ethiopia, bloody civil wars in Somalia or Yugoslavia, human rights violations in Mexico thus become the personal responsibilities of all good, non-parochial citizens of Main Street; supposedly complementing their local involvement in reducing garbage, homelessness or junk food in their own neighborhoods. Global Samaritans may fail to see that when their local actions are informed, shaped and determined by a "global frame of mind,"[10] they become as uprooted as those of the globalists they explicitly criticize.

To relearn how to "think little," Berry recommends starting with the "basics" of life: food, for example. He suggests discovering ways to eat which take us beyond "global thinking and action" towards "local thinking and action." Global thinkers and think tanks, like the World Bank, disregard this wisdom at the level of both thought and action. Declaring that current food problems, among others, are global in their nature, they seek to impose global solutions. Aware of the threats perpetrated by such "solutions," the proponents of "Think globally, act locally" take recourse to the tradition of Kohr et al. only at the level of action, as a sensible strategy to struggle against the "global forces." By refusing to "think little," given their engagement with global campaigns, the Worldwatch Institute and other "alternative" globalists of their ilk inadvertently function on their enemies' turf.

How do we defeat the five Goliath companies now controlling 85 percent of the world trade of grains and around half of its world production? Or the four controlling the American consumption of chicken? Or those few that have cornered the beverage market? The needed changes will wait for ever if they require forging equally gigantic transnational consumers' coalitions, or a global consciousness about the right way to eat. In accepting the illusory nature of the efforts to struggle against "global forces" in their own territory, on a global scale, we are not suggesting the abandonment of effective coalitions for specific purposes, like the Pesticides Action Network, trying to exert political pressure to ban specific threats. Even less are we suggesting that people give up their struggles to put a halt to the dangerous advances of those "global forces." Quite the opposite. In putting our eggs in the local basket, we are simply emphasizing the merits of the politics of "No" for dealing with global Goliaths: affirming a rich diversity of attitudes and ideals, while sharing a common rejection of the same evils. Such a common "No" does not need a "global conciousness." It expresses the opposite: a pluriverse of thought, action and reflection.

All global institutions, including the World Bank or Coca Cola, have to locate their transnational operations in actions that are always necessarily local; they cannot exist otherwise. Since "global forces" can only achieve concrete existence at some local level, it is only there – at the local grassroots – that they can most effectively and wisely be opposed. People at the grassroots are realizing that there is no need to "Think Big" in order to begin releasing themselves from the clutches of the monopolistic food economy; that they can, in fact, free themselves in the same voluntary ways as they entered it. They are learning to simply say "No" to Coke and other industrial junk, while looking for local alternatives that are healthy, ecologically sound, as well as decentralized in terms of social control. Among the more promising reactions in the industrial world is the movement towards Community Supported Agriculture (CSAs), inspired by both local thinking and action. This growing grassroots movement is teaching urban people how to support small local farmers who farm with wisdom, caring for local soils, waters and intestines. In doing so, local communities simultaneously ensure that unknown farmers from faraway places like Costa Rica or Brazil are not exploited with inhuman wages and left sick with cancer or infertility. By taking care of our own local food, farms and farmers, those of us who are members of CSAs are slowly learning to overcome the parochialism of "industrial eaters": who are "educated" to be oblivious to the harm done by purchasing from multinational agribusiness and others who "Think Big," destroying millions of small family farms across the globe.

Those of us supporting CSAs are trying to abandon the global thinking with which "industrial eaters" enter their local grocery stores: buying "goods" from any and every part of the earth, motivated solely by the desire to get the "best" return for their dollar. Of course, re-learning to think locally about food (among other "basics") we are also frugal: we also want the best return for our dollar. But for us this means much more than maximizing the number of eggs or the gallons of milk with which we can fill our grocery bags. We are interested in knowing about the kinds of lives lived by the hens whose eggs we eat; we want to know what type of soil our lettuce springs from. And we want to ensure that not only were the animals and plants we bring to our palate treated well; we are critically examining our eating habits so that the farmers who work for us will not die of deadly diseases or become infertile because of the chemicals they were forced to spray on their fields. We have now read enough to know why these ills occur every time we buy grapes from California or bananas from Costa Rica. We also know that when our food comes from so far away, we will never know the whole story of suffering perpetrated unintentionally by us, despite the valiant efforts of journals like *The Ecologist* or scholars like Frances Moore Lappé (1991); nor, for that matter, once we get a partial picture, will we be able to do much about it. Therefore, by decreasing the number of kilometers which we eat, bringing our food closer and closer to our local homes, we know we are "empowering" ourselves to be neither oppressed by the big and powerful, nor oppressors of *campesinos* and small farmers who live across the globe; and we are also reskilling ourselves to look after the well-being of members of our local community, who, in their turn, are similarly committed to our well-being. In doing so, we are discovering that we are also saving money, while being more productive and efficient: saving on manufactured pesticides, fertilizers, packaging, refrigeration or transportation over long distances.

Self-sufficiency and autonomy are now new political demands, well rooted in the experience of millions of Indians, *campesinos*, "urban marginals" and many other groups in the southern part of the globe. Rerooting and regenerating themselves in their own spaces, they are creating effective responses to the "global forces" trying to displace them.

DOWNSIZING TO HUMAN SCALE

The time has come to recognize with the late Leopold Kohr that the true problem of the modern age lies in the inhuman size or scale of many contemporary institutions and technologies. Instead of trying to counteract such inherently unstable and damaging global forces through government or civic controls that match their disproportionate and destructive scale, the time has come "to reduce the size of the body politic which gives them their devastating scale, until they become once again a match for the limited talent available to the ordinary mortals of which even the most majestic governments are composed" (Kohr, 1992, p. 10). In other words, said Kohr,

> instead of centralization or unification, let us have economic cantonization. Let us replace the oceanic dimension of integrated big powers and common markets by a dike system of inter-connected but highly self-sufficient local markets and small states in which economic fluctuations can be controlled not because national or international leaders have Oxford or Yale degrees, but because the ripples of a pond, however animated, can never assume the scale of the huge swells passing through the united water masses of the open seas. (Kohr, 1992, p. 11)

This is sound advice not only for dealing with the WTO, the European Union, NAFTA or the World Bank in the political arena; that is, to put public pressure on governments with regards to the reorientation of their policies. It applies equally to every local struggle. Kohr's alternatives cannot be constructed from the top down, creating gigantic dikes to stop such oceanic waves or struggling to "seize" such powers in order to give them a different orientation or to dismantle them. In the struggle against global forces, there is a need to keep all political bodies at a human scale.

This is exemplifed by the Zapatistas. On January 1, 1994, a few thousand poorly armed Indians started a rebellion in the south of Mexico. We elaborate on this Zapatista movement in different parts of this book.[11] We explain both how it has precipitated the end of the old authoritarian regime[12] of a country of 90 million, and how it continues to articulate the struggles of many local groups. No other call of the Zapatista movement was more successful than "Basta!" ("Enough!"). Millions of Mexicans were activated by it, shaping their generalized discontent and their multiple affirmations into a common, dignified rejection. The movement was able to encapsulate new aspirations in ways that affirm and regenerate their local spaces. They show no interest in seizing power in order to impose their own regime on everyone. Their struggle for a radically democratic governance attempts to take some of the political procedures of formal democracies, while combining these with those prevailing in their own traditions, in their communities. In their commons, the Zapatistas and other Mexicans are trying to govern themselves autonomously, well rooted in the spaces to which they belong and that belong to them. While affirming their dignity and their hope of flourishing and enduring according to their own cultural patterns and their own practices of the art of living and dying, they are joining in solidarity with all those liberating themselves from the parochialism of the "Global Project."

ESCAPING PAROCHIALISM

Global proposals are necessarily parochial: they inevitably express the specific vision and interests of a small group of people, even when they are supposedly formulated in the interest of humanity (Shiva 1993). In contrast, if they are conceived by communities well rooted in specific places, local proposals reflect the unique "cosmovision" that defines, differentiates and distinguishes every culture: an awareness of the place and responsibilities of humans in the cosmos.[13] Those who think locally do not twist the humble satisfaction of belonging to the cosmos into the arrogance of pretending to know what is good for everyone and to attempt to control the world.

There is a legitimate claim to "universality" intrinsic in every affirmation of truth. However, people who dwell in their places[14] do not identify the limits of their own vision with that of the human horizon itself. Among Indian peoples, for example, all over the American continent, the notion of "territory" is not associated with ownership, but with responsibility. If the Earth is the mother, how can anyone own her? Indian peoples feel a genuine obligation to care for the portion of the cosmos where they have settled and they affirm the truth of their notion of human relations with their Mother, the Earth. But they do not transform that conviction into the arrogance of knowing, controlling and managing planet Earth, seeking to impose their own view on everyone.

Growing coalitions of local thinkers/activists are learning to effectively counteract the damage of global thinking and action through a shared rejection. Their shared "No" to their "common enemies" (whether a nuclear plant, dam or Wal-Mart) simultaneously affirms their culturally differentiated perceptions, their locally rooted initiatives and modes of being. When their shared "No" interweaves cross-cultural agreements or commitments, they retain their pluralism, without falling into cultural relativism. They successfully oppose globalism and plurality with radical pluralism, conceived for going beyond western monoculturalism – now cosmeticized and disguised as "multiculturalism" inside as well as outside the quintessentially western settings: the classroom or the office. And they find, in their concrete practices, that all "global powers" are built on shaky foundations (as the Soviet Union so ably demonstrated in the recent past); and may, therefore, be effectively opposed through modest local actions. The very size of gargantuan, disproportionate and over-sized "systems" make them out of balance and extremely fragile. Saying "No," in contrast, may be one of the most complete and vigorous forms of self affirmation for communities and organizations of real men and women. A unifying "No," expressing a shared opposition, is but the other side of a radical affirmation of the heterogeneous and differentiated beings and hopes of all the real men and women involved in resisting any global monoculture. Saying "No, thanks" to mindless jobs or the medicalization of society is the negative aspect of the affirmation of a wide variety of autonomous ways to cope with globalist or nationalist aggressions upon people's communal spaces.

CLOTHING THE EMPEROR

Two million French workers in the streets and several weeks of massive strikes did not stop the "neoliberal" design for France. A million farmers of India demonstrating against GATT did nothing to stop the threat the latter is posing to their lives. In contrast, Gandhi's Salt March, the simple decision of the oppressed to make their own salt in their streets and neighborhoods, could be considered decisive in ending the global British Empire. The rebellion of a few hundred Indians, poorly armed, could begin the end of the nation-state of Mexico. All these cases help us to understand the nature of modern power. However, they illustrate two distinct modes of power struggles: those that clothe the Emperor in contrast with others that disrobe him. Examining the reasons for their differential outcomes may help to see how real men and women can successfully exercise their power to pursue their own purposes; or, alternatively, be highly counterproductive in their confrontations with the "global forces" threatening them.

With the Salt March, Gandhi rendered naked the inhumanity of colonial domination. By doing so, he also revealed to the "common" men and women of India their own power to liberate themselves from colonial oppression. When Gandhi mobilized the people for "self-rule" (swaraj) through initiatives that involved taking over their own production of salt in deliberate violation of oppressive British laws, the colonial government deliberately refused to put him in jail, having learned from past experiences that every incarceration only increased Gandhi's power to disregard his "rulers." Ignorant of the possibility that millions of oppressed Indians would follow Gandhi's initiative by producing salt in every corner of India in order to regain their own autonomy and power, the Viceroy discovered his miscalculation too late. By then, it was obvious to the colonized "social majorities" that their minority colonizers did not have enough jails to incarcerate all those audaciously disregarding their oppressors' laws. The tax imposed by the British on salt production was economically irrelevant for both the government and the people. But it had symbolic value and critical importance as a means of establishing minority control over the majority. The simple decision of the latter to reject such control broke a fundamental principle of colonial government. In autonomously producing salt for themselves or weaving their traditional clothes – instead of buying British textiles – India's masses rediscovered their own strength and power. Nothing else has proved to be more effective in dismantling an entrenched, "powerful," well-established, politically oppressive regime.

The French workers will probably succeed in their struggle to slow down the actual materialization of a plan depriving them of their "rights" to jobs, pension plans or personal security. But even if they kill the Juppé plan, and even though they have helped to throw Juppé himself out of office, they will only get more or less of the same from the machinery of the state to which they are presenting their "rights" or demands. By claiming from the state what the state has (or does not have), they are strengthening it; further feeding the myth of its centrality, its importance to their lives. Following its logic, the government will negotiate with the unions and a "good" agreement will finally be reached: a compromise between what the workers want to protect and what the government needs to dismantle. But the very basic "issue," the evil threatening people's lives in France and everywhere else, will remain untouched.

"What resists, supports," once observed an old Mexican politician, taking his metaphor from engineering: resistance of materials makes for sound construction. By strongly *opposing* Juppé's plan, French workers are, at the same time, legitimizing its authors; revealing how much they need them; engaged in a power dispute in which "the people" remain the weaker party. Gandhi's radicalism lay in the philosophy and praxis of simply ignoring British "power" – its laws, its technology, its industry. Turning away from political structures that weaken "the people," he moved the struggle for power to spaces where they can exercise their capacities for self–rule; governance that renders redundant rulers "on top." Affirming the liberation of "the people" from their rulers, he was underscoring the opposite: the dependency of the "rulers" upon the "ruled" for maintaining the myth that the former possess power, or that power is concentrated at the top of pyramidal structures.

Failing to take paths like Gandhi's in their own liberation, those resisting recolonization today through GATT and other "global forces" are not overcoming the real threats these pose for the "social majorities" across the world, including millions of farmers in India. By concentrating their attacks on the institution, on the emblem of those arrangements, they render even more opaque the technological system that maintains the myth of global power. This opacity hides the nakedness of the Emperor. In this darkness, it is easy to maintain the pretence that the Emperor is clothed. All the energy used for the massive demonstrations organized by the prestigious activists of India has not only proved to be sterile; it has further added bureaucrats to the heavy structure of GATT, reinforcing the feeling of powerlessness "the people" experience before such Goliaths.

Real men and women, like monuments or pacts, are often the symbols of a complex evil: a whole set of social relations and institutional arrange-ments. Destroying them can have a powerful symbolic impact, when that action reveals their nature and weaknesses, while enriching "the people's" awareness of how to deal with them. The Bastille, the Winter Palace, the Berlin Wall, are now classic examples that demonstrate the end of an era through the final destruction of some of its main symbols of power. The opposite can happen, however, if the assaults are launched against the priests, the ghosts, the rituals, the clothing, of the identified evil, while leaving the latter intact. Rather than weakening or destroying it, the action may strengthen it; rather than awareness, it may generate blindness.

What is usually called "the western project" attempts to universalize all its institutions; that is, to impose everywhere the same set of behaviors, attitudes, arrangements, norms and rules. The best model is still the Catholic Church ("catholic" means universal). Its paradigm has shaped and molded most modern institutions. GATT is but a contemporary manifestation of the "western project." Like all its predecessors, it is but a collection of rules and arrangements to be imposed everywhere. The long process of negotiations in the Uruguay Round and its conclusion (the WTO) propitiated an unprecedented concentration of specific "forces," which adopted a common charter to promote their personal and collective interests. GATT or the World Bank are emblems, symbols or paradigms that serve to express both a set of arrangements and a balance of forces. They are unbeatable at the abstract level. For, in the abstract, they represent, no more and no less, most governments of the world, most corporate interests, etc. To struggle against them at that level tends to strengthen them. To identify the implications of GATT, to be fully aware of what it means in specific local struggles everywhere, is extremely useful. To transform such awareness into organizing principles for concerting a world struggle against GATT or the World Bank, at their headquarters or their jamborees, seems to be useless or counterproductive. They are unbeatable on their own turf – as the UNCED, in Rio, aptly demonstrated. Moving beyond their turf to the local level makes it possible to see their irrelevance. In that seeing, their nakedness becomes impossible to hide. Opacity is easier to maintain when the institution is acknowledged as a global force to be contended with. Local operations and their functionaries are easier to see through; their nakedness more difficult to hide. Here, local struggles can make them irrelevant at the localized level; and an accumulation of local struggles may well produce the formulation of a new set of arrangements.

Acquiescence to the assumption that "global forces" have the power only serves to clothe their nakedness, thereby supporting them; feeding and strengthening them. Every transnational corporation, every imperialist government, every coalition of the Big and the Powerful, has an abstract, emblematic, illusory existence in the real world; they are but "virtual realities" (non-realities). Coca Cola or Marlboro have no "real existence" or power where people ignore them; they have no more power than the power people give to them by "believing" in what they offer. In most cases, people defeated colonial governments by turning against them the logic of their operations (transforming the benefit into a loss); doing so by dismantling the prevailing belief in their power, through either violent (Vietnam) or non-violent (India) means. The power of a colonial government ends at the very minute that the colonized cease to believe in it. Sooner or later, the force it can still apply to exert its domination will vanish, or it will be impossible to use it, if no power is given to it by the ruled.

The Catholic Church seemed in its time even more powerful, in relative terms, than the modern arrangements of the western "Global Project." It was able to resist any attempt to destroy its symbols or operators, following its own beginnings: killing Christ was not the end of Christianity, but its beginning. But it failed in its fundamental purpose, even in the places where the Cross came with the Sword. No global challenge to its world-wide domination ever succeeded. But sooner or later, most local challenges to its domination can and do succeed; for example, through local disregard for the parish priest's admonitions and injunctions in the name of the Pope.

In advancing both local thinking and action, we are also explicitly advocating initiatives for interconnecting local struggles. These interconnections, more likely than not, are easier forged around the politics of "No"; a common rejection which defines diverse affirmations. We are not advocating blindness, parochialism or anti-intellectualism. "Global thinking" is not abstract thinking; it is an oxymoron. There is often a clear need for abstract analysis in order to know as much as possible about the logic shaping those "global forces." Local thinking should be capable of identifying the nature of these forces existing at the local level.

Clearly, to counter the current situation, mythopoetic capacities are urgently needed. For it seems necessary to generate new myths as a substitute for those that have dominated the imagination of people for such a long time and are now losing their meaning and, therefore, their hold. But myths should not be taken as if they were descriptions of reality. By bringing differentiated myths to the forefront, and exposing them to critical awareness, their power can be undercut: they cease to function as myths or presuppositions. "A myth is precisely what escapes our awareness. It is the un-thought. The moment we become aware of it, it disappears and remythicizes or transmythicizes itself" (Raimón Panikkar, quoted by Vachon, 1995a, p. 13).

THE POWER OF THINKING
AND ACTING LOCALLY

Local initiatives, no matter how wisely conceived, prima facie seem too small to counteract the "global forces" now daily invading our lives and environments. The whole history of economic development, in its colonialist, socialist or capitalist forms, is a terrible true tale of violent interventions by brutal forces "persuading" – with the use of weapons, economic lures and "education" – small communities to surrender. Furthermore, some of the contemporary threats, as Chernobyl illustrated in a horrifying way, do not respect any frontier – national, communal or ideological. The wise decision taken by the Austrians, to ban nuclear plants in their own territory, becomes irrelevant when some are operating 50 kilometers from their frontiers.

Innumerable similar cases give ample proof that local peoples often need outside allies to create a critical mass of political opposition capable of stopping those forces. But the solidarity of coalitions and alliances does not call for "thinking globally." In fact what is needed is exactly the opposite: people thinking and acting locally, while forging solidarity with other local forces that share this opposition to the "global thinking" and "global forces" threatening local spaces. For its strength, the struggle against Goliath enemies does not need to abandon its local inspiration and firmly rooted local thought. When local movements or initiatives lose the ground under their feet, moving their struggle into the enemy's territory – global arenas constructed by global thinking – they become minor players in the global game, doomed to lose their battles.

The Earth Summit is perhaps the best contemporary illustration of this sequence. Motivated by global thinking, thousands of local groups flew across the world to Rio only to see their valuable initiatives transmogrified into nothing more than a footnote to the global agreements, conceived and now being implemented by the Big and the Powerful. Prescient of this failure of "Thinking Big" or global, Berry (1972) accurately predicted that the global environmental movement, following the "grand highways" taken by the peace and civil rights movements, would lose its vitality and strength, uprooted out of its natural ground: the immediate spaces of real men and women who think and act locally.

NON-PROVINCIAL LOCALISM: FORGING HUMAN SOLIDARITIES

Our contention that global powers may be effectively opposed through modest local action is affirmed by carefully documented evidence. *The Ecologist*'s book, *Whose Common Future?* (The Ecologist, 1993) is an outstanding example of a growing genre. Instead of an illusion, we have before our eyes the real enfleshed experience of millions, documented in a wide variety of circumstances. But this does not mean that success always accompanies local struggles or that the "global forces" are being dissolved by these initiatives. In many cases, the results are ambiguous.

The World Bank and the Japanese government abandoned the Narmada project, thus scaling down one of the most damaging development projects conceived by those "global forces." Such success was based on local actions, well articulated for many grassroots networks which offered an active solidarity for that purpose. But the very nature of that "global threat" became finally evident when the Indian government, and particularly some provincial governments of India, assumed the project and are currently implementing it. Local initiatives were able to modify the local balance of forces, thus forcing the Goliaths involved to abandon the project. But they were not able to reach the point of displacing the "intimate enemy": the local, colonized agents, whose global thinking is now being imposed on "the people" (Esteva and Prakash, 1992). In other cases, successful struggles, constituted of modest local actions, have only relocated the projects of "global forces," moving them to places where they confront less resistance.

The Ecologist also offers substantial evidence for our conclusion that it is an illusion, both arrogant and counterproductive, to fight against those "global powers" on their own territory: the "global scene." Its account of the Earth Summit is a sad testimony to the wasted efforts of the best independent environmentalists, now trivialized in charters that the Big and the Powerful are using to protect and promote their own interests. As we have mentioned, "global powers" can only have material existence, and do the harm they are doing, in their local incarnations. David overcame Goliath in his own territory and won; he did not need to adopt the strength and technology of Goliath for his victory, but used his own tools, which he mastered so well. For the very logic of those "global powers" forces them to leave places where they confront persistent, rooted, fiery local opposition. Every local initiative can give good use to the information that others, with similar concerns, may provide to them. They may also benefit from their alliances with other men and women struggling against similar threats in their own spaces. The solidarity they may obtain through these linkages can be of critical importance for their concrete struggle. But groups linked through solidarity must not fall into the arrogance of growing too big for their own boots; escaping from the human scale to become like their enemies in the deleterious arena where the latter dominate. The British Green Party is just one among many grassroots groups that have begun to ape their global enemies in the false hopes of thus overcoming them on the latter's turf (Papworth, 1995a, 1995b, 1995c).

Their mistakes are wisely avoided by those who choose to live, to think and to act on the appropriate scale: in proportion to the human capacity for knowledge and comprehension. It is a wisdom reflected by the best known local initiatives. The Zapatista movement, once again, offers a very good case in point – even if their international fame at this juncture might make them appear like globalists. The Zapatistas successfully activated thousands of initiatives of people who disseminated their manifestos and communiqués through the national and international communication networks, thus bringing world attention to the resistance of local communities in Chiapas against their oppression by the state, and by different national and international organizations.[15] Within hours of their uprising organized for January 1, 1994, the Zapatistas made global news. Publics as far away as in India and Hong Kong were discussing the letters of Marcos and the other spokespersons for the Zapatistas. True, the Zapatistas won the battle of public opinion, as Octavio Paz recognized. By spreading their message across local and national boundaries, they created a national and international solidarity between grassroots organizations. This morally and politically prevented the national government from stifling their movement in the manner of the sixties or the seventies repressions. Such success was not the result of their mastering global thinking or global tools, but exactly the opposite. The media success of the Zapatistas in fact came from the very nature of their struggle and discourse: local and truthful, so distant from any pretension to sell themselves to others or involve others in some grand transnational ideology. This instantly made them both exceptional and a media event.

Despite the global emergence of solidarity for their cause, and despite the global relevance as well as spread of their message to oppressed and abused groups in every nation-state, it would be a mistake to present the Zapatistas as engaged in global thought. Their concern for injustice across the globe, their sense of solidarity with the marginalized of the earth, does not come with the vast baggage of some universal conception of justice. By proposing conceptions of self-governance following their own indigenous traditions, they are simply opening the door for others to escape the monoculture and homogeneity of the model of governance imposed by nation-states world-wide. The doors they are opening lead to a wide diversity of cultural routes, and a celebration of multiculturalism destroyed by even the best-intentioned "global thinking."

Global forces, in their local incarnation, were challenged by the Zapatistas. Local initiatives spread that challenge around the globe, forging resistance against other local incarnations of those global forces, forcing the latter to take the first step back. The "Zapatista journal," started by a librarian in California and disseminated through e-mail, has a "local profile," used by many local people, actively exerting local pressures upon the local incarnations of global chains. The group Acción Zapatista, of Austin, Texas,[16] has started to regenerate the old art of pamphleteering, while at the same time giving highly sophisticated use to state-of-the-art techniques and technologies of "internetting." Corporations and governments are investing millions of dollars in R&D to mimic what grassroots groups of this kind are doing, attempting to mastermind ways of stopping them. There is no single "global tool" for a "global confrontation" associated with the Zapatistas – although thousands of pages are being written and circulated about them, while an incredible amount of video footage is now being transmitted or shared around the globe.

SETTLING IN A PLURIVERSE

Liberation from the logic of "global forces" implies "rethinking the world." It requires a shift in focus from the goal of living in One World, a universe. In its stead, the door is opened for settling in a pluriverse. The importance of the Zapatistas for that endeavor can be attributed to the content and scope of their struggle. Well rooted in their tradition, while fully aware of contemporary reality, they are discovering veins of hope, of alternatives, even in the middle of the fin-de-siècle turbulence and the bankruptcy of dominant ideologies. They are awakening, moving and stimulating the creative imagination of many others, who were already involved in similar concerns and struggles but often found themselves at a dead end.

What is happening in Mexico is not just a "democratic transition," analogous to what happened in Spain a few years ago. It is more than an answer to neoliberal policies which merely tries to soften the impact of the globalized economy and the free trade catechism. It is the revolution needed for the creation of new or post-modern commons. It is the first revolution of the twenty-first century, tearing apart the frame of the economic society and the nation-state, after its rupture with the fundamental premises of the modern era. "With the EZLN movement," said Marcos, its speaker, "has come something you have never in your life dreamed of." It is still vague and diffuse. It is taking shape in the horizon as a rainbow. Like a rainbow, it is impossible to reach it and useless to try to give it precision. We will not attempt to do that. We know that the lenses of radical democracy, of cultural autonomy may help to appreciate it ... and to better enjoy it.

The word "autonomy" does not exist in any of the hundred languages spoken by the Indian peoples of Mexico. Autonomist struggles are not part of their tradition. By including autonomy in their current agenda, they appealed perhaps to one of their traditions for struggling against their oppressors: using the language of the dominant society to restrain its force. They thus elicited confusion and resistance. Their claims for autonomy do not imply separatism or fundamentalism. But neither can they be reduced to a mere search for democratic decentralization of the functions of government. While many groups, particularly in the government, resist considering any form of autonomy for the Indian groups, many others do not only support the latter claim, but are also finding that it may well represent what they are looking for, in their own contexts. The grassroots global distribution of the writings of the Zapatistas is not only the result of the genius, humaneness and historical density revealed and expressed in them. It comes because of the relevant resonances that their movement has for the concerns and hopes of many people around the world. They invite others to liberate themselves, opening windows of hope.

Local autonomy is the only available antidote for the "Global Project." Just as locally autonomous persons started bringing down the Berlin Wall brick by brick, similarly locally autonomous communities can exert their powers to say "No" to all global agendas that destroy their natural and cultural spaces. The current struggle for autonomy in Mexico[17] mainly looks for recognition and respect for what Indian peoples already have. Autonomy is not something that we need to ask of someone or somebody can give us, observed an Indian leader. We occupy a territory, in which we exercise self-governance and justice in our own ways, he clarified, noting furthermore that his peoples have capacities for self-defense. We now claim recognition and respect for what we have already conquered, he stated firmly.

This leader's vision and approach is illusory or reactionary for the "social minorities" who "manage" the modern state, in Mexico and everywhere else. The lands and forms of government, justice and self-defense of Indian peoples suffer continual interference by market or state forces, and have been severely damaged. To struggle to conserve what they have would be like condemning them to their present marginality; and to enclose them in their battered modes of living or systems of government. The question now seems to be to give Indian peoples full access to what modern nations claim as part of the state's jurisdiction, thus widening and strengthening their autonomy.

This is a central issue. Indian peoples are not abandoning their old claims to recover whatever has been taken away from them; they present them with more firmness than ever. But by centering their claim in recognition and respect for what they have, they allude to a capacity for cultural self-determination which challenges the foundations of the universalist assumptions of modern thinking and cannot be contained within the confines of autonomist traditions, in Europe and elsewhere. Despite the decimation and annihilation they have suffered, the Indian peoples of

Mexico have succeeded in giving historical continuity to their condition. They want to continue being themselves in the contemporary world.

In the modern English tradition, "self-government" and "local autonomy" have become interchangeable. Both the terms are misleading: rather than self-determination and local freedom, they express the outcome of a process of absorption and integration of local or indigenous patterns of government by the nation-state. Decentralization became the mechanism used by the centralist state to impose itself over the independent exercise of local freedoms, to enforce its control over them and to make more effective and efficient its oppressive administration. In England, the enclosure of the commons affected the material, social and political bases of villages and parishes, dissolved through the reform of the Poor Laws in 1834. The intervention of state powers in local spaces was completed through the Municipal Corporations Act (1835), the Public Health Act (1848), the legislation on compulsory (1876) and free (1891) schooling, and with the Local Government Act (1888). Administrative decentralization, self-administration (local election of state officials) and democracy (citizens' participation in orienting public policies), propitiated the integration of local life to the centralized administration, whose increasing complexity continually weakened the decentralized management of local affairs and reinforced their dependence on the administrative center (Cammeli, 1982).

These traditions and tools of domination, in the continental European version, were established by the Spaniards in the territory of what is called Mexico today. The municipality had a clear centralist character, as a decentralized form for the implementation of colonial administration. The resistance of Indian peoples to that institution, hostile and alien to them, whose excluding character and vertical design were maintained in Independent and Revolutionary Mexico, compelled them to consolidate and enrich non-formalized political styles for their own government, constituted as the opposite to centralized institutions. In time, when Indian peoples succeeded in their appropriation of some of those state apparatuses, they gave them new functions. They transformed them into hinges for their relations with the state, in and through which all of their contradictions with it were reflected.

Current grassroots struggles for radical democracy are not looking for a more democratic access to the existing structures of the modern state, supposedly or conventionally democratic. Respecting their own political styles and designs, they seek to go beyond the decentralization of state structures. They radically differentiate this from decentralism, for the latter refers to authentic government by the people themselves. It cannot be reduced to the modern cliché of "self-government" – a euphemism for the democratic integration of everyone to state rule. De-centralization has as a premise a notion of power which centralizes it at the top – delegating it from the top down through levels of competence. Decentralism, in radical contrast, retains power in the hands of "the people" – re-creating, regenerating and relying upon political bodies on the human scale, constructing from the bottom up mechanisms for delegating limited functions to the state for concerting the harmonious coexistence of local units.

In Canada, some years ago, we had the opportunity to attend a debate between the government official in charge of Indian affairs and a Mohawk chief. This debate illustrates the meaning of contemporary post-modern struggles and their difference from conventional percep-tions of decentralizing power and control. "You must understand," said the official with some impatience, after many hours of discussion, "that the Canadian government will never accept the sovereignty of the Mohawk people." "We have no interest in getting sovereignty," firmly answered the chief; "for us sovereignty does not imply building frontiers with 'No trespass' signs. In our language, to be sovereign is to be free like the wind. That is what we want."

At the end of August 1995, Marcos, the speaker of the Zapatistas, pointed out in an interview:

> The proposals of the government ... want to conclude the Conquest of Mexico ... [through] a process of absorption and destruction of what make our peoples Indians: their culture ... The problem, for us, is not seizing power, but who exerts it.... We bring the problem of power to another space, more plural, more unselfish, where positions of force do not play. And there, in that new space, we hope to build something new.[18]

That is the issue in the current struggle of Indian peoples. It unites them in solidarity with indigenous peoples on all the continents, no longer begging for handouts or charity by the state and its global alliances.

BEYOND THE NATION-STATE

Like other indigenous peoples, Indians have ceased to assume the current design of the state as a point of reference for their political dreams. They can deal with state representatives coming into their spaces to handle some inter-communal conflicts or to present their claims – something they accepted or settled for in the past with all dominant structures. But they do not adopt state systems as their own: they do not assume these as the horizon of their own political conceptions. Furthermore, in making explicit their rejection of the present state regime, Indian peoples do not feel the need to have a blueprint of the new political design. They think that alternative paths will be made even as "the people" walk along the way towards their liberation from the oppressive structures of the state; that it will be enough to walk new paths towards more or less diffuse notions, like rainbows, of socio-political or cultural regimes that will be substitutes for the present one.

Marcos recently clarified that the alternative they are looking for will not come from the government, the political parties or the EZLN, but from "something new." The source of this alternative is not yet clear, hence the need to talk with others, those with whom the Zapatistas seem to have been syntonically linked since January 1994. And thus Indian peoples, well rooted in their diverse traditions, fluidly articulate themselves with some of the most advanced trends of contemporary political thinking. These dispense with the vision of "the society as a whole" as a premise for political action (Foucault, 1977). That is why the Zapatistas continue to find active solidarity across the globe for their surprising initiatives.

The radical rejection of the nation-state, as a politico-juridical design, may seem romantic and illusory to "realists" who fail to see in current trends any possibility for its dismantling. Seeing, in fact, the opposite, believers in the myth of the self-regulating market continue to under-score the need for nation-states as essential for controlling the social order. The more the "free market" will reign over the world, the more those means will be needed.

Critical debates about the nation-state,[19] however, offer good rea-sons for its demise. Their structures were conceived and implemented to administer national economies, and are rapidly losing their capacity to perform that function, both because no economy can any longer be called truly "national" and because the means of control of the na-tional and international statist structures of the postwar era have been reduced or dismantled. The erosion of credibility and influence of those structures has caused a pervading sense of impotence. One of the best formulations for this perception comes fom David C. Korten: "We are experiencing accelerating social and environmental disintegration in nearly every country of the world – as revealed by a rise in poverty, unemployment, inequality, violent crime, failing families, and environ-mental degradation ... governments seem wholly incapable of respond-ing, and public frustration is turning to rage" (Korten, 1996, pp. 11–12).

Nation-states will probably last for many generations to come. They can adapt to new conditions. They still embody not only powerful vested interests, but also the hopes of many people, who find in them a funda-mental sign of identity. Many others, however, have started to advance in the construction of alternative structures. The latter endeavors should be clearly distinguished from those who struggle against the current nation-states, but only to create their own, through peaceful or violent means, like in Czechoslovakia or Yugoslavia. What grassroots groups are doing, as reflected in the initiatives of the Zapatistas, is renouncing the frame of reference of the nation-state, without falling into the myth of globalization. By rooting themselves in their local spaces and weaving webs of solidarity with others like them, they are effectively applying *the* necessary antidote for the "Global Project:" local autonomy.

There is a growing body of literature, moving now from the marginal press to mainstream publications, to describe those heterogeneous experiences.[20] Many of them have as a common denominator a radical departure from any form of global thinking, and a courageous effort to delink themselves from the "Global Project." We have already alluded to the movement of Community Supported Agriculture, rapidly spreading, with many different variants, in all industrial countries. There are growing numbers of experiments with "alternative currencies," which create local control of the exchange of goods and services, promote self-sufficiency and social justice through reducing the dependency on the market or the state.

They do not have the visibility of massive mobilizations, like that of the French workers. Prima facie, they seem to have no effect upon the power structures of the market or the state. However, they are effectively undermining the dominant system and the "Global Project" – at the only level where these can be undermined. Conventional power disputes, in contrast, barely modify the balance of forces and the current trends. Local autonomy has a hundred, a thousand, a million incarnations. In a pluriverse, there can be no one dominant notion of autonomy. In a pluriverse, there are local spaces for endless diversity. Initiatives for autonomy and independence taking place in an isolated village in the south of Mexico seem to have no relation to the struggles of peoples in downtown Mexico City, and even less with those in Vancouver, Philadelphia, Bangkok, Boston, Paris, Delhi or Chapel Hill. But they belong to the same ilk. They are independent initiatives, applying ingenuity and courage, taken by people who are succeeding in relearning to rule themselves. Seeing through the grand myth of global power, they recognize that autonomy means not "needing" the bill of goods, the "gifts" being promoted by "global forces." In these ways, "the people" are regaining confidence in being themselves.

The drive for autonomy reflected in all those experiences is now also defining many social movements. Their claims are no longer concentrated in demanding that the state meet their needs. Instead, their quests for liberation are defined by exercising their freedoms. Many Greens are recovering their original critique of industrial society, and using their energy to locally reorganize attitudes and practices, rather than national marches and sit-ins in state capitals. As Betty Friedan pointed out at the International Women's Conference in Beijing in 1995, many feminists are turning their attention to local affairs, identifying women's struggle with community well-being. In each and every case, people are giving to autonomy the specific meaning appropriate for their localized contexts and concerns, always expressing an attempt of self-determination, braking and breaking the homogenized commands of the "Global Project."

The struggle for autonomy seems to be but the new name of an old notion of power: people's power, exercising unprecedented impetus in its contemporary forms at the grassroots.

BEYOND GLOBAL NEOLIBERALISM: THE INTERNATIONAL OF HOPE

On January 1, 1996, the Zapatistas launched their Fourth Declaration of the Selva Lacandona, which reflects the slow process of affirmation and flourishing of their movement. In Chapter 5, we will examine the political theory and proposals implicit in the Declaration. We want to end this chapter with the First Declaration of La Realidad,[21] launched a few days later. It is an invitation to local groups in different parts of the earth, calling them to organize an Intercontinental Encounter "For Humanity and Against Neoliberalism."

All across the globe, communities and grassroots organizations are resonating with it and responding to the call. For some observers, it represents not only global thinking but an attempt at global action. The initiative, however, reveals an alternative paradigm to both. It offers an excellent illustration of a local initiative based on local thinking which liberates all those across the globe touched by it precisely because it escapes the oppressive parochialism of global thinking.

The Declaration of La Realidad starts with a Náhuatl poem:

> Now I have arrived
> Now I am here, present,
> I the singer.
> Now is the time to celebrate,
> Come here and present yourself,
> those who have an aching heart.
> I raise my song.

It addresses "the people of the world" in the following terms:

During recent years, the power of money has presented a new mask over its criminal face. Beyond borders, without regard to race or color, the power of money humiliates dignity, insults honesty and assassinates hope. Renamed "Neoliberalism," the historical crime of the concentration of privileges, riches and impunity has democraticized misery and hopelessness.

A new world war is being unleashed, but now against all humanity. As in all the world wars, what this one seeks is a new division of the world.

They call this modern war "globalization," it assassinates and forgets. The new division of the world concentrates power within power and misery within misery.

The new division of the world excludes the "minorities." Indigenous people, the youth, women, gays and lesbians, people of color, immigrants, workers, campesinos; the majorities that make up the world basement are seen, by the power, as dispensable minorities. The new division of the world excludes the majorities.

The modern army of financial capital and corrupt governments advances, conquering in the only way it is capable: by destroying. The new division of the world destroys humanity.

The new division of the world only has room for money and its servants. Men, women and machines are equal as servants and disposable beings. Lies govern and multiply in means and manners.

A new lie is being sold to us as history. The lie of the defeat of hope, the lie of the defeat of dignity, the lie of the defeat of humanity. The mirror of power offers us an equilibrium: the lie of the victory of cynicism, the lie of the victory of servility, the lie of the victory of neoliberalism.

In place of humanity, they offer us the stock market index. In place of dignity, they offer us the globalization of misery. In place of hope, they offer us emptiness. In place of life, they offer us an International of Terror.

Against the International of Terror that neoliberalism represents, we must raise an International of Hope.[22] Unity, beyond borders, languages, colors, cultures, sexes, strategies and thoughts, of all those who prefer a living humanity.

The International of Hope. Not the bureaucracy of hope, not an image inverse to, and thus similar to, what is annihilating us. Not power with a new sign or new clothes. A flower, yes, that flower of hope. A song, yes, the song of life.

Dignity is that country without nationality, that rainbow that is also a bridge, that murmuring of a heart regardless of the blood within it, that rebel irreverence that scoffs at borders, customs agents and wars.

Hope is that rebelliousness that rejects conformism and defeat.

Life is what they owe us: the right to govern and to govern ourselves; to think and act with a liberty that is not exercised at the cost of the slavery of others; the right to give and receive what is fair.

Because of all this, together with others who, beyond borders, races and colors, share the song of life, the struggle against death, the flower of hope and the breath of dignity...

Struggling for the protection of their own spaces from the cultural imperialism of neoliberalism, the Zapatistas speak:

To all those who fight for the human values of democracy, freedom and hope.

To all those who make the effort to resist the world crime called "Neo-liberalism" and whose aspiration is that humanity and the hope to be better become synonymous in the future.

To all the individuals, groups, collectives, movements, social organizations, citizen and political organizations, to the unions, neighborhood associations, cooperatives, all the lefts that have been and are to be, non-governmental organizations, solidarity groups with the struggles of the peoples of the world, gangs, tribes, intellectuals, indigenous people, students, musicians, workers, artists, teachers, campesinos, cultural groups, youth movements, alternative means of communication, ecologists, settlers, lesbians, gay men, feminists, pacifists.

To all human beings without a house, without land, without work, without food, without health, without education, without liberty, without justice, without independence, without democracy, without peace, without a country, without a tomorrow.

To all those who, without regard to colors, races or borders, turn their hope into a weapon and a shield.[23]

While we were writing this chapter, the Encounter was held in the Selva Lacandona, following preparatory meetings held in five continents. Thousands of people across every continent reacted with imagination and creativity to this call, launched from the middle of the jungle by a small group of Indians surrounded by 50,000 troops. There was no "Steering" or "Central Committee" to organize or manage this World Conference. As all other communiques of the Zapatistas, the invitation to the Encounter, and some practical recommendations for those interested in attending, were published in the local press and circulated through the world-wide web of communication since January 1994.[24] Their struggle will not be "the bureaucracy of hope, not an image inverse to, and thus similar to, what is annihilating us." It will not be "power with a new sign or new clothes." It will be "a flower, yes, that flower of hope. A song, yes, the song of life."

This song is not beginning to be sung by some gigantic New Age coalition, a countervailing "power" to "global forces." Neither is it an event for holding hands across the world and chanting a New Age mantra. It is one of many profoundly practical initiatives to share knowledge and experiences of myriads of local experiments all over the globe, struggling to resist and survive, liberate themselves and flourish by refusing to submit to the Goliath of global neoliberalism. The International of Hope is only one initiative among others forging human solidarities needed to succesfully oppose the International of Terror, without moving on to its turf. It remains quintessentially local thinking and local action.

The Agenda for the meeting was simple: it invited "the people" to discuss how life is "under neoliberalism, how it is resisted, how to struggle and which are the proposals to continue struggling against it and for [human]kind," examining economic, political, social and cultural aspects. At the end of their call, the Zapatistas say:

> Brothers: Humanity lives in the breast of every one of us, and, like the heart, prefers the left side. We need to find her; we need to find ourselves.
> There is no need to conquer the world. It is enough that we make it again. We. Today.

Yvonne Dion-Buffalo and John Mohawk recently suggested that colonized peoples have three choices in response to colonization: become *good subjects*, accepting the premises of the modern West without much question; become *bad subjects*, always revolting against the parameters of the colonizing world; or become *non-subjects*, acting and thinking in ways far removed from those of the modern West.[25]

Like other grassroots groups, the Zapatistas are revealing what it means to be non- subjects, affirming their own forms of local thinking and action in their particular cultural spaces. They refuse to buy or sell global ideologies, political platforms, revolutionary plans or the appropriate way to participate in conventional politics and to struggle for power. They refuse to transform themselves into any form of enlightened vanguard or to reduce their action to a force game or to mere numbers in a "statistical democracy," trapped by the ballot box. At the beginning of the negotiations with the government, 150 people, representing a wide ideological spectrum and a diversity of qualities and experiences, accepted the invitation of the Zapatistas to be their advisors in that process. They were invited to La Realidad to talk with them. "What is your orientation?" asked one of those invited. "What is your conception of autonomy? What do you want from us?" "You are the ones to tell us," Marcos answered, smiling, and continued:

> We have our own notion of autonomy and we exert it in our spaces. But we know that it is not the only one, and it is not necessarily the better one. We are inviting you to bring your own experience, your own vision, to this common space, to weave there a consensus and to identify divergences, in order to explore what we can do together. You are the ones to give us alternative orientations. We are just committing ourselves to defend the positions emerging as a consensus as our own.

And so, for the first time in the history of this part of the planet, Indian peoples coming from all over the country, to the Dialogue of San Andrés or to the National Indian Forum convened by the Zapatistas, were able to weave a new fabric of ideas and actions, uniting them without dissolving them into a unique ideology, platform or bureaucratic organization. The new organization has no precedents. Before the Conquest, the Indian peoples inhabiting the territory of what is Mexico today had no need to come together in a single political body. During the colonial period, the struggle of resistance kept them separated. And in Independent Mexico, particularly in the second part of this century, all the efforts to unite them came from the top down. Precisely for that reason, all of them failed.

While planting their flowers of hope, grassroots movements like those of the Zapatistas are casting seeds that are flying freely with the wind to faraway places. There, in countless communities all over the immense earth, others are also striving to grow by escaping national and global "neoliberal" projects and designs; learning from each other's struggles how to evolve their own cultural notions of "a good life" lived in thriving local spaces.[26]

NOTES

1. "An assumption is … a principle I set at the base of my thinking process in a more or less explicit way. A presupposition, on the other hand, is something I uncritically and unreflectively take for granted. It belongs to the myth in which I live and out of which I draw material to feed my thinking" (Panikkar, quoted by Vachon, 1995a, pp. 12–13).

2. To study the different reasons Wendell Berry offers for opposing "global thinking," see Wendell Berry (1972, 1991a, 1991b). Also see Madhu Suri Prakash (1994). For other critiques of "global thinking," see Wolfgang Sachs (1993).

3. One good example is the recent case of an officer from Bavaria, Germany, who forced "global" censorship of some programs disseminated through the Internet, for local, parochial reasons. See John Perry Barlow, "Thinking Locally, Acting Globally," in *Time*, January 15, 1996, p. 41.

4. For the past three years at the Pennsylvania State University, we have been studying with Ivan Illich how, for the many millions raised on TV, Mickey Mouse has become as real as Ronald Reagan; that, worse yet, both are in fact larger than "real" life itself – as are TV phenomena like Michael Jackson, Madonna, among others. For his discussion of the destruction of the senses in the age of La Technique, see Illich (1994a, 1994b).

5. For a classic exploration of reductionism in science, see Caroline Merchant (1980).

6. See "One World," in Wolfgang Sachs (1992).

7. For a long time, a "problem" was a logical construct in geometry or mathematics which has a "solution" – usually only one. In today's world, a "problem" is a technical way for diagnosing personal and collective predicaments, shaping them in such a way that only the professionals and experts who construct the "problem" can offer the "solution" to it. See Uwe Pörksen (1995).

8. We are calling "alternative global thinkers" all those theoreticians and practitioners who explicitly oppose conventional global thinking, epitomized by the World Bank, while committed to global alternatives to it. The Worldwatch Institute,

David C. Korten, James Robertson, Greenpeace, exemplify such alternatives. David C. Korten is the founder and chair of People-Centered Development Forum (14 E 17th Street, Suite 5, New York, NY 10003, USA), which disseminates a regular column and promotes seminars, global campaigns, etc., on alternative developments. Among his books: *Getting to the 21st Century: Voluntary Action and the Global Agenda* (West Hartford, CT: Kumarian Press, 1990) and *When Corporations Rule the World* (West Hartford, CT: Kumarian Press, 1995). James Robertson is an active member of The Other Economic Summit, developing the 'Schumacher school' of economics. He publishes a newsletter, *Turning Point 2000* (The Old Bakehouse, Cholsey, Oxon OX10 9NU, UK). Among his books: *Future Work: Jobs, Self-Employment and Leisure After the Industrial Age* (London: Temple Smith/Gower, 1985) *Health, Wealth, and The New Economics: An Agenda for a Healthier World* (London: TOES, 1985).

9. "La ciudadanía planetaria, una lejana esperanza," interview with Leonardo Boff, in *Reforma*, January 24, 1996.

10. It is a real challenge to describe a "global frame of mind". What global corporations and imperialist governments engage in cannot be called thinking, as Wendell Berry warns. But many people have started to adopt the same attitude, the same approach, by reducing the Earth to its statistical descriptors. We call that attitude a "global frame of mind."

11. For an analysis of the post-modern Zapatista movement signalling the end of the modern era in Mexico, see Gustavo Esteva (1994a, 1994b). Also see Autonomedia (1994). For analyses of other important local movements, see Esteva and Prakash (1992); The Ecologist (1993).

12. Even if the regime does not recognize it, publicly or privately, the change is an undeniable one for the people.

13. See Raimón Panikkar (1990a, 1990b). For his discussion of radical pluralism, see Raimón Pannikar (1979).

14. For the important differences that distinguish "dwellers" of places from modern "residents," see David Orr (1992). Global citizens are the antithesis of dwellers, participating in the project of destroying the places of the latter.

15. There was a spontaneous and rapid diffusion of the demands of the Zapatistas and reports on its actions through computer communication networks which connect vast numbers of people interested in events both inside and outside of Mexico. "This diffusion, which flashed into conferences and lists on networks as Peacenet, Internet and Usenet, was then collected, sorted, compiled and sometimes synthesized and rediffused by particularly interested parties in the nets. For example, the Latin American Data Base at New Mexico State University began to issue a regular issue Chiapas Digest. The Mexican Rural Development discussion group of the Applied Anthropology Computer Network began to compile news and analysis and make it available through an easily accesible gopher site: Chiapas-Zapatista News. The Institute for Latin American Studies at the University of Texas has duplicated those files at its own Lanic gopher site." See Harry Cleaver (1994).

16. For the most complete and the most recent publications on the Zapatistas, contact this network at the following e-mail address: nave@uts.cc.utexas.edu. For the Zapnet collective contact zapnet@actlab.utexas.edu (e-mail) or 311 Tom Green, #405, Austin, TX 78705, USA (mail). Their Web site is at http://www.actlab. utexas. edu/zapnet.

17. At the beginning of 1995, a group of independent organizations created the

National Indian Plural Assembly for Autonomy (ANIPA is its Spanish acronym) to elaborate upon a proposal for creating autonomous regions whose control remains in the hands of Indian peoples. The proposal was finally approved in the third meeting of ANIPA, on August 26–7, held in Oaxaca, a province where the majority of the people are Indians. The debate in this meeting, even more than the approved document – which is a contradictory instrument for negotiation and has suffered many changes afterwards – reflects the current state of the discussions about autonomy, now being held everywhere in Mexico. The issue has been a central theme in the negotiation between the Zapatistas and the government, but the debate is not confined to it. While all Indian peoples have been active in their internal discussion about their autonomy, many non-Indian groups are also participating in the public debate, in order to define what this political word means for them. In this and the following sections, we are drawing upon what was said in some of these meetings and other recent fora, as well as published pamphlets, manifestos, declarations and other materials.

18. *La Jornada*, August 25, 1995.

19. See, for example, Jean Marie Guéhenno (1995), who concludes that even the most powerful of nations, such as the United States, no longer have the capacity, in a global world, of protecting the peoples whose destiny they claim to embody from the uncertainties of the outside world. His arguments for the demise of the nation-state seem unpersuasive, and his prediction of an "imperial age," controlled by communication networks rather than by politics, does not have firm grounds. But his diagnosis of the current condition of the nation-state can be widely shared. Furthermore, some of his insights about the future role of state-less ethnic or religious communities in a world without national walls is attractive for all varieties of "communitarians." He thinks that they will provide a sense of belonging which the contemporary nation-states no longer furnish.

On April 23, 1982 a new republic was created in Key West, Florida, declaring its independence from Washington after a conflict with the federal government. When its "authorities" reached an agreement with the US government, the republic declared itself in a "latent state." It came again to life in November 1995, when the US government partially stopped its operations, due to its conflict with the Congress, and the "republic" announced that it was still in operation. The episode, which seems more like fiction than reality, illustrates the new forms of exacerbated nationalism or localism, emerging not only in the former Soviet Union or the Balkans, but even in the US.

Among the most insightful critiques of the modern nation-state is Leopold Kohr's *The Breakdown of Nations* (1986). Also see Fourth World Review, particularly John Papworth (1995a, 1995b, 1996).

20. See Gustavo Esteva (1993); also Pat Lauderdale (1991); Little Bear Leroy (1982); Robert Vachon (1991–3).

21. La Realidad is a small village in the middle of the Lacandona jungle, in the area occupied by the Zapatistas, where they have learned not only how to survive, but also to regenerate their cultures and commons.

22. "International of Terror" or "International of Hope" are not conventional formulations either in English or Spanish. Given the frequent use of historical expressions for the symbolic content to their current struggles, we are inclined to assume that the Zapatistas launched these peculiar idiomatic constructions to allude

to the nature of their endeavor. On the one hand, these peculiar titles remind us of the international conferences that for many years dominated both the thinking and the actions of the socialists and the communists (the First, the Second, the Third, the Fourth "International"). Yet these Zapatista reminders also side-step and go beyond that tradition, escaping both from a universalized ideology and from a world organization which is doomed to become a new bureacracy: "an image inverse to, and thus similar to, what is annihilating us." How can the "flower of hope" be organized by a bureaucracy?

23. *La Jornada*, January 30, 1996.

24. Given the unexpected response to their invitation, the Zapatistas could not host all the people who wanted to come to the small villages where the Encounter was held. They were finally forced to ask some friends to operate "national committees" so that quotas allocated for every country were not exceeded. Old habits of exclusion and internal political conflicts reproduced in some cases traditional patterns of selective inclusion. Whenever the Zapatistas were informed of such cases, they opened the door to the excluded. Other friends in Mexico assumed the tasks of local logistics – lodging, transportation, etc. – exercising their own initiatives. And thus, in a very informal way, without formal or hierarchical structures, through the independent initiatives of hundreds solidary with the Zapatistas, the International of Hope moved one step further along in a long, unpredictable, surprising and unfolding process of change.

25. Yvonne Dion-Buffalo and John Mohawk (1994), quoted in Frederique Apffel-Marglin (1995).

26. For a more extended discussion of the ideas presented in this chapter, see Gustavo Esteva and Madhu Suri Prakash (1996).

THREE

BEYOND THE INDIVIDUAL SELF: REGENERATING OURSELVES

I worry about minds, hearts and social rituals being infected by development, not only because it obliterates the unique beauty and goodness of the now, but also because it weakens the "we." … The multiple we was traditionally characteristic of the human condition; the "first person plural" is a flower born out of sharing in the good of convivial life. It is the opposite of the statistical "we," the sense of being jointly enumerated and represented in a graphic column. The new voluntaristic and empty we is the result of you and me, together with innumerable others, being made subject to the same technical management process – "we drivers," "we smokers," "we environmentalists." The I who experiences is replaced by an abstract point where many different statistical charts intersect. (Ivan Illich, conversation with Majid Rahnema, Bremen, December 13, 1994)

A person is always a personal existential reality, concrete, communal, a centre of the universe (a microcosm), and a whole, that is, holistic.… An individual (self) is always an abstraction, an impersonal unit of an impersonal collectivity, a particular aspect of some general definition, theory or system, or aggregate. It is always part of an abstract globe. (Robert Vachon, 1995b, p. 56)

Woe betide any man who depends on the abstract humanity of another for his food and protection. (Michael Ignatieff, 1984)

DIS-MEMBERING

Our son wants to celebrate his seventh birthday at McDonald's with his classmates, minus his extended family. After two years at school, he has successfully learned this norm, along with others regarding what is "cool." His first six birthdays have been communal feasts; with almost everything on the festive table prepared and served by his many uncles and aunts, grandparents, brothers, sisters and friends of our extended family: all those and others who were by our bed during or immediately after his birth; and have since cared for him. His affection for them notwithstanding, his school norms are already molding him to celebrate this annual rite outside the home, without the extended family; to prefer partying with his own age group at one of the commercial institutions of the "social minorities." Despite our desire not to taint his fascination with the world that surrounds him (which unfortunately includes McDonald's and other "industrial eating" establishments), we are concerned that not so long from now that same childish fascination will be transformed into "mature" habits, needs and addictions to what is now considered "normal" by millions.

Without embracing the anti-fast-food and related fundamentalisms of the "good parents" we know, how do we protect him from norms with ramifications as far-reaching as those of global tourism: setting up the same pre-fab units in far-off jungles, deserts and beaches to satisfy consumers who "need" the same Bed and Breakfast in foreign lands that constitutes the "norm" "back home"? How do we shelter him from the industrial eating which ensures that french fries are standardized to taste the same 10,000 miles apart: in India, Mexico or the US?

However banal our questions, they help us take our first timid, tentative steps into a dark and troubling realm: the crisis of modern identity. How do we explore our profound concerns about the "identity crisis" of the modern individual self shaped early in life by industrial eating, while escaping the banality of over-dramatizing the little take-out box of french fries manufactured for "the masses"?

The modern individual self is created as much by the food he or she is fed from birth, as s/he is by the school texts, computers, automobiles and other "goods" manufactured by and for industrial eaters. The making of modern identity, we are told, is "an achievement, an ensemble of ... understandings of what it is to be a human agent: the senses of inwardness, freedom, individuality ... at home in the modern West" (Taylor, 1989, p. ix). While celebrated by the "social minorities," the modern "individual self" suffers an anguish increasingly remunerative for their "shrinks." Studying this shrunk self, we have also started to learn from the "social majorities" how they escape being dis-membered: cut up into assuming the shape of an individual.

Our journey into the dis-memberment of modern men, women and children begins with the least understood aspect of contemporary life: the dehumanization of the most basic human act — the communal breaking of bread. "Consumers" educated by Ralph Nader, Frances Moore Lappé or the other watch-dog groups proliferating today to raise public awareness about "health," "physical fitness" and "good nutrition" have already been exposed to millions of pages of newsprint, revealing the social and environmental violence perpetrated not only by "fast food" but by the entire agri-business empire that lures and traps industrial eaters with promises of ease, speed, convenience and slender "health." Their struggles to have labels for calories, salt, fat and preservatives or other improvements in "consumer awareness" are moving ahead in conjunction with other environmentalisms (analyzing the comparative recyclability or decompositional quality of tetrapak vs styrafoam, or sixties-style campaigns for global justice that measure how many bowls of grain can be fed to the starving billions in exchange for one T-bone steak). Leaving to others to "manage" these campaigns for "health," "environmental education," "low-fat diets," "recycling vs incineration" and other "public interest" problems created by industrial eating, we shift our attention towards concerns cultural and agri(soil)-cultural; to *ethnos* and identity.

By destroying communal food, industrial eating transmogrifies peoples into "consumers," who consume commons in pursuit of the illusion of being an "individual self." Among the "dearest liberation" sought by "industrial eaters" is a "minimal involvement" with the growing or cooking of food. Convenience, ease, speed, saving time and energy for consuming food offer modern "freedom": to pursue the goals and activities that define modern identity.

Reflecting on this identity, Berry notes that an "educated" sixteen-year-old learns about making babies, but remains totally ignorant about growing the potatoes he or she daily eats. For the

> food industrialists have by now persuaded millions of consumers to prefer food that is already prepared. They will grow, deliver, and cook your food for you and (just like your mother) beg you to eat it. That they do not yet offer to insert it, prechewed, into your mouth is only because they have found no profitable way to do so. We may rest assured that they would be glad to find such a way. The ideal industrial food consumer would be strapped to a table with a tube running from the food factory directly into his or her stomach. (Berry, 1990, p. 146)

Dis-membered from communities, from rituals for the communion of food, the "passive American consumer" sits down to

> a meal of prepared or fast food, confronts a platter covered with inert, anonymous substances that have been processed, dyed, breaded, sauced, gravied, ground, pulped, strained, blended, prettified, and sanitized beyond resemblance to any part of any creature that ever lived. The products of nature and agriculture have been made, to all appearances, the products of industry. Both eater and eaten are thus in exile from biological reality. And the result is a kind of solitude, unprecedented in human experience, in which the eater may think of eating as, first, a purely commercial transaction between him and a supplier, and then as a purely appetitive transaction between him and his food. (Berry, 1990, p.148)

Behind the mirage of industrial eaters' "dearest liberation," Berry discerns death: throttled communal bonds which hold together peoples and their soils. Agri-business destroys agri-culture; replaces the traditional "we" with the modern "I": with eyes glued to TV screen, disconnected from the mouth masticating a microwavable meal. Industrial eating rips people apart, not only from each other, but even from their own senses. The mechanics of industrial cuisine (whether "exotically ethnic" or mundanely provincial) destroys the pleasures of eating, which are profoundly sensuous.

This results in two kinds of modern deserts: physical and cultural. Without the tending of human hands, top soil is being blown away, along with the stories, rituals and practices that make cultural soil. Soil (agri) culture gives way to machine "culture." To re-member people, joining them in communion with their place, commons and culture, their "we," Berry (1990, p. 152) remembers William Carlos Williams:

> There is nothing to eat,
>   seek it where you will,
>   but the body of the Lord.
> The blessed plants
>   and the sea, yield it
>   to the imagination
> intact.

Customs and rituals surrounding the growing, preparation and serving of food are at the heart of community and communion – "the profoundest enactment of our connection with the world" (Berry 1990, p. 152). Delving deep into these connections, we discover how eating "is a profoundly social and ecological event that connects us in the most intimate and primary way to others, to our land, water, and soil, to the future, and to other species.... Eating provides our most intimate association with the other" (Blair, 1996, pp. 297–8).

This communion of growing and cooking communal food is alien to "industrial eaters," using the metallic sound and plastic screen images of their TV sets to fill the void and loneliness of humans without commons; with senses numbed, eating in exile from their ancestral "we." Converts to the modern religion of convenience smell fast cash opportunities in the Global Project, spreading the plague that destroys sense and sensibility.

This plague has yet to kill the soil cultures of the "social majorities." To reflect on communion and commons for post-modern re-membership, we remember afresh some of our journeys amidst the "social majorities." "Education" that teaches the "dearest liberation" from growing or cooking food has not yet tainted them. Celebrating

communion and community through their mundane or highly ritualized celebrations of/with food, they enjoy the sensual pleasures of eating;
keeping alive their carnal bonds, physical and cultural, to their places.
With these glimpses into the communal food of the "social majorities," this chapter deepens our understanding of the annihilation and
dis-memberment that creates modern identity. We traverse the concrete
industrial highways moderns travel to enter the trap of the individual
self. How do modern institutions and technologies construct this self
by destroying the traditional "we," the "first person plural," the flower
born of the good of convivial life? How do the "social majorities"
stave off these modern giants, regenerating the traditions of their Dead,
strengthening their different "we's"?

In "deconstructing" some of the key elements used to contruct the
individual self, we speak to people who are beginning to find the prison
of the modern individual self as unbearable as we do; who are looking
for ways to escape the modern mindset, with its ideals of privacy that
separate us from each other; who wish to learn from the commons of
the "social majorities" diverse ways of rejoining and re-membering their
"we." Our grassroots journeys have convinced us that no real "we" (as
distinct from sociological or statistical abstractions like that of "classes" or
"masses") can be constituted by summations or additions of the individual
self; that real men and women must go through terrible mutilations and
distortions in order to think and to behave as an "individual self"; to
believe that they are atoms; or that they are unique juxtapositions or
compilations of diverse atoms "fused" into one person: "I am a woman,
an Iranian, an economist, with black eyes, an Aryan nose and a Ph.D.,
a reader of Foucault, a fan of the Beatles, a citizen of Australia, etc."
Douglas Lummis aptly reminds us of de Tocqueville, who defined individualism as a "failure of understanding"; that is, as an illusion. He never
described the US as a country of individuals, but as a people under the
illusion that they are individuals. Being under this illusion, they behave
in ways that leave them more "ragged" than "rugged" (Dewey, 1962).

On our venture of regenerating ourselves, escaping the modern myth
of the individual self, we display a few intuitions, hunches, anecdotes
and stories, in the way dealers place cards on the table. The images on
our cards differ from those found in the standard industrial pack. In the
game of liberation, dealing our way out of the standard industrial pack,
we begin with one of "the basics" of human life: food. In our quest to
regenerate ourselves, we bring into our midst foods that help re-member;
to rejoin in membership; reclaiming the types of different and diverse
"we's" by which non-moderns define themselves; such that no "I" could
possibly be understood without a "we," enfleshed, carnal and sensual. To

compare those traditions with contemporary experiences and reactions, we study the modern "I": the owner of a mind; whose memory and other mental functions have the capability of clicking on to Microsoft Windows '97; who is in the process of mutating from being a text to a screen, surfing ahead of the rest in the dawning Information Age.

RE-MEMBERING

Our explorations of community, communion and re-membering begin with one of the most basic or fundamental aspects of each culture, shaping from birth the persons initiated into it. While all humans eat, notions of personhood and personal identity vary so widely because of the equally wide differences in cultural patterns for growing, cooking, eating or celebrating their foods.

Our journey starts with the culture of *comida*. *Comida* belongs to an *ethnos*, but it can never be reduced to ethnic food. By crossing over the chasm that separates the first from the second, peoples are transmogrified into modern industrial eaters. *Comida* disappears where people buy, prepare and cook food to nourish the myth of the "individual self." Regenerating ourselves means, among other things, escaping the prison of industrial eating and ethnic foods.

To contrast the individual self (who consumes industrial food, ethnic or other) from the "we" of *comida*, we find ourselves remembering the beautiful small town of San Andrés Chicahuaxtla. In this town, situated in the northern mountains of Oaxaca, a fog sits most of the day, most of the year. Here people live, quite literally, in the clouds. They are Indians of the Triqui nation. All the women wear magnificent homespun huipiles, with horizontal rows of red and white in creative, very personal designs, conceived and woven by their wearers. They have magnificent stories. They love to tell of the time when a terrible plague of enormous grasshoppers devastated whole areas of Oaxaca, arriving finally at San Andrés. There, the plague ended. For they eat grasshoppers in a thousand forms. They are experts in capturing them. The kids, particularly, know how to skillfully play the hat in the grass for the capture. An expert will complacently agree that the grasshoppers are rich in protein; but, apart from that modern concern, they are in fact very tasty. When the plague of grasshoppers came to San Andrés, the Triquis ate them all. Now they have a prayer, begging them to return.

We remember when we first met doña Refugio, the mother of a friend who invited us to visit him. Since the 1940s, her husband, don Marcos was the leader of the town. He first brought peace to it, wisely conciliating with its neighbors all conflicts about limits. Every year, he leads the march around those limits, during which the whole town dances, sings and celebrates ... not to build walls, but to peacefully remember and affirm their agreements in a joyful encounter with their neighbors.

When development came to Oaxaca and the fantasies of the Triquis (like the fantasies of most of us, "underdeveloped" peoples) were captured by its promises, he conducted the successful struggle to bring to their town a road, a school, a health center and all the other development "marvels." Don Marcos' sons and a daughter followed the pattern of the times to participate in the ritual of "superior education." After completing or abandoning the university, all of them resigned from their urban careers and returned to the town.

In its constant struggle with the educational authorities, for many years the local school departed from the official curriculum, concentrating upon apprenticeships in skills that are locally needed – in agriculture, carpentry, craftmanship and other areas. One of the sons of don Marcos was responsible for this venture.

No doctor appeared in the Health Center, thus protecting the town from the usual medical interventions that disable traditional communities' healing capacities. Their ultra-modern building of the Center became a House for Guests. (Their decision may be seen as a reversal of the modern processes that have transformed hospitality into hospitals, as we will soon see in later sections of this chapter.)

When another son of don Marcos finished his studies as a doctor, he succeeded in getting the commission to work in the Health Center-cum-House for Guests. He clearly respected both the guests and his local traditions when he concluded that no "hospital beds" were really needed. Similarly, he transformed the operating room out of respect for the local women, who maintain their traditional squatting position when giving birth; and he refused to obstruct the women of the community from being there to assist with labor; while he stayed around, to be called only when needed. Rarely was he called; nevertheless, he became, in fact, quite famous in the region for his success in assisting births.

Marcos, the third son, was selected to give the main speech to Spain's royalty when they came to Oaxaca. Full of respect and hospitality, he welcomed them to this old land, "where we conserve," he said; "we live together and we resist, in our own ways of life, which were created by the wisdom of our ancestors and which we continue re-creating."

He added:

> We use this occasion to tell the western world that our way of life has been essentially communitarian, solidarian, with a profound respect for the land, our mother, which protects and nourishes us; that is why our heart suffers when we see how it is damaged, destroyed by greed and ambition, when it is

denied to their ancestral dwellers, when its natural equilibrium is broken with so many industrial products.

We have been studied with the western perception, in its different forms, but we have not been understood; it is still imposed on us with the Western form of development, its civilization, its way of seeing the world and relating to nature, thus denying all the knowledge generated by our different peoples. We have domesticated the corn, that sacred plant which gave us existence and we continue improving it. But even so, whenever an agronomist comes to our towns, he tells us that the corn numbered and produced in his research center is better; if we build a house with our knowledge and materials, an architect comes to tell us that a dignified house can only be built with industrial products; if we invoke our old gods, someone comes to tell us that our faith is superstitious.

During our visit, we were recalling all these family events when it came time for the meal. We entered the very warm place of doña Refugio, his mother. She was squatting on the floor, at the very center of the room – her place of cooking. We sat down around her, chatting with her and her family for more than two hours. Hand-to-hand, she gave us each a piece of chicken – which she cooked because she knew there were guests – or served a delicious soup of guías de calabaza, one key element of the traditional *milpa*. We were chatting and chatting, exploring why this woman was still here, and happy to be in her small town. She had refused to ever move out of San Andrés, except for short visits to the neighbouring town of Tlaxiaco: a place of five thousand people defined by her as a "big city." She also refused the "convenience" of a Lorena stove (which would "save" her from squatting), along with many of the other "comforts" of modern society. That morning, she offered us many reasons why she cooks and lives in the ways taught to her by her place, her people.

All her "reasons" reveal how profoundly her whole world is embedded in the "we" of a soil culture. Why did she not want to leave? What were her reasons for refusing so many "comforts" she was offered by her sons when they were still in the city? Prima facie, some of her reasons seemed unusual. She said, for example, that Lorena stoves are bad for the back, for they force you to be on your feet to cook. Other women argue in favor of the Lorena stove precisely for the reasons rejected by her, maintaining that the posture of standing while cooking is good for the back. Like doña Refugio, other women of San Andrés also oppose the modern stove: "If I have one," they say, "I will become a servant of my family. Sitting in front of my fire, I am a queen." We do not know if these queens of their tradition are right. But if you can imagine doña Refugio in her home, perhaps you can suspect why she said that there is no reason for her to leave … since she has "everything," as she says. And more.…

The fire is at the center of the warmest room of the house. And doña Refugio is there, every day, at the very center, surrounded by her whole family, talking with her husband, children and grandchildren; discussing personal difficulties or the predicaments of the community. That fire and doña Refugio are at the center of their conversations; and, in fact, at the very center of family life. And family life is the center of the community. The whole community's life is in fact organized around such fires, the center of kitchens, the source of *comida*. The very essence of the *milpa* is here, and not in the corn emerging in the fields – the only element of the *milpa* researched by the experts, the agronomists. The essence of their "we," their *milpa*, is precisely here: around the communal fire, in the very heart of the family.

Some time ago, we proposed using the word *comida* to differenti-ate doña Refugio's "we." In contrast, *alimento* is reserved for profes-sional, institutional or industrial use, referring to the foods (whether ethnic, gourmet or mainstream) eaten by the "individual self." To eat, to care for *comida*, to generate it, to cook it, to assimilate it: all these are the activities that do not belong to industrial eaters; to individual selves who define themselves with abstract "we's." *Comida* belongs to non-modern men and women and is usually associated with gendered activities. Almost the whole life of doña Refugio and the men, women and children she is surrounded by in San Andrés Chicahuaxtla can be described around these activities of *comida*. *Alimentarse*, in contrast, is to purchase and consume *alimentos* (edible objects) designed by professional "experts," while being produced and distributed through institutions for the convenience of industrial eaters: those millions of modern "I's" whose "dearest liberation" is part of the contemporary social ideal of minimal involvement in the growing and cooking of food.

We can make this distinction in Spanish to explain the difference of the "we" defined by *comida* from the "I" that consumes *alimentos*. We can find in the reality of doña Refugio, as well as in all peasant groups, differential behaviors that correspond to both conditions. We can document that *comida*, among many peasants, still refers to a very complex cultural relationship with their land, their *milpa*; which is not equivalent to the technical activity of producing maize, as the *milpa* is described by industrial agriculture. We can document the differences between their attitudes and behaviors and the ones of middle-class stu-dents in Mexico City. They must be *alimentados*; they consume *alimentos*; and they are completely dependent on the institutions that give or sell them these *alimentos*. It is difficult for their "I" to understand the "we" inherent in *comida*; using the word, as they do, to refer to the *alimentos* they purchase, just like other industrial eaters all over the modern world.

There are other languages, like German, in which we can make some of these distinctions. But the corresponding words do not represent differential realities to the same extent. In contrast, we may offer a lot of examples from the South, where the communal cultural practices referred to by the word *comida* still abound. We cannot, however, make this distinction in English. Food is *alimento*, not *comida*. Nourishment, and other words of the family are referred to only as food. Meal is a cultural word, like *comida*. Perhaps it originally meant *comida*, like Mahle, in German, of the same root; but now it refers only to the time and condition of taking food. Nourishment is a technical word – like nutrition, *nutrición*, *nourriture*, *Nahrung* – which refers to the contents of food, as defined by professionals. There is no English word for *comida*. It is not easy to explain why. Thinking of that makes us feel sad. While "feast" comes closest in its implication of eating together, it refers only to a special occasion, while *comida* is eaten by the "social majorities" in the "normal" course of every day. Perhaps we need to recall that the Anglo-Saxon world was the cultural space in which the industrial mode of production was established first and foremost. There, vernacular activities related to *comida* have been suffocated or suppressed.

Those who have recently tried to regenerate such activities have confronted great difficulties. This situation has institutionalized the permanent scarcity of *comida*. This scarcity does not refer to underfed (vs overfed) minorities in the First World; nor to "malnutrition": the technical expression that enroots the idea of a "recommended diet," established by institutions, professionals or alternative sects. Rather, we are reflecting upon a general condition of industrialized societies where individual selves are dependent on the private or public institutional apparatus that creates the addiction to food "services"; where needs are delinked from capacities; where capacities are considered equivalent to buying power; while needs are projected on to all peoples by the reigning modern myths of "preference curves" or "consumer sovereignty." The homogenization that prevails is hidden beneath the illusion of differential consumption (marketing "ethnic," "gourmet" or fast foods), fooling the genuine hunger for differentiating autonomy: allowing for real, not mythical or ideological, freedom of choice. The worst, perhaps, is that this world inhibits industrial eaters from even perceiving the absolute lack of *comida*; the chronic scarcity of food that defines the "I" in the midst of a "we." "Industrial eaters" daily suffer the illusion of abundance in their supermarkets. According to their common perception, hunger – the absolute lack of food – can appear only in backward countries, like Ethiopia; in America, as President Reagan used to say, only ignorants can suffer hunger. Some people have identified many hungry Americans (20 million or more, they say) and associate it with many things, except ignorance. But few industrial eaters genuinely sense the lack of *comida*; not the physical hunger of an empty belly, but the hunger of "I's" who lack their "we."

In the Dominican Republic's Monte Bonito, a beautiful small town in the northwestern part of the country, Erik Duus, a Norwegian, has been recording an extensive practice of the local women called *impostura*. While *comida* and *impostura* are rooted in radically different worlds of commons, both create "we's" in and through the communion of food embedded in soil (agri)culture.

While studying many of its forms, Duus has never attempted to define *impostura*. It has a symbolic meaning and is, at the same time,

> an informal contractual relationship, where the partners make an implicit promise to each other to exchange part of their meal with each other. The woman's ability to seal such a partnership with another woman, without the interference of the males, seems to depend on how consistently activities and responsibilities are kept gender-specific. Locally, the responsibility of the man is to provide for fresh food, while the responsibility of the woman is to prepare the meals. Many women would go as far as saying that what goes in the kitchen is none of their husbands' business, as long as the meals are served at the customary table. However, there is no absolute division between men's and women's work when it comes to direct tasks. Men can commonly be observed peeling manjok and preparing meals; while women can be seen carrying the machete to the fields, to take part in the agricultural tasks.

The main characteristic of the relations between the sexes within and outside the household seems to be that men behave and relate to other men in their attempts to comply with their responsibilities, and that women relate to other women to address theirs. Phrased differently, men and women rely on patterns and designs of social relations, only partly segregated. Just as men support each other with labor and often with raw food, the majority of the women help each other with cooked food or prepared meals on a regular basis. Some women might have developed this to the point where they give each other some part of everything they prepare throughout the day, from coffee in the morning to the three daily meals. However, it is most common to pass only the *comida*, a meal that ideally should consist of rice with cooked beans or peas and, preferably, a small piece of meat.

Duus discovers that *impostura* is a matter of complex interpretations and acts and gestures, diving into the creation of rich meanings and symbols in social interaction. He offers a wide variety of expressions used by women to talk about *impostura*.

We will quote three of his examples:

(1) To me, *impostura* means affection.... For example, you and I, we have affection for each other. You send me your *comida* and I will send you mine. But in this no one is looking for any advantage ... only affection. Because, perhaps you will send me your *comida* now, before mine is ready, and I will eat it and take away my hunger, you see? But perhaps there will be days when I can send my *comida* also to you, when you are hungry. This is what we are searching for.

(2) Impostura means togetherness and that we treat each other good in the neighborhood.... Impostura is having good friends and being considerate each day as poor people.

(3) Impostura we use here like perhaps one day I do not have anything to give my children, and then one *impostura* arrives, and I will be able to fill them ... that is *impostura*. The *impostura* is something we got used to as friends and neighbors, you see? ... that's how it is – that if there are neighbors, we like to believe that if we have *impostura* we shall treat each other better.

Erik Duus elaborates on these expressions very beautifully. He perceives the three main issues about *impostura* in them. Giving away food, he thinks, is understood beyond the act itself, to express sentiments of communal unity, consideration, togetherness and kindness. Such solidarity is partly a question of economic position. "But it is also related to the female world of responsibility and solidarity. As mothers and women who are responsible for bringing up the children, they emphasize collectivity and mutual help to secure this."

Duus also observes that there are many acts similar to *impostura*: gifts of food are made on many different occasions, at marriages, births, etc. "Impostura has a reserved meaning where it becomes identified as being different from these other quite similar acts." In the whole range of uses and meanings of the word, *impostura* may reflect an act as abstract as a "custom" or the very particular piece of meal prepared. It is thus very difficult to make a distinction between *impostura* and those other acts that look so similar. However, an uneven reciprocity, the kind that cannot be quantified and whose basic rules are not evident or stable in time and space, seems to be a built-in component of *impostura*. Duus illustrates this point through a short conversation with a woman:

A. I find that if I give you today, tomorrow, the day after and so on forever, and you do not give me because you cannot afford it ... no, that has nothing to do with *impostura*.

Q. But what if I give to you a big plate every day and you only give me back one small one, is that *impostura*?

A. Yes ... oh, yes, that is *impostura*. Because you give me a lot because you have a lot, and I will give you just a little, because I have just a little.

For a hundred pages, Duus continues carefully examining the world of *impostura* in many of its highly complex nuances. We cannot present all the richness of his stories here. But we can present one more description of *impostura*:

> Look, when God gives me one pound of rice and there won't be enough to portion it out with a ladle, I will take one of the tin spoons, one of the smaller spoons, and give everybody a little. The idea is that I live sharing.... That is how we poor people live. (I would say) Oh God, how hungry I am. Then immediately people will arrive, and the woman over there will cook her pound of rice and she will send me a little, perhaps she over there will also send me a little, that's two and my stomach will start getting full, but then the woman over there will also send me a little, then I am getting filled up, and then, when Juana sends me her part I am already satisfied. When you arrive, I can therefore say: Look, mister, you have this little meal. God gives to me and to everybody.

The whole context of Monte Bonito supports these communal attitudes:

> Agricultural activities are the backbone of the village and the community economy ... Commuting by foot or donkey is a daily affair ... The major crop orientation in the peasant agriculture is that of rice, manjok, plantains, sweet-potato and other roots for direct consumption, while peanuts, peas, and beans are often cultivated as cash crops. This does not mean that the peasants of the area make a clear distinction between cash and subsistence farming. It is quite common to retain a rather large proportion of the beans and peas for personal consumption in the period of the harvest. On the other hand, it is fully accepted for one to sell parts of the rice, manjok and other roots in the market.

Duus also observes that,

> the present emphasis on subsistence cropping and production for domestic consumption must rely on a combination of both cultural and economic perspectives. On the one hand, one can detect a certain reluctance to seek more market-oriented agricultural engagements. Peanuts, the most secure crop, give only marginal economic benefits in terms of labor input. The production of peas and beans is very risky, with little prediction for success or failure. These peasant households can therefore not be characterized as having completely "withdrawn" from a more market-oriented production. On the other hand, one must understand that the production of rice, plaintains, *manjok*, sweet-potatoes, and other roots belong intrinsically to their way of life. These products are virtual symbols of self-reliance and autonomy; they are products that greatly "liberate" time for other purposes and play an important part in the local exchange system. With *manjok* in the ground, the men have complied with one of the basic household responsibilities and are "free" to participate in social and public life in a "proper" way.

We are telling this story to reveal the scarcity that appears in the world of the individual self, of *Homo oeconomicus*. "Food" is a word immersed in the economic world of the industrial eater: the individual self who is doomed to live with scarcity; not natural shortages or absolute lack of food, but scarcity in its technical sense of the relationship between limited means and unlimited ends. This technical "economic problem" of professionally allocating resources dooms the industrial eater to permanent or chronic scarcity.

Comida alludes to practices and rituals in the worlds of "we's" where economic scarcity is staved off; where the arts of their elders, their dead, are still sufficiently vital and alive; preventing scarcity from appearing – despite the global epidemic of economics. In Monte Bonito, *impostura* does not relate possessive, invidious subjects or individual selves. Rather, it connects affectionate people, full of neighborliness; not "managed" by institutions, but free, alive and autonomous precisely because of their personal bonds; with their roots nourished by their traditions; in worlds where commodities play a marginal role and the environment is largely occupied by the commons.

But this story about *impostura* in Monte Bonito is just one among thousands of closely recorded anthropological accounts that reveal how the "social majorities" escape the isolation of modern individual selves, enjoying the solidarity of *comida*. For more than a decade, we have been enjoying our discoveries of many forms and shapes of *impostura*, of *comida* – the heart of commons and communis still alive and beating even within the giant ghettos of New Delhi or Mexico City. In Monte Bonito, *impostura* is the natural continuation of a long-established tradition. "Observers" may dismiss it as mere reminiscence; what has survived from the past; that is, an interesting but marginal practice in rural, "primitive" towns. In Mexico City or New Delhi, one needs to deal with the question of how and why these kinds of practices are again being regenerated. Flourishing in some of the most modern gigantic urban settlements, are these practices of eating mere reminiscences, or, worse still, steps backwards into underdevelopment? Alternatively, are these examples of grassroots post-modernism? Do they demonstrate the ingenuity of "the people," regenerating indigenous knowledge, making and remaking their cultural soils?

REMAKING THE SOIL OF CULTURES

Tepito is a *barrio* in downtown Mexico City: 72 blocks occupied by 120,000 inhabitants. In 1945, it was one of the worst places to live in Mexico. Its houses were really ugly; in fact, they were rooms, not houses, each approximately 13 to 25 square meters, built around dusty yards, without sanitation facilities and made of very poor materials. Ten, twenty or fifty of these "houses" constituted a *vecindad*.[1] Only delinquents of every kind accepted living there.

After World War II, the government of the city "froze" the rent of low-cost housing. "The people" struggled to keep it low-cost, in spite of countless attempts by lawyers, politicians and developers to eliminate it. Those living in Tepito, enjoying the lowest rent in the city, continued "conquering" their spaces with ingenuity. They created second floors by building in the interior of their houses. Their houses serve as workshops during the day and as homes at night. Patios are common spaces with multiple purposes. Step by step, the Tepitans continue "invading" their streets, transforming them for trade, creation and recreation. The trade of used clothes flourishes next to that of new clothes produced in Tepito. Shoe repairers prosper next to workshops that produce new shoes. Tepitans remake, remodel and transform a thousand mechanical and electrical gadgets thrown out by their rich or middle-class owners. The quality of the objects reformulated by Tepitans is now famous.

During the major earthquake of 1985, 40 percent of their weak houses collapsed. Lawyers and developers thought that their opportunity to get rid of the Tepitans had finally arrived. Tepitans fought to stay, to rebuild their homes. A whole struggle started. An obscene trade of charities – of churches, political parties and NGOs – attempted to capture and "help" a portion of the "victims." In solidarity, many of us became involved in their struggle of resistance against "aid" from America and Europe. The experiences of the Tepitans taught us how "aid" does the opposite of "helping" (Sachs, 1992). To resist the international flow of aid that replaces *comida* with the food of industrial eaters or individual selves, we recounted stories like the following.

Twenty-four hours after the earthquake, the UN's Food and Agriculture Organization (FAO) representative in Mexico received a call from Rome: "You have a million dollars to help the victims. You must expend the funds in the next three months." The representative immediately created a Commission, with French, German and Chilean experts. They "happened" to have a ready-made aid project, establishing more than a hundred restaurants to sell subsidized food, while "educating" the "victims" of Tepito how to consume a balanced diet. The Tepitans were profoundly offended, angry and concerned. "Thirty years ago," they reminisced, "we used to eat *escamocha*: leftovers of friendly restaurants, given for free to poor people. We cooked everything in enormous pots in the streets and shared the final product, *escamocha*." They added: "We don't want industrial *escamocha*. We eat very well, everything we want, in our own way." They are right. Tepito offers every kind of *comida*, in the most diverse styles. In the streets, the children – "dirty" with playing or working – look robust. Well-intentioned social workers will find it difficult to identify "malnutrition." Tepitans were especially concerned with the FAO and other "aid" projects. One-third of them make a living by cooking and selling *comida*. Many could be ruined by the "aid" of subsidized, industrial food. Like all development aid, this project was counterproductive. Tepitans opposed this "food aid" in the same vein they previously opposed the development of their spaces.

The earthquake revealed to us the world of Tepito's *comida*. Those cooking and selling *comida* are not simply engaged in "business" or in "income generation." They are but the top layer of a far from frozen, extended web of very complex activities. Something like *impostura* is alive there. It is a thousand times more complex than that in Monte Bonito. Erik Duus would have a far greater challenge trying to write anthropological accounts of the *impostura* of Tepito, where many of "the people" maintain close connections with the rural communities from which they first emigrated. These connections are channels for a constant flow of people and goods in both directions. This "trade" remains a key element for the regeneration of the rural communities. It keeps alive a very active web for mutual help and solidarity. It is not a mere "commercial operation," seeking profit or "comparative advantage." It modulates migration in both directions. It hosts people at both ends of the web to receive proper support within diverse clusters of communities occupying multiple spaces, in both rural and urban areas. These types of linkages now also operate between rural communities in Mexico and groups living in the US. Michael Kearney (1996a) describes them as "transnational communities."

Inside Tepito, exchanges are made in the most fantastic, complex and even "efficient" ways. In the *vecindades*, a kind of *impostura*, comprising a lot more things than *comida*, frequently prevail. Outside the vecindades, there are literally hundreds of associations – by street, by line of activity, by trade or skill. Since many families spend most of their time on the street – for their trade or work – they do not cook at home. They have concerted special arrangements with "establishments" where friends or relatives are cooking and selling *comida*. In their turn, the latter have arrangements with the workshops, the market and most Tepitans. If we trace all the aspects and shapes of *comida* in Tepito, we may find that it embraces perhaps the whole range of human activities – from rituals and prayers to the *milpa*, street dancing or electronic gadgetry.

Tepito's earthquake offered but a clue to what we keep on discovering among "the people" at the grassroots – in rural areas and the popular *barrios* of cities. Every so-called economic "crisis" in Mexico reveals to us how "marginals" or lower-middle-class employees complement their incomes and enrich their lives through *comida*. They could "educate" the middle or upper middle classes – previous role models for the "poor" who lost part or all of what they considered the "privileges" of development – teaching them ten thousand tricks that the "poor" master so well for a living. Today, we understand better why people have not killed each other in Mexico City – that monstrous settlement of 16 million inhabitants – even in the middle of what the experts call the worst economic crisis of the century in Mexico. At this point, we do not know if Tepito will survive as a *barrio*. Developers, in spite of strong resistance from "the people," continue dismantling Tepito's original ways of subsistence. Yet, Tepitan culture continues exploding into the surrounding *barrios* of the city, each with its own *comida*.

Comida cannot be removed, displaced, or replaced. In urging *comida*, we are not advocating that women squat around the fireplace all over the world. Nor are we suggesting that *comida* is a bed of roses. We deeply admire the central place doña Refugio has in San Andrés. Our desirable society also has women at the center. But we also know too well that matriarchy can be as oppressive as patriarchy. We see, however, that real men and women have the power to change such modes of oppression. For in the world of *comida*, all predicaments, good and bad, are on a human scale.

Anything that can be eaten is an object of power, observed Elias Canetti (1966) at the end of his long exploration on the foundations of modern power, and the close relationship between the masses and power. Individual selves are taught to feel powerful *qua* "masses." With the myth of "consumer sovereignty," they are "educated" in the illusion that a mass of consumers control and determine the patterns of the market and the corporations; or that the mass of voters, controlling and determining political life, give political form to the rational interest of each individual (the "democratic myth"). In spite of its radical resonance, the word "mass" needs to be traced to its origin in the Church and the bourgeoisie. In being reduced to "a mass," real men and women are transmogrified into material things: measured in terms of units of volume. By accepting the activities of the masses – eating in McDonald's or voting at the ballot box – real men and women give up their real power; as they do their common sense, lost in operations that disregard the human scale.

Comida defines a social condition in which power remains in the hands of the people. It is their source of solidarity and conviviality; their antidote to ragged, lonely individualism. Every post-modern group has to rediscover its own cultural ideal of *comida* – in its attempts to rediscover sustainable living and agri-culture. In this search, this adventure for rediscovery, going beyond the deprivation, sadness and monotony of modernity, we may find secret hidden stocks of a still unknown class of *comida*. Do not look for industrial *comida*, the "social majorities" teach us. It is a contradiction in terms.

COMMUNAL MEMORY:
REMEMBERING TO ESCAPE DIS-MEMBERING

Cultures may be seen as memories. Ways of recalling establish fundamental differences between cultures, even when people are recalling the "same substance."

For the "social minorities," the vast chasm that separates organic from industrial memory is not sensed. In their other worlds, still separate from the monoculturalism of modernity, the "social majorities" depend only on organic memory. Like their dead, they have escaped the growing dependence of the "social minorities" on industrial memory.

Comida illustrates well the difference between industrial and organic memory. The second is necessarily communal. Like any living language, *comida* reflects the living memory of routine or ritualized practice. Comida is not prepared following the recipes published in a book for gourmets; it cannot lie passive in published print. It is alive in the flesh; in the hands, hearts and tongues of those who partake of it. Only through the practiced rituals of growing, preparing and serving *comida*, this memory is passed on; each generation re-members those that precede; regenerating the "home economics" (Berry, 1987) of households, commons and communities, of the neighborhood or the local region.

A very different memory of Mexican cuisine is "passed on" to chefs of "ethnic foods," graduating from schools of hotel and restaurant management. This industrial memory, unlike the first, depends upon a complicated economy: of publishing "houses," professional schools and global tourism. Passed on through texts, written and taught by professionals, this memory does not re-member or remember any community (even when it extends the membership of professional associations, bringing throngs of members to its annual meetings). Wherever industrial memory replaces organic memory, it destroys and dis-members communities; replaced by the careerists of professional associations. Without the stories and rituals of community and commons, organic memory dies. Industrial memory, on the other hand, needs only the texts of educational and other institutions designed for mobile "careerists." In the profound differences that separate these two distinct types of memory – one industrial and the other organic – lie clues for understanding how commons are dis-membered and transmogrified and individual selves are constructed.

For many centuries, memory was perceived as an art associated with personal training – which varied with every culture. Memory was alive and changing. In each telling of the history of the place and the people, the narrator added and subtracted, even as the mood and spirit of the audience varied. No two tellings of the *Ramayana* or the *Iliad* constituted a repetitive invariant record or compact disc.

The alphabet, the book and the text modified this situation, particularly in the West. The alphabet created the word. Originally, the Greek language had no word for "a word," singly identified. Talking was not viewed or taught as learning to pronounce a collection of words, in a specific order. And for the Greeks, as Plato stressed, "living recall is superior to memory based on the reference to dry letters which cannot protest when their sense is twisted around by the reader" (Illich, 1993, p. 40).

Memory associated with those "dry letters" of a book suffered a profound transformation around the twelfth century in the West. Prior to that change, it was assumed that the light emanating from the page helps the reader to recognize him- or herself. For some time, that self was still deeply embedded in a religious cosmos: the new sense of individuality could be interpreted only through its organic insertion in that mental universe (Cougar, 1973). But the modern, possessive individual was already in the process of being broken and reshaped, an extention of the new technologies and tools that were being produced. One among several steps towards this shaping occurred when the text was created as an object, something distinct from The Book. Furthermore, the book itself went through a major transformation: from a pointer towards the cosmos, it became a pointer to a privately owned mind.

> The book was no longer the window into nature or God; it was no longer the transparent optical device through which the reader gains access to creatures or the transcendent. Out of the symbol for cosmic reality had arisen a symbol for thought. The text, rather than the book, became the object in which thought is gathered and mirrored. (Illich, 1993, p. 119)

In and through processes akin to those which transformed The Book (shared and studied together by a community of scholars by virtue of being rare, unique or not easily reproducible) into the text (possessed by and published for thousands, even millions, reading in the isolation of places like the private bedroom or bath, minus any community), the individual self has been cut out of the cloth of modern beliefs. Produced by industrial technologies, this cloth bears no resemblance to the fabric of traditional commons and community. Just as his Walkman has broken him off from hundreds gathered to listen together to "live" music, transmogrifying him into the solitary "fan" jogging alone on I-80, so the memory of the modern reader has been broken off from communal memory, becoming an extension of the text, mass manufactured for the private consumption of the individual self. For textual selves, remembering is no longer a living expression of experiences that affirm intimate connections between dwellers (Orr, 1992) and their places. The memory of textual selves is like their family videos or photographs: substitutes for the living and continually changing memory of shared events and stories, daily told and retold in communities, making and remaking communal soil. Mnemotechnic tools are no longer devices to organize the castle of memory and visit it in all of its conditions, annually, monthly or even weekly, mutating with the seasons of nature. Instead, they are mummified; or like castles transformed into museums, with visiting hours specified for tourists. The memory of modern men, women and children is increasingly an extension of their lap-tops and other private mnemotechnic possessions, on which they depend more and more to find or save the text files of their lives.

In the context of "self as text," speaking becomes a form of reading aloud; and a good speaker is someone whose utterances flow with the precision and mechanical order of a text. Even real people at the grassroots – including our friends or well-known acquaintances – are transmogrified from the lively story-tellers of their communities into frozen, mechanical texts whenever they are placed in front of a video camera by researchers doing an "interview" for some abstract public. Living ideas, stories and complex forms of expression, heard and enjoyed many times by a community, are suddenly frozen into poor versions of the dominant discourse – when they are forced to speak in publics created by loudspeakers, TV cameras or hyper-text. Confronted with an abstract public, the vibrant, vivacious story-tellers we have encountered in every community begin to stare into global hyper-space, mimicking Barbara Walters and other famous performers. Recast for an abstract audience, their stories lose the power of spoken and lived words: remembering community, re-embedding the "I" embedded in the "we"; always changing with every telling; weaving into one continuous web times past and present in ways that makes their social fabric unique; like no other; always in-the-making, unfinished, incomplete and alive, unlike a published text that is complete, dead and finished.

The dominant style of public discourse, increasingly invading family and community via satellite, constructs a veil, even a wall, between real women and men. This wall prevents them from facing each other as I–Thou (Buber, 1970); from talking person-to-person. Asked to speak in the absence of the familiar faces of their own communities, common men and women no longer say what they actually think, feel or recall. Instead, facing the unknown national or global audiences of media networks, common men and women, posturing like "talk show hosts," say what they think their audiences want to hear. Back on their own feet, in the real worlds of their communities, speaking face-to-face rather than trying to "communicate" with someone "out there" on the globe – researchers, officials or some abstract public – they regain their real voices, rich with the local flavors of idiomatic speech (Esteva, 1991).

Like all modern people, we once possessed our individual memory; a repository of the mind we owned. To have a memory in this sense is best described or conceived as a storehouse. The person who possesses that memory – any and every "I" – is its appointed watchman. One can click on the memory function and read it, whenever the need arises. Sometimes we still fall into that illusion. Less and less able to think of ourselves as individual selves, however, we are also losing our previous tendency to conceive of texts, photographs, and videos as the repositories of memory. What and how we recall today can hardly be described in terms of a memory possessed by an individual self. From our friends and other teachers at the grassroots, we are understanding how personal identity is shaped by memories that are commons; shared stories of ways in which people name and treat each other.

In a recent National Assembly of Indian peoples in Mexico, there was intense discussion about their current claim: respect and recognition for their *usos y costumbres* (customs and traditions) by the Mexican Constitution and the official authorities, particularly those in charge of the administration of justice. At some point in this discussion, a lawyer argued that, for purposes such as these, it is necessary to put those customs into writing, creating the form of a charter that will be the internal law in every community, every people. The Indians reacted to this suggestion with strong opposition: Our customs, they said, cannot and must not be written. Every case of stealing two turkeys is different. You cannot have a general rule. We all know what is involved and we apply the pertinent principles. We demand from our authorities that they do what must be done in each and every case. Furthermore, if we translate our customs into a law, we will freeze them; we will kill them. And we want them to remain fully alive. Our people know and remember well all the customs, the "rules" to be applied for orienting their own behavior or to protect the community against their violations.

At this assembly, one participant observed that the original meaning of the word *jurisdiction* comes from *juris* and *dicere*. Rather than defining an administrative division for the enforcement of the abstract law, through professionals and bureaucrats, the word originally alluded to a social condition in which ordinary men and women ruled their own interactions, strengthening their bonds, based on trust. In radical contrast, in modern trials, as epitomized by that of O.J. Simpson, the judge, prosecutor and lawyers try to define and present a collection of "facts," constructed as if they were texts; and as frozen. At this trial, like others, the prosecutor and the lawyers were, of course, concerned with the "emotions" of the jury. They were trying to elicit in them, as in the public, the proper "emotions" by inviting the witnesses or the experts to remember what actually happened. Alan Dershovitz synthesizes the spirit of the American judicial system by arguing that the role of the lawyers for the defense (who, he claims, are usually hired by guilty individuals) does not consist in discovering the truth or making justice, but in exonerating their client, no matter if he or she is innocent or guilty, by using all the instruments or resources allowed by the law.[2]

These are two irreconcilably different ways and kinds of remembering words or events. In fact, there is such heteronomy between these two sets of experiences that we do not think that we can use the same word, "memory," to refer to them. If we want to keep the word for our memory as modern men and women, we need to use another to speak of that collective way of remembering that occurs when people's lives are living memories: continually changing, shared with neighbors, friends and relatives, with a past and future that constitute a "commons" and not a "private collection." The remembering that is a part of the "memory" of a village story-teller, telling thousands of times the same story, each and every time with a difference, is critical for the re-membering without which there can be no community. In contrast there is the remembering of a student, digging into her "memory" to present the important facts on the final exam in order to get the best grade, her personal ticket for upward mobility. Unlike the first, the second "liberates" persons from their communities, promising progress and upward mobility for the individual self, "free" to belong to the community of his/her own choice – which means, in fact, having no community.

We are not arguing here against mnemotechnic tools or the use of written memory for different purposes. We are attempting to understand the specific transformations we have been getting a whiff of among the people at the grassroots. In their process of regeneration, they seem increasingly concerned with both the need to relearn to appreciate their living recall and to take a distance from abstract memory, coming from a text or "written" in "the mind," "The Book," or the Law. They are keeping the parentheses when they use abstractions: being fully aware that they separate things from reality and sequestrate them. Putting these abstractions within brackets, they avoid confusions in their daily life. In contrast, the "facts" presented to the Simpson jury, the "economic facts" disseminated by the media to foster expectations or to reduce frustrations, the media descriptions of the Persian Gulf war, are as "real" as most other certainties by which modern men and women orient their daily behavior. They are derived no longer from practical experiences (what really happened to me, or what I learned from my mother, etc.), but from abstractions whose "brackets" (revealing their nature) have been suppressed or forgotten.

In making such claims, we are renouncing one of the fundamental assumptions in which we were "educated": the presumption that "there is some originative and independent source of order that, when discovered and understood, will provide a coherent explanation for the human experience" (Ames, 1993, p. 46). We were educated in the need to seek for the "real," the stable structure of the changing world, as well as in the adoption of some of those "realities" as our own point of reference; to orient ourselves in the adventure of living. Within academia today, there are different attempts to redefine knowledge – given the increasing challenge to what was previously assumed as reliable forms of knowing. There may be some value in dealing with these issues of redefinition through exploring the origin of the words in use for that purpose. Their etymology can provide a taste of the historical transformations that should be examined. In Latin, *cognoscere* is "to know by the senses," and its implicit meaning is familiarity, experience, communion, recognition; scire is "to know by the mind," and its implicit meaning is separating, dividing, splitting. To know, *conocer*, or knowledge, *conocimiento*, in English and Spanish, come from *cognoscere*. That original meaning, however, has almost disappeared and the content of scire, "to know by the mind," now predominates. The roots of "mind," in turn, are associated with memory, with remembering and thinking. Memory is the first meaning of "mind," according to the Oxford English Dictionary. Some of the implications of this for our discussion are immediately evident. By forgetting to know and remember by the senses, with all the rhythms, fragrances and tastes of the diverse oral traditions, modern men and women have fallen into a form of knowledge and remembrance that fails to re-member precisely because it separates, divides and splits (following the same patterns by which the alphabet divides the speech into letters and words), ignoring or forgetting what they are doing. They lose the precision of the Greeks, who recognized in abstract analysis an operation which separated the idea from reality; who kept the brackets, the awareness of the sequestration of reality that they practiced when they were abstracting. The dominant contemporary mode of knowing and thinking identifies reality with abstraction. The most extreme example of this comes from the public who conclude that what is on the screen of their TV set "really happened" because they "saw" it. At that same extremity, a modern man or woman identifies himself or herself, his or her own being in the world, with the individual self into which he or she has been dis-membered.

Tools redefine and reshape the human condition. Modern tools have transformed their users and operators into extensions of or in the image of the machine. And no other tool seems to have had a more profound impact on the human condition than the alphabet. It transformed men and women, during a long historical process, into texts – unisex texts, we must say. And our young contemporaries are now being transformed into screens. An invisible wall separates modern men and women, who can only face each other as if they were what they are not and cannot be: individual selves shaped in the mold of a text or a screen. Products of the tools that they fabricate, modern individual selves are the proud owners of the textual mind. In the process of being upgraded today by Windows '97 or WordPerfect 6.0, post-modern academics and others "surfing the Internet" are mentally muscling up to become owners of the textual mind's latest successor: the cybernetic mind – a screen with windows that are clicked open.

Our journeys into the worlds of the "illiterate" or "uneducated" "social majorities" teach us how to remain outside the trap of becoming extensions of our Apples and IBMs – cybernetic spaces within which we find millions of our cohorts, colleagues and acquaintances caught without even sensing it. While these journeys into the spaces of the "social majorities" are our prophylactics, protecting us from the "viruses" that plague the minds of moderns and academic post-moderns, they also serve to remind us that we are not pre-text people. This "manuscript" reveals that we are bookish persons, even though we are "writing" our book on Toshiba 1900 lap-tops.

We are a part of neither an oral nor a pre-screen culture. We do not know how to speak or see in the way oral men and women do, or did: we suppose that not one of them is still alive. We can only imagine how they were. Both literate and illiterate people now live in the reign of the alphabetic mind (Illich, 1987a). If we go to a village of "illiterate" people and start a conversation about their land conflicts among neighbors, the village elders usually run to their huts, producing "legally recognized" deeds that they obtained from the Spanish Crown and the Mexican government. Their relations with their neighbors are no longer based on words, the mutual trust of a long shared past and traditions, but, instead, on a paper, a text. They cannot read, but they are subordinated to the reign of written texts, alien texts. (This does not mean that the oral cultures themselves have died: we find them fully alive among the "social majorities." What we are underlining is the profound transformation they have suffered, after their subordination to power structures where the text reigns sovereign.)

Furthermore, our excursions into the spaces of the "social majorities" teach us how much we do love books. We have discovered in and through them some of our best friends. We have regular encounters with them. While we are trying to live in the non-textual ocean of real life – constituted of singular, real, face-to-face relationships of I–Thou – we thoroughly enjoy our excursions into the island of the alphabet. We know that our perceptions, even our very being, cannot be sharply separated from the books and the texts we have come to cherish, which often have offered us the key, the clues, to better articulate, in yet another text, what we are perceiving at the grassroots.

At the same time, we can no longer describe ourselves as "text people." With this expression, we are alluding to the types of persons whose minds have been shaped and constructed as if these were texts. The alphabet existed before the text. Plato struggled against the division between orality and literacy, and examined the transition from the always new act of remembering to the literate memory. The latter divides speech and thinking. But the text, as an object in itself, different from the book, appeared simultaneously with the possessive individual, and is its counterpart. A text is radically uprooted from any concrete, living experience. This is the case no matter how much it evokes living and concrete experiences, or is written or read in a very concrete and alive situation. The textual mind is constructed according to that model. The liturgy of the Catholic Church generated the faith and the reality of the community as a church, which is the object of such faith. In the same way, the learning of texts in privileged places like schools generates the modern textual mind, radically uprooted and homeless. Men and women of the text era think that speech can be frozen; memories can be saved and recovered; secrets can be engraved in the conscience for future re-examination; experiences can be described and inscribed for the history books of posterity. In the course of writing these books, men and women of the text "look" for proper words to express what they want to say; to fix for ever in the lines of the page the events that have occurred – in their lives, their jobs, their countries – mummifying them for the purpose of their resurrection by historians and social analysts of future years.

A text is past speech in a very real sense. It is speech that has suffered a transformation so radical that perhaps it can no longer be called speech. The alphabet allows people to register past speech; even to conceive that record as a "language" that can be used to speak; particularly to transmit to others the text one has in the mind. A textual individual is a self whose speech is an attempt to delve into the mind, looking for the proper words, the text, to "communicate" (rather than converse) – a quintessentially modern urge. The individual self can no longer speak without looking for the appropriate text, the one capable of capturing every thing s/he wants to communicate. S/he looks for the best way to transmit that text; to imprint it in the minds owned by others. The present of the individual self is constructed by the text. The materials for constructing the present are continually pulled out from a memory bank. They are deposited and stored there from all the previous texts, learned "by memory."

Before the text, men and women learned to abide by their words. After the text, they have the need to rely on words. People's struggles at the grassroots involve reclaiming the original meaning of "jurisdiction": the condition in which the word of a person is valued; once accepted, it rules. The radical transformations separating the original meanings of words and their modern use can only be fully grasped in and through the contrasts that separate the worlds of oral peoples from the peoples of the text. In the world of orality, where the oath is law, all the words are alive and fluid; as alive and fluid as all else in their contexts; as changing as their speakers who utter words; with meanings as mobile as the intonations with which they emerge; being transformed in and through the human exchange and interchange. The words of modern men and women have also to be understood in context. The word "context" still describes the weaving of words, the connection between the parts of a discourse, the parts around a "text" which determine its meaning. But more and more today, the contexts that connect minds that are texts are not constituted of living words. Modern individuals' contexts are defined increasingly through connections made by the inert words of texts. Their minds are constructed in the shape of uprooted texts. It should be no surprise that the modern self feels such unbearable despair, loneliness and homelessness.

No, we can no longer describe ourselves as text people. But to introduce ourselves here as post-text people, we need to step back a little; to react with anguish and confusion whenever we find ourselves thinking and talking like an "educated" person: taught to be an individual self. We also want to immediately separate ourselves from other post-text men and women. We encounter them among our contemporaries, especially young people bred on electronic text composers. "Text" means something entirely different to them: a series of binary bits. Their eyes are trained to compete with WordPerfect's search command, to "interface"

by surfing the Internet through hypertext; their gaze is a form of scan-
ning (Illich, 1994a). And their sense and sensibility? We acknowledge our
inability to talk with those people in the same way we are conversing
with the friends we have symbolically invited to our table for writing
this book. And we stop ourselves in horror as we imagine the kind of
transmogrification that is occurring to the Being, the souls, of digital
men and women. That Becoming is an unbearable, unspeakable nightmare. It is too painful to endure watching. As we gaze with Illich, we
begin to understand the virtue of "guarding the eye in the age of show"
(Illich, 1994b). Meanwhile, the mind of the individual self continues to
be retooled for the twenty-first century, evolving from text to screen.

The "uneducated" or the "illiterate" have not lost their human
capacities to know by the senses. They keep their common sense, their
consciousness of parentheses when they are abstracting, even though they
may be subordinated to the text (living as they are in a world where it
"rules," only to be displaced rapidly by the screen). Those incorporated by
the literate world have not yet been transmogrified into texts. They have
started resisting their own subjugation at the very time of their "final"
incorporation to the modern world through the "Global Project." They
are transforming their old struggle of resistance into a struggle for liberation. The liberation of their cultural and physical spaces depends upon
resisting the apple of modern freedom: to break and destroy communal
memory for the economic "goods" offered to the mobile "individual self."

WHO AM I? FROM CALLING CARD
TO KNOTS IN NETS

"Who am I? Here is my card. My cellphone number and my e-mail
address need to be changed. May I suggest…"

First meetings between two persons in the modern world are radically
different from those that occur among peoples living at the grassroots.
These differences offer critical clues to the chasm of personal identity
that separates the world of living communal memory from the world
where persons *qua* texts or screens "communicate," increasingly in
virtual reality.

In the modern world, there is an "interface" between individual
selves who are the possessors of calling cards; classifying them in terms
of the statistical "we" – the name preceded by the title, followed by the
credential, the institutional affiliation, the phone and fax numbers, and
address and location, e-mail or other. I am a professor of philosophy,
teaching Ancient Greek Thought in an Ivy League university. During
the course of ensuing talks, this individual self offers additional clues

for her identification as an individual self: her nationality – she is from Turkey, Japan or India only by birth, while currently owning a Canadian passport; reading or writing particular books, visiting certain museums, or appreciating classical music as well as jazz; either struggling for or affirming her sexual identity; celebrating her color, culture or racial identity with her passion for eating "ethnic gourmet food"; attending the annual professional meetings of APA, AERA and similar associations...

In villages and other spaces of the "social majorities," introductions take a completely different course. Keeping away from abstractions, they focus on what is known face-to-face, in the flesh and in the web of personal relations by which people define themselves and others. An introduction proceeds with stories of personal relationships, along with those unique, even idiosyncratic features that distinguish and differentiate:

> Here is Juanito, the man who speaks with the plants by their names. Oh, you know what he did last week? He was puzzled by a herb growing in his *milpa* that he had never seen before. He took a handful of it and walked to the next village to consult his uncle, who is a very wise old man. He once stopped a feast just with a look of his eyes. He cannot sleep if he does not know the name of a plant. Juanito is following in his uncle's steps. He has named his daughter Gardenia, because he finds her as surprising and mysterious as an unknown flower. Oh, this Juanito, he is such a good chap...

During the course of the conversation that follows this introduction, many other stories about Juanito will naturally emerge. These will not offer any list of abstract categories, but of shared memories and experiences with a person in the flesh. That explains, in part, why the individual self with the calling card finds it so difficult to "get down to business" with peoples at the grassroots; invariably failing to understand why meetings with them are "so slow"; why non-economic, communal beings seek to establish relationship, not business; why the monetary exchange is only a small part of what they hope to create in their encounters with others.

At the grassroots, the meeting occurs between persons who define themselves by concrete "first person plurals" – those flowers "born out of the sharing in the good of convivial life." Their lives at the grassroots are constituted by the living communal soil: memories of shared stories, told and retold in endless mutations; of the births, weddings, funerals, harvests, and all else that punctuate and shape the dailyness of daily life; of rites of passage whose meaning demands and depends upon the participation of the community, centered on ceremonies – not the least of which is the communion of bread broken together.

An individual self, increasingly defined by abstract institutional affiliations, suffers an "unbearable lightness of being." A communal person "suffers" heaviness: of being in soil with the "we" of membership, memory and re-membering; a knot in a net of relations; this knot, not any other knot. To know that someone is a citizen of a specific country, a passenger of a specific flight, a member of a specific profession, a consumer of a specific collection of products, a reader of a specific set of books, does not tell us anything about the substance or being of this person in the flesh and blood. We only have an abstract approach to his or her concreteness: constituted of a collection of abstract categories in which he or she can be classified. Anyone pretending to be an individual, that possessive individual constructed in the West, can only describe himself or herself through the "individualization" and juxtaposition of those abstract categories. His/her daily life usually is a continual passage from one "role" to the next.

All of these roles are but abstract, genderless conditions that modern men and women are forced to adopt, in order to fit into the modern world. He or she will move from being husband or wife, to driver, waiter, consumer, boss, employee, passenger... It is expected that they will "behave" professionally; that is, avoid being himself or herself *qua* real, enfleshed persons, and, instead, following what is expected, perform as abstract, homogeneous, genderless individuals, with behaviors prescribed for every "role." "Role" is "a concept by which, since Ralph Linton's *The Study of Man: An Introduction* (1936), sociology links the social order to the characteristic behavior of the individuals who comprise it. Role is the device by which people become part of a plural that can then be analyzed by genderless concepts" (Illich, 1982, p. 80).[3] Role-modelling is now a fundamental element of the "educational process": children and young people are taught to adopt appropriate role-models, which means reducing and in fact eliminating their concreteness as real persons, a boy or a girl, transmogrifying them into the standardized genderless individuality of all the individuals of the corresponding role. People are educated to live their lives performing a series of "acceptable roles"; that is, shaping their lives in the mold constructed for individuals in every role. If "role" was, in the time of Linton, a technical term to be used as a descriptive device for a new kind of behavior, emerging in the industrial society among certain people in specified situations, it now operates as a social norm, that is, the criteria to discriminate between normal and abnormal behaviors of people reduced to role-performing individuals.

After a conversation with Juanito, little will be known about the categories into which he can be classified. Little will be known about the "roles" he plays, if any, in his own community. Much, however, will be known about the shape of this specific knot, inside a specific net of relations. Thus, Juanito becomes a real person for the friend of his friend to whom he is introduced.

For many years, we were continuously perplexed by our inability to express what we were experiencing in the types of *barrios* and villages that are inhabited by the "social majorities" of peasants and urban marginals. It took us most of our adult years to start discovering how our experiences were imprisoned by the formal categories in which we were "educated." The glasses constructed for us by modern education severely distorted our perceptions of the experiences of people living at the grassroots. It was puzzling to also discover that those glasses, constructed to enrich and expand our vision beyond traditional provincialism, had actually imprisoned us in the more severe prisons of modernity; with the global provincialism of certainties published and promulgated world-wide by the "experts," including economists, political theorists and professional educators.

Discovering the bars of our modern prison was a first step in our continuing search for ways to escape; to learn to liberate ourselves from the culture of the experts; to use again our own "eyes" for discerning the wisdom our own cultures had to offer. On this quest, we are discovering whole new, rich, diverse worlds. Cleansing ourselves of the "education" that made us spurn our traditions, we are learning to renovate our hopes about the so-called "poor," the "marginal," the excluded and the "underdeveloped." Rather than being left-overs of the epic of development, as our previous "eyes" suggested, our own peoples and other "social majorities" now appear to us to be beyond development.

It has not been easy to share our experiences with others. Whenever we have tried to do so, we have found ourselves in a difficult predicament. All too often, we are affectionately warned that we may be, at best, discovering and identifying some exceptions: either mere anomalies or a few fast-disappearing remnants from the past. Recently, a colleague gently chided us:

> In the real world, most people want to be developed. If the so-called "social majorities" are given the option, they will vote for what appears in popular magazines: more pornography and sports; more TV than reading; bigger homes with lawns, and cars rather than bicycles. The millions, if not the billions, struggling to abandon their Third or Fourth World villages in order to enter the US and Europe, offer us proof of one "fact": the quest for what is still called "the American dream" is global.

These conventional lenses for viewing the "social majorities" of the world, time and again, still make us doubt our own eyes. Yet, the more we see, and the more closely we learn to look beyond the categories of "professional experts," the more transformed become our images of the "underdeveloped" people we encounter; of their notions of self and other.

RETURN AND RE-MEMBERSHIP:
REGENERATING SOIL CULTURES

> A human community, then, if it is to last long, must exert a sort of centripetal force, holding local soil and local memory in place. Practically speaking, human society has no work more important than this. Once we have acknowledged this principle, we can only be alarmed at the extent to which it has been ignored. (Wendell Berry, 1990, p. 155)

In the worlds of "marginals," people are continually rediscovering the nets in which they are knots; the many relations crossing through them. They are continually trying to repair the painful and damaging transmogrification they have suffered when being individualized in the course of colonization and development. In recent years, they have started to regenerate themselves, in their own spaces, by demonstrating what is involved in abandoning the fundamental assumptions of the alphabetized mind. More and more, they refuse to construct themselves as "the individual self."

Domingo's story is typical of the refusal to settle for the "success" that dismembers the individual self. A friend and a postman in Mexico City for twenty years, he came to us to celebrate his recent promotion: selected from among six thousand colleagues to a rank a numbered few ever rise to in the postal hierarchy of Mexico. Designated Postal Inspector, he was ecstatic. However, just a few months later, he came to say good-bye. He had just resigned his new position. With his family, he was returning to his small community in a distant province. Remembering his recent phenomenal success at work, we expressed our surprise and our concern. Why was he "sacrificing" his career and his old-age pension at this point in his career? He laughed when he heard our puzzled queries.

> My people called me back. Once they learned that I was Post Inspector, they had full proof of my reliability and sense of responsibility. They are honoring me as the municipal authority of the community for the next year. Therefore, I must return immediately. Yes, I am giving up all the privileges I have here. I will no longer enjoy the new status I have at work. I will not have my pension. But after all, what does that mean compared to being in my community as a responsible elder? Where will we find our community in Mexico City? What does it mean to have a pension and institutional dependence in this urban desert? If I do well in fulfilling my functions in my village, and I assure you that I will do my best, I will be someone amongst my own people. That means being cared for till the day I die, after which my family will have our whole community's support. That is why I am going back to my people.

We do not know how many share Domingo's success in abandoning the opportunities available to individual selves. But we do know that there are many who are experiencing the losses of moving from a "we" to the life of an "I," an individual self. They are trying hard to regenerate their "underdeveloped" communal spaces. Increasingly disenchanted with goverment bureaucracies, state agencies and other modern institutions, more and more among the "social majorities" are returning to "the village," their own people and commons (Bradford, 1991).

Take, for example, the case of Francisco. We discovered Francisco in Las Juntas – a beautiful village in the mountains of Guerrero, in the south of Mexico. To reach this village, it is still necessary to drive five hours on a dirt road and another two sitting atop a perverse mule. Nobody knows why they call it Las Juntas (Together), for the fact of the matter is that Las Juntas is a collection of dispersed houses, every one at the top of a small hill. The little valley at the center where the community meets for its fiestas and celebrations cannot be described as the center of a town.

On the very day of our arrival, there was a big celebration in Francisco's honor. A member of this village since birth, he was returning to it after ten years of absence in New York. Later, we had the opportunity to talk with him. We could not but ask him why he abandoned his job and life in New York, only to come to live in this place; a village where they have neither the electricity nor any of the comforts to which he had become accustomed.

He first laughed. Then, with his brilliant smile, he replied:

It is not so difficult to understand. Gringos think all Mexicans want to immigrate into their country. I never had any plans of emigrating. I went to the US, like many of my friends, to earn some extra money, and to have some adventures; to know another world; but never to stay away from my own people. After a few months of working here and there, I found a job in Queens. But, of course, in a Mexican restaurant. I had friends there. It was a good job. So I stayed. Every year, I came back to Las Juntas, to see my people, visit my family, my friends … my novia [fiancée]. We married and she came with me to New York. We stayed and stayed. Year after year. A few months ago, I was celebrating my tenth anniversary in the restaurant! My boss, a very gentle American, came for the celebration. That night he suggested that I was eligible for receiving American nationality.

I could not sleep the entire night. For the first time, the idea of living forever in the US became a reality. I suddenly realized that if I did not take a decision right now, I could end up spending my whole life there. A week later, I resigned from my job. My boss was completely surprised by my decision. He could not understand. He was sure I would return. And, yes, I intend to do that for a few months, from time to time, to work in his restaurant, thus adding a few bucks to my income.

But my real life is here. This is my place, among my people. Look at my wife and children! Look at their joy in being amidst our own people. I know every centimeter of this place. I know every tree, every house, every corner of Las Juntas. And every member of this community knows me. Here, I am someone. I am a person. I am appreciated because I always kept one foot here: sending some money, from time to time, for the works that had to be done in the village; for the fiestas; during the holidays. I always kept a contact with my people here. Step by step, I will have my own house here; all the comforts.... My wife, children and I will be cherished and respected here. In New York, who am I? Who will care for us? Who will care for my family if I suddenly die? It is not difficult to see why I am coming back to my place.[4]

Among our friends who constitute the social majorities, we learn that there are more and more Franciscos attempting to go beyond modernity's attempts to place everyone in the anonymity of the "global village."

The following story illustrates that even in urban settlements, "the people" of "cultures of the soil" are struggling to recover and regenerate the soil of their cultures.

Fernando Díaz Enciso invited us some years back to a very special event: the inauguration of his cultural center. He also wanted us to comment on a book he had just published: *A Thousand Stories of Santo Domingo de los Reyes*. Fernando collected them himself. In these stories, "the people" of Santo Domingo, a neighborhood in the south of Mexico City, next to a modern "university city," tell of their experiences of struggling for land – against the rocks, as well as against the authorities.

During the ceremony, Fernando also planned to announce the opening of an "ecological park" in their settlement. After adding a few "tourist" attractions, the people of Santo Domingo want to attract the kind of weekend tourism which responds to the increasing environmental consciousness of the inhabitants of Mexico City – especially those who cannot afford the "getaway" to Cuernavaca, Tepoztlán or other nearby cities in search of spaces where their children can run around, breathe slightly less polluted air, and enjoy themselves for a while. They foresee that this "ecological park" will generate some income for the people of the settlement, and should also get them some financial support from "the authorities" to improve their spaces. In addition to a modest increase in their income, they hope that this will also generate creative interactions with others – conversations about their experiences which enable "the people" to learn from each other about creative initiatives that can help to improve the urban monster they all share.

Fernando Díaz Enciso is a short man, brownish and robust, with timid gestures and brilliant eyes. It would not be possible to distinguish him from the other thousands in the crowds of Mexico City. Still, it is not possible to ignore his presence when he walks in any of the streets of his *barrio* or enters into any of its homes or spaces. He is obviously his people's leader. We will not even attempt to explain the secret of his charisma – something we intuitively sensed without being able to fathom it for ourselves.

A quarter of a century ago, Fernando was among the leaders of one of the biggest urban land invasions of Latin America. In one single night, 25,000 people, colloquially called the *paracaidistas* (parachutists), floated in and took over several hectares in the south of Mexico City. Other thousands arrived in the following months to a place that could not be more hostile: its soil, of volcanic rock, resisted treatment; even cacti refused to grow there. Only scorpions, spiders and snakes found this bleak plateau to be a hospitable habitat.

Who would fight for such a miserable piece of land? Yet, in hindsight, it is easy to see the wisdom of their desperate decision to invade that hostile land. Even the city authorities were forced to accept their invasion, but without the offer of any official support or services; the government's compromise for accepting the invasion without eviction.

That was only the beginning. The invasion continued. To cut the story very short: 500,000 people now live there. Everything has been done, literally, "of, by, and for the people": the building of the houses, the streets, the shops, the common spaces, including their own system for disposing of their garbage. And most of it had been done by women.

"Since the time we started to build our neighborhoods," reminisced doña Chonita, "we women have worked and worked. For we have been in the neighborhood, in our homes, the whole day. If a roof falls, we put it back in its place; if there is the need to cover a hole in the street, we do it; all these things outside the house as well as attending to the needs at home, the husband and the children." For a moment, she stopped to put the handful of radishes she had just collected into a big steel pot, next to which sat other women, young and old, cleaning the romeros and vegetables "they have 'extracted' from the land." Her smile shows signs of tiredness. She continues:

> And it is because the husband needs to go out to work; then you cannot wait for him to return to solve all the problems we confront. What you need is just your hands and the will to do the same thing that the señores usually do. It was like that since the beginning. The construction of the *barrio* was the task of the women every day of the week. We did the building and cleaned the streets. And we also dealt with the children, to see that they can reach farther than we have done. We took care of the family economy and, above all, confronted the constant challenge of eviction. The men spent their time obtaining permissions for their trades; otherwise the police break our stalls and shops and persecute us in other ways.
>
> But the land, the once-wretched land, gives us everything. It is good to one, if you work it. That is how no one here is really a *pobrecito* (a very poor person). We are working hard. We know that there is no free lunch.

After the dramatic overnight takeover of land, every other step has been hard and slow. Step by step, they organize everything in their community by themselves, with a pittance from the government once their settlement had a name, a shape, an identity. Like most others among the "social majorities," they have no expectations of state authorities: "Before, we were waiting for the authorities, to see what they will do for us," said don Antonio; "but they always promise everything, and give us nothing."

The Cultural Center of Santo Domingo de los Reyes has a surprising entrance: the façade is like the arcade of a cathedral, 15 meters high. But there is no church behind the arcade. It gives access to a patio, around which there are a variety of spaces: for children, for adolescents, workshops, a library, a documentation center, a theater for communal assemblies and feasts. On the main wall, they have a mural painted by Daniel Manrique, the painter of the *barrio* of Tepito. Their whole *barrio* expresses that they are living in the center of the world, of the cosmos; that they are aware of it; that they are proud of being at its center and that they accept full responsibility for keeping it alive. That day of the inauguration also revealed the diversity of the people with whom they are solidary: the members of other *barrios*; technicians and social workers of public agencies; volunteers of NGOs, university professors, as well as a "high official" complete with necktie and his cellular phone who has offered "hidden support." These are their "contacts," the threads of their wide social fabric, keeping the most polluted city in the world alive.

Contemporary cities belong to the poor, observes architect John Turner. For centuries, the life of marginals in Mexico City was based in multi-functional, self-contained *barrios*; each a complete culture, more or less self-reliant and autonomous. The city grew by dissolving such *barrios* and building specialized spaces: to work, study, buy, sleep or be entertained in. "The people" who built the modern city remained there: the peasants expelled from their commons by the Green Revolution, as well as those who were compelled to seek work as masons, carpenters, janitors, etc. They neither had a place in the buildings they built with their hands and skills, nor could they return to their devastated communities. They remained. After painfully learning the rules of the urban, industrial, political game, they survived by creating their own spaces; defining their own forms of urban identity, of living together. In a single night, they have created whole settlements where, only the day before, there were wastelands. Neither bulldozers nor the police, at the service of development, were able to stop them. Confronting the impotence of Third World authorities, new *barrios* were constantly established, joining up with the older *barrios* of resistance. The modern city is besieged by these *barrios*.

Modernization tried to replace people's traditional practices and skills by creating "needs" (for houses built by "experts," to take one example) and their "satisfiers" (a housing industry whose "boom" invariably creates a growing deficit of houses). They modernized Mexico City, accommodating cars, factories, shopping centers and freeways; yet failed in their stated goal of "housing the poor." The norms and regulations of "international standards" skyrocketed costs, rendering the industrial "solution" inaccessible to the "social majorities." Marginals forced the government to accept their improvised solutions, including the virtual elimination of the market for land, labor and money (as Polanyi would have described the arrangement) by limiting the encroachments of the economy.

More than half of the currently existing houses in Mexico were built by their owners. There are no "homeless people": even the most destitute may "invade" a plot and assemble the four sticks needed to start a house. The social fabric of the city took its peculiar shape from the fact that more than half of its inhabitants had to struggle with the police to "settle down," beyond the law and based on their autonomous organizations for community, solidarity and struggle. Instead of rural urbanization (which never came), the city was "ruralized." Instead of abstract, impersonal, modern norms and unfeasible techno-industrial regulations, marginals created their own autonomous forms of social regulation for the flexibility needed to survive the machinations of developers, professionals, bureaucrats and their market.

The quality and the ingenuity of these settlements, fostering conviviality and expressing dignity and autonomy, came to be widely recognized over the years. Yet doubts existed about their technology and engineering. The 1985 earthquake in Mexico City cleared up those doubts. The collapse of Nonoalco-Tlatelolco, a development that was the pride of American and Mexican engineers, circulated in postcards as the very image of modern Mexico, imposed a heavy death-toll. Many modest houses also collapsed, but rarely did their inhabitants die. Most houses built by "the people" proved themselves to be more lasting and appropriate to local conditions than some of the most sophisticated products of modern engineering. That same earthquake posed a special challenge for Mexico City. Almost 100,000 "houses" had to be built in a short time and in very restricted places downtown. Developers were motivated to use the calamity to redefine national housing policies. With the backing of national and foreign professional institutions, they pressed for typical industrial "solutions." While these remained stalled within bureaucratic channels, thousands of earthquake victims, in record time and quality, built themselves two- and three-floor dwellings, appropriate for the kind of conviviality they enjoy in their neighborhoods.

Their experiences illustrate the new political forms of social movements coming from the margins in response to the "crises" of economic man. This "lead" actor of the economy, lacking feasible answers with which to cope with economic "crises," frequently reacts with desolation, exhaustion, even desperation. He constantly falls for the political and economic game of carpetbagging the present for the future, transmogrifying hopes into expectations. In contrast, the "lead" actor of the new commons, the common wo/man, dissolves or prevents scarcity through imaginative efforts to cope with predicaments imposed upon her. She looks for no more than free spaces. With limited support for her initiatives, she invents political coalitions increasingly capable of reorienting policies and changing political styles. The new awareness emerging at the margins, awakening others at "the center" while broadening coalitions, offer hopes for arriving at those critical points through which inversions of economic dominance become feasible.

In spite of the economy (national or global), common men and women have been able to keep alive another logic, another set of rules. In contrast with the economic logic, theirs remains embedded in the social fabric; confining the economy to its place: a marginal one. The margins alone can teach others what they are doing to regenerate their places beyond the reign of economics, reinventing ancient traditions of hospitality.

FROM TOLERANCE TO HOSPITALITY

For "global citizens," the globe is not large enough to support both their own endless "needs" (for rapidly obsolescent "goods") and the families of marginals. Even those opposed to xenophobic campaigns (such as Peter Wilson's in California, partially generated by the turbulence associated with NAFTA and other globalizing events) find it difficult, if not impossible, to accept that people at the grassroots struggle to stay in their own places; trying to keep or recover their own worlds. Anxious to protect the shrinking job market, they seek to close national doors, preventing "human surpluses" from becoming "resident aliens" or immigrants. The choices of Juanito, Francisco or the people of Fernando Díaz Enciso in Santo Domingo de los Reyes are read by the modern minorities either as "exceptions to the rule" or not "freely" made at all. They remain convinced that the persons of our stories remain the exceptions; unique rather than the common rule.

Juanito's, Domingo's or Fernando's stories are, of course, unique. They are not, however, exceptions. They reveal important patterns. The Miztecs constitute by far the largest group of Mexicans living in New York, a rapidly growing "minority." Of those who have succeeded in accommodating themselves to that inhospitable context, many are actually building houses in their original communities in Oaxaca for their return. Most of New York's Miztecs are taking steps in that direction (Valdés, 1996). Migrants to California, coming from the different Indian cultural groups of Oaxaca are dissolving the traditional opposition between "modernity" and "tradition," organizing "transnational communities." These "socioeconomic fabrics spread between Oaxaca and the United States and points in between," are defined by political expressions like the "transnational Oaxacan indigenous organizations" (see Kearney, 1996a, 1996b).

We seek neither to elaborate upon such sociological diagnoses of indigenous persons' patterns nor to predict whether or not these peoples will succeed in their current endeavors. We simply seek to understand their struggles and predicaments, respecting them rather than reducing them to the latest variety of social science theory – such as Kearney's – about what "the masses" are predictably or probably going to opt for. Their current actions, however, nourish our hopes for the continual regeneration of spaces where real people enjoy a shared memory, maintaining hospitality. It is no secret that the "social minorities" are rendering the planet inhospitable, for humans as for all living creatures. Environmentalists have documented this inhospitality in detail. Our interests depart from theirs, focusing on threats posed to cultural conceptions and practices of hospitality. It is very difficult if not impossible for individual selves to be hospitable. Traditions of hospitality are kept alive only by those who enjoy and participate in communal memory. Individual selves are better, perhaps, at tolerating rather than hosting others.

Tolerance is but the "civilized" form of intolerance. The tolerated person is told that s/he is not the way s/he should be; and that, however, the dominant group or culture is so generous and civilized that s/he can stay – in spite of his/her difference. Hospitality is something radically different. Hosting the other has no implicit content of comparative judgement. It includes a principle of levelling (which comes with the root meaning of hospitality) by which the foreigner, the stranger, the "Other," is given a place within the "we" hosting him/her.

We know first hand the radical differences that separate and distinguish the experiences of being tolerated or hosted. We are not talking here of being hosted by friends or family in different countries: we may be foreigners for them, but not strangers. Friendship or family ties dissolve any feeling of estrangement. Our ideas or habits may be merely tolerated by an uncle hosting us, who disagrees with or even hates them; but he does not see us as strangers – that is, real foreigners. In reflecting upon hospitality here, we are alluding to the attitudes we have observed when we are among peoples with whom we have no specific ties of family or friendship. Such experiences now bring us to elaborate upon the absence of hospitality among the "social minorities"; on the impossibility of individual selves being hospitable. Our reflections probe the differences we have experienced between the "Hospitality Room" at an international airport of the "social minorities" and the Cultural Center of Santo Domingo de los Reyes; or between the human context of a modern hospital and the House for Guests into which the Health Center of Chicahuaxtla was transformed. These experiences compel us to go deeper in exploring the inhospitality of the "Global Project" to the "social majorities."

Every culture, every group, has its own practices and expressions of hospitality. From as far back as the ancient Greeks, we can trace practices of hospitality that radically differentiate the eastern world from the western. The history of hospitality in the West is arguably the history of its substitution by institutions that only took the name of this ancient human tradition (hospital, hospice), while its content vanished.[5] Hospitality remained alive in the East.

> An experience related by the late Cardinal Jean Danielou simply captures this complex historical truth. A Chinese friend of his, after becoming a Christian, made a pilgrimage from Peking to Rome on foot. In central Asia, he regularly found hospitality. As he got into the Slavonic nations, he was occasionally welcomed into someone's house. But when he arrived among the people of the western churches, he had to seek shelter in the poorhouse, since the doors of homes were closed to strangers and pilgrims. (Illich, 1987b)

A pilgrim starting in Bolivia or Peru, travelling to the north in the American continent, would probably tell a similar story. The "poorhouse" now has many names in modern societies: hospice, hospital, shelter, asylum. Financed by governments, churches or the voluntary sector, all these "caring" institutions have one central feature in common: they "care" for specific classes of people excluded from a "normal life," which is the opposite to what hospitality previously meant for strangers. In recent times, furthermore, the Stranger is no longer hosted, even in the poorhouse or its equivalents: s/he is immediately captured by the police and sent away. "Globalization" is xenophobic.

In the western tradition, hospitality could only be extended to an "other" who is not completely "other": someone with whom it is possible to practice the levelling implicit in hospitality.

> The stranger (*xenos*) is any needy man who speaks a Hellenic tongue. Zeus makes all Greeks alike, levelling them. "To level" is the root meaning of ghosti, the root from which guest, host and hostility are derived.... The second part of the word, pit or pot, means "power", more precisely the "power holder", the master of the house, the clan, the place.... The hospitality extended to

guests is always based on xeno-philia, the love of xenos, the other Greek. It cannot be offered to the *barbaroi*, babblers, who speak no language a Greek can understand...

Genuine hostility, like that of Menelao against Pisander, "can only occur with the kind of equals who are received as guests" (Illich, 1987b).

Western travellers continue to experience that speaking the language of the host is not a condition to be a guest in non-western cultures. Even today, visiting foreigners fully appreciate the hospitality they are offered in arriving in most villages of the southern part of the globe, in spite of their exposure to the processes of modern deterioration.

There is, of course, nothing more treacherous than that which violates hospitality.[6] Too many, if not all, colonizing ventures started with an episode of abused hospitality. The story of Cortés trapping Montezuma, who was hosting and honoring him as a distinguished guest, is not the exception but the rule of hospitality abused by colonizers. The destruction of hospitality is but one of the consequences of the long process of embodiment of the individual self, as a specific western construction. (The very fact that such destruction did not occur or occurred to a different degree among the "social majorities" is one of the reasons for their specific capacity to resist individualization and regenerate their commons.) The enclosure of the commons (Marx); the disembedding of economy from society and culture and its constitution as an autonomous sphere (Polanyi); the transition from the reign of gender to the regime of sex and the creation of the text (Illich): those and many other historical changes are landmarks of that process.

In our continuing travels crossing over between the worlds of the "social minorities" and the "social majorities," we have learned that every modern institution of hospitality – hospital, hospice – is rooted in the long tradition of intolerance masked as the "ideal" of "tolerance" that defines modern hospitality. This hospitality is shaped by the same mindset that breaks commons and communities, replacing them with the lonely privacy and competitive public corporations of "homeless" minds; individual selves doomed to the futile search for home.[7]

When Michael Ignatieff (1985) starts his long journey to explore "the needs of strangers," he tells a daily life story so common in industrial countries that it has become invisible. It deserves quoting at length:

> I live in a market street in north London. Every Tuesday morning there is a barrow ouside my door and a cluster of old-age pensioners rummage through the torn curtains, buttonless shirts, stained vests, torn jackets, frayed trousers and faded dresses that the barrow man has on offer. They make a cheerful chatter outside my door, beating down the barrow man's prices, scrabbling for bargains like crows pecking among the stubble.

They are not destitute, just respectably poor. The old men seem more neglected than the women: their faces are grey and unshaven and their necks hang loose inside yellowed shirt collars. Their old bodies must be thin and white beneath their clothes. The women seem more self-possessed, as if old age were something their mothers had prepared them for. They also have the skills for poverty: the hems of their coats are neatly darned, their buttons are still in place.

These people give the impression of having buried their wives and husbands long ago and having watched their children decamp to the suburbs. I imagine them living alone in small dark rooms lit by the glow of electric heaters. I came upon one old man once doing his shopping alone, weighed down in a queue at a potato stall and nearly fainting from tiredness. I made him sit down in a pub while I did the rest of his shopping. But if he needed my help, he certainly didn't want it. He was clinging on to his life, gasping for breath, but he stared straight ahead when we talked and his fingers would not be pried from his burdens. All these old people seem like that, cut adrift from family, slipping away into the dwindling real of their inner voices, clinging to the old barrow as if it were a raft carrying them out to sea.

My encounters with them are a parable of moral relations between strangers in the welfare state. They have needs, and because they live within a welfare state, these needs confer entitlements – rights – to the resources of people like me. Their needs and their entitlements establish a silent relation between us. As we stand together in line at the post office, while they cash their pension cheques, some tiny portion of my income is transferred into their pockets through the numberless capillaries of the state. The mediated quality of our relationship seems necessary to both of us. They are dependent on the state, not upon me, and we are both glad of it. Yet I am also aware of how this mediation walls us off from each other. We are responsible for each other, but we are not responsible to each other. (pp. 9–10)

At the end of his long journey, Ignatieff looks desperately around, to avoid nostalgia, fear, cynicism or despair.

We think of belonging as permanence, yet all our homes are transient. Who still lives in the house of their childhood? Who still lives in the neighbour-hood where they grew up? Home is the place we have to leave in order to grow up, to become ourselves. We think of belonging as rootedness in a small familiar place, yet home for most of us is the convulsive arteries of a great city. Our belonging is no longer to something fixed, known and familiar, but to an electric and heartless creature eternally in motion. (p. 141)

His only hope: to find words, "a language adequate to the times we live in ... to keep us human. Without a public language to help us find our own words, our needs will dry up in silence" (p. 142). Unable to see beyond the individual self, after his profound insights in its story and tragic evolution, he concludes that "the problem is not to defend universality, but to give these abstract individuals the chance to become real *historical individuals* again, with the social relations and the power to protect themselves" (pp. 52–3, emphasis added).

What Ignatieff does not, or, perhaps, cannot consider is that there are no "real historical individuals"; that individual selves are nothing but modern abstract constructs. Ignatieff identifies himself with the "we" of the "social minorities," living in the welfare state. They are trying to escape from sentimentalism: seeing everything through rose-tinted spectacles, not seeing, being blind to what is happening with them and their societies; despair: giving up all hope; cynicism: accepting the unacceptable, bearing the unbearable; religious faith: a move to transfer the hope out of this world; superstition: transferring the religious faith to an idol, like development, progress, science, technology (Lummis, 1996, p. 147). No matter within which of those categories they fall, they seem to share a feeling of impotence, powerlessness. What can I do? Even those fully aware of the current disaster, refusing to adopt any hypocritical slogan or to become cynics, fall into the despair of individual impotence: What can I do? No longer trusting that their individual votes, their letters to their representatives or their personal activism will effect any relevant change, they are confronted by the persistent question: What can I do?

At the grassroots, we seldom find the sentimentalism, despair, cynicism, superstition or the feeling of impotence described by Ignatieff. Common people learn to trust each other and be trustworthy in ways that are rapidly vanishing among the "social minorities." Their common faith is seldom deposited in abstract causes or phantoms, like humankind. Instead, it is entrusted to real men and women, defining the place to which they belong and that belongs to them. Rather than the private hope and public despair of the "social minorities" (some hope for their personal lives, no hope for public affairs) (Lummis, 1996, p. 154), we usually find expressed among them a common hope in their own capacity to deal with their predicaments, whether good, bad or indifferent. Given that condition, they can be both hospitable and responsible.

A specific attitude to the "other," the one coming from outside, the stranger, was embedded in the traditional practices of hospitality. In the *Iliad*, when Ulysses arrives in Ithaca, transformed by Minerva to the point that he cannot be recognized by his subjects, Emmaeus the swineherd leads the stranger into his hut.

> He bade him sit down. He strewed a thick bed of rushes on the floor. On top of this he threw a shaggy chamois skin, a great thick one on which he himself used to sleep at night. He said: "Stranger, though a still poorer man than you might come here, it would yet not be right for me to insult him. All strangers and beggars are from Jove. Take from me what you can get and be thankful." (Illich, 1987b)

Why am I behaving like the rich, who cannot offer help or hospitality to the hungry and naked stranger for fear of being robbed, ponders Tolstoy's humble peasant in "What Men Live By." But it is not only in Tolstoy or the pages of the *Iliad* that we see genuine expressions of "common" women and men's hospitality. Today, we continuously discover this hospitality even in the dust, squalor and destitution of the millions who inhabit the urban ghettoes we have walked through or visited, such as the one by the railway station of Nizamuddin East, at the center of monstrous New Delhi. For the social planners and sociologists, "the people" who have built their homes there in two rows on the pavement are "urban squatters"; illegally making houses no higher than four feet – if that; with dimensions enough for the family to crawl in to escape the night chill of December in Delhi or the monsoon squalls. Humble, these dwellings still reflect the simple pride of those for whom they are real homes. On our morning walks, we have marvelled at their beauty, freshly covered with *gobar* (cow-dung) and hand-painted with rangoli designs and even decorative domicile numbers for their easy identification; as we have also marvelled at the shining utensils in which they prepare their early breakfasts on the pavement. Not to be intrusive, we have walked through without looking directly at the convivial cooking going on in the neighborhood. On the occasions that they have caught us admiring their beautiful decorations on doorways, we have been immediately welcomed with smiles, and a warm invitation: "Come, sit with us and share our chappatis." To make us comfortable, they have indicated that we do not have to join them on the pavement floor, immediately emptying the only family *charpai* or bed, covered with rolled up bedding, to make room for us to sit raised up.

We cannot but recognize the hardships and extreme deprivation of these people, the severe restrictions they are daily confronted with as "oustees" of their rural spaces. But we can no longer see their hospitality as a "plot" to either pickpocket or squeeze out money from us – as we have often been cynically warned; or even as "folkloric," "quaint," and idiosyncratic behaviors that modernization and development will dissolve in the course of the "global project." We are slowly learning to appreciate their gestures of kindness, generosity and hospitality as expressions of their traditions' vitality, so far successfully resisting the modern processes of destruction that reduce peoples into societies of strangers. Such traditions of hospitality, notes Rabindranath Tagore is "the product of centuries of culture" (Tagore, 1961, p. 93). Reflecting on how long it takes to evolve cultures of hospitality, he shares stories of travels in his own land:

> Once there was an occasion for me to motor down to Calcutta from a place a hundred miles away. Something wrong with the mechanism made it necessary

for us to have a repeated supply of water almost every half-hour. At the first village where we were compelled to stop, we asked help of a man to find water for us. It proved quite a task for him, but when we offered him his reward, poor though he was, he refused to accept it. In fifteen other villages, the same thing happened. In a hot country, where travellers constantly need water and where the water supply grows scanty in summer, the villagers consider it their duty to offer water to those who need it. They could easily make a business out of it, following the inexorable law of demand and supply. But the ideal which they consider to be their *dharma* has become one with their life. They do not claim any personal merit for possessing it.... To be able to take a considerable amount of trouble in order to supply water to a passing stranger and yet never to claim merit or reward for it seems absurdly and negligibly simple compared with the capacity to produce an amazing number of things per minute. A millionaire tourist, ready to corner the food market and grow rich by driving the whole world to the brink of starvation, is sure to feel too superior to notice this simple thing while rushing through our villages at sixty miles an hour. Yet ... that simplicity is the product of centuries of culture. That simplicity is difficult of imitation. In a few years' time, it might be possible for me to learn how to make holes in thousands of needles simultaneously by turning a wheel, but to be absolutely simple in one's hospitality to one's enemy, or to a stranger, requires generations of training. (Tagore, 1963, pp. 92–3)

We see these traditions of *dharma* and other cultural gestures as powerful "weapons" of regeneration, shedding light on the blessings the "social majorities" still enjoy as they daily create and re-create their post-modern initiatives for protecting their commons' hospitality. Such cultural traditions of communal hospitality keep them laughing and human in the midst of the inhuman conditions created by Manpower Planners; bringing the "social majorities" away from their villages into the streets and ghettoes of New Delhi, Mexico, Rio de Janeiro, São Paulo ... where they are the "human surpluses" of the "social minorities." We are alluding here not to the demographic definition of the current predicaments of the world (for reasons ecological or other),[8] but to "human surpluses" defined in economic terms. They were born with capitalism, with the industrial mode of production, which, "by producing too many useful things, ends up producing too many useless people" (Marx, 1954). Capital is not an amount of means of production, commodities or money, but a relationship between the owners of those means of production and their workers. The history of capitalism reveals "the masses" expropriated of their own means of subsistence, and who cannot be absorbed in the production process controlled by the owners of the means of production. The "Global Project" is accelerating that process in unprecedented ways: first, because of its scale; second, at a historical moment in which the old "solutions" (like massive migrations – to what is now the US, for example) are no longer possible; third, because the corrective mechanisms, constructed in the last two centuries and basically associated with the welfare state, are being dismantled by the same forces accelerating the process. The "Global Project" clearly implies a radical redefinition of the "social majorities," now expressed as the "population problem." Both during the colonial and the postcolonial period, they were a source of accumulation: slaves, serfs, servants, workers. They are rapidly becoming disposable: in the era of the globalization of the economy, capital has more appetite than ever for cheap labor, but no stomach to digest the current supply – at any price.

Here, we cannot deal with the technical implications of this situation. All that we want to make evident are some of the contemporary reactions of "the people" now being excluded from the economic system: those who ceased to be on a payroll and are unlikely to ever regain that status; those who are losing, at the same time, their jobs and their retirement plans or funds; those who can no longer find use for their skills and capacities and are not able to acquire new ones ... Some of them are attempting the old escape routes: migration, retraining, deceleration of technical advances, etc. But many others, particularly among the "social majorities," are rejecting the social minorities' definition of their condition: "human surpluses." Not being fools, they are all too aware that their "incorporation" into the "global economy" implies their "inclusion" as castoffs – in real words, being excluded. They are no longer enamored with how castoffs are "tolerated" in the worlds of the social minorities: through, for example, the undignified condition of those living on "welfare," collecting a check to survive from the society denying them opportunities for useful and creative living. They also know by experience that the social remedy for their condition is through regenerating their elders' traditions of hospitality – hosting those who are the rejects of welfare and other related systems for dealing with surpluses in the worlds of the "social minorities." They now know better the virtues of their own traditions: to count their blessings, including the forms of hospitality they still enjoy.

BEYOND WASTE: COMPOSTING, REMAKING COMMUNAL SOIL

When people lose their communal soil (cultural or agricultural), no longer can or do they rely on each other in the neighborhood. They depend, instead, on abstract institutions, including elaborate modern legal systems, manned by armies of lawyers. This conglomerate produces obsolescent "goods," all too soon headed out as countless truckloads of waste bound for landfills and incinerators – preferably where the "social majorities" have homes. Mourning this tragedy, Wendell Berry (1990) also unveils the one that remains hidden: the wasted lives of the waste-makers; humans bound for mindless factory jobs and plastic offices, carefully sealed off from nature; while elders and children are kept deliberately unproductive by institutions and professions supposedly designed for their care. Reflecting on all these wasted lives used up in manufacturing shoddy, obsolescent "goods," Berry reflects on the "good work" of commons not destroyed by the individual self's economy. At the heart of productive communion and commons, keeping them whole, healthy and organic, Berry identifies the pleasures of eating, growing and preparing food. In diverse worlds, each defined by the activities of producing their own *comida*, people are "productive," and not human surpluses or waste. And where humans are not wasted, nor is other matter. What is not worn or eaten does not travel thousands of useless toxic miles to arrive at a landfill. Taking different paths, it re-enters the organic cycle in which everything returns to the soil out of which it emerged. From dust to dust.

Following Berry's organic cycle, we end our reflections on regenerating ourselves by tracing the movements of *comida* from the mouth to the other orifice: the anus. At the point of departure, we arrive deliberately – at the other end, literally and metaphorically. At the grassroots, we have come to appreciate not only how the people escape industrial eating but also human waste. Like industrial food production and consumption, modern defecation and urination alienate, disconnect and dis-member. Learning to disembowel as an individual self, moderns are educated to believe that, like the "dearest liberation" from an intimate engagement with their food, they must disengage from their human wastes.

This modern certainty has transformed the luxury Mr Crapper invented for the King of England (Reyburn, 1971) into a "basic human need" of "the masses." Mr Crapper's nineteenth-century creation to help royalty gain further distance from their own waste, the Water Closet, took hold of the industrial world after World War II. It totally reformulated the urban environment. Today, the WC and its sewerage system are the very expression of a modern city; of development or progress itself. Modern identity is defined by it. We have been informed about numbers of draftees honorably discharged because they suffer from the inability to perform an essential human function in the absence of their water closet.

As a "basic human need," the WC is being offered or imposed upon the "social majorities" as one of the promises of progress; a mode of privacy and convenience they ought to aspire for and achieve. While schools, critical for forging a national identity, are joining other institutions in reducing the number of spoken languages in the world from 5,100 to 100 (Sachs, 1992), modern sewerage is reducing diverse traditions for communal defecation to the one universally prized by the individual self.

Bharati Mukherjee's Jasmine takes us out into the fields with the village women of the Punjab, giving us a glimpse of the conviviality they enjoy as they defecate together in the soft darkness yet-to-be dawn. Like the traditional communal smoking enjoyed by peasants, it is not a solitary activity, but convivial in its very essence. This communal activity – filled with tales of joy and sorrow, husbands and lovers, kind or terrible mothers-in-law, and all else that constitutes the dailyness of daily life – is gendered like the majority of grassroots activities. It creates close bonds between the women on this side of the village, as also between men who go out together to the opposite side.

In another part of the planet, poet Gary Snyder attempts to recover the communal conviviality of other ancient traditions. In comfortable latrines built in lovely cabins, with windows from floor to roof that open to the vast vista of his garden and Californian woods, Snyder's guests enjoy nature and the natural. While not defecating together, Gary Snyder's guests are not entirely alone and closed off; they can see and be seen. Hospitable to guests unaccustomed to such communal practices, he has also constructed a modern flush toilet for privacy.

The ideals of privacy defended by individual selves often come with the faith that by pulling the flush toilet handle, they are handling their responsibility; scientifically and hygienically "solving" the "problem" of disposing of human waste. Their education keeps them innocent of the ways in which the WC, like other modern technologies, efficiently hides the problems it creates. Promoting convenience today, it is inconveniencing those yet to be born, absorbing vast proportions of the water piped into modern homes, involving a high consumption of energy, modern sewerage creates scarcities of drinking or irrigation water for the "social majorities." Distanced, like the royalty they prefer to mimic, "educated" men and women are kept ignorant of how "black waters" are one of the main sources of planetary pollution; how modern human waste, mixed with water, pollutes by transmogrifying nature's springs into industrial water: H_2O plus the chemicals of treatment plants.

Modern sewerage, like industrial eating, ties up people's intestines to other centralized bureaucracies. The individual self, shaped, defined and dis-membered from community by the water closet (and his or her other industrial inventions) is forced into increased dependencies on the market or the state. This dependency was rendered naked during the disastrous earthquake of 1985, when two million people were left disconnected in Mexico City, after their sewerage pipes broke. Disconnections like these reveal the nexus between a technology designed for the privacy of individual selves which "down the tubes," so to speak, transforms them into "the masses." WC users are reduced by urban planners to a unit of volume: the amount of faeces generated per head. Instead of a communal responsibility that belongs to people's commons, "human waste" is transformed into a state matter, controlling all citizens who follow its regulations. Their privacy prevents individual selves from identifying the hidden strings that pull them into conformity with state norms, every time they pull the chain for what they believe is another modern "liberation." The private water closet, tying the self to the vast and intricate system of the state's sewerage pipes, is a metaphor for the logic of contemporary socio-politics.

The "social minorities" will likely continue their dependence on such damaging factors in the foreseeable future. The implementation of alternatives requires such radical changes of habits and modes of thinking that few dare to suggest them.[9] For "the people" who constitute the Two-thirds World, the water closet emerges as a "need" only when urban friends or relatives come to visit them in their villages, and cannot accommodate themselves to "primitive" local conditions. (That was one of the reasons why the people of San Andrés Chicahuaxtla included a flush toilet in their House for Guests.) Some members of the "social majorities" have undoubtedly been "educated" that the water closet is a "basic human need," and, therefore, a legitimate political claim. While a few have succeeded in getting their claims met, most others are not even waiting for a "solution" to an artificially created predicament. By now, many have learned the hard way the consequences of this scientific "improvement." Living in the places where the "social minorities" transport their "black waters," the "social majorities" are learning how these pollute their soils and rivers, creating "problems" for which they do not have "solutions" rooted in their own traditions. Furthermore, the "social majorities" are learning fast that, despite the "sincere" promises of the authorities seeking election (or re-election), sewerage remains a radical impossibility for "the masses" in the foreseeable future. They know that state budgets for water or energy are not sufficient to provide them the privileges taken for granted by the "social minorities." No doubt some "marginals" resent this fact, while the others look for alternative solutions; those that help them to recover their sense – particularly their sense of community. Options like dry sanitary toilets offer practical and feasible solutions for the disposal of "the masses'" excrements. Instead of spreading environmental contamination or the dis-ease of the individual self, they are spreading the contagion of grassroots autonomy. Those using dry toilets and other alternatives to the WC's sewerage system are rediscovering nature's ways for transforming their "waste" into valuable community soil, participating with full autonomy in the organic chain of life. With dry latrines and other alternative technologies, they do not need to use expensive water and energy to transport and treat their faeces; for they are not producing waste (shit, black waters) but life (compost).[10] Being inexpensive and "environmentally friendly," these allow "the people" to enjoy a renewed sense of (local) responsibility.

San Luis Beltrán became a *barrio* of the city of Oaxaca during the last two decades, when the city's growth extended itself into neighboring hills and valleys. Like other suburbs of Oaxaca, it "lacked" the modern sewerage system. In 1987, the people of this *barrio* learned of the experiences of other communities which, confronting shortages of water, had opted for dry latrines. We worked together in building the first twenty-five. To construct the remaining two hundred, they needed no outside help; they had each other. Once dry latrines began to be publicly discussed in Oaxaca, villagers visiting the city, eager to learn the best available techniques for building and using this specific tool, began to arrive in San Luis Beltrán, now quite famous in the region for its dry latrines. In 1992, city authorities announced that San Luis Beltrán was being included in the government's plans for extending the sewerage system of Oaxaca. The peoples of San Luis Beltrán opposed that plan, knowing that Oaxaca lacks a treatment plant; that its black waters are contaminating everything, including the Atoyac river – which, for many centuries, used to be the source of enjoyment and pleasure for all the inhabitants of the city. Their community explored the consequences of transporting their sewage onto the lands of neighboring communities. Their response to the city authorities: "No, thanks." Following that specific decision, they confessed that their original acceptance of dry latrines was only provisional: till the time they succeeded in acquiring modern facilities. After their experiences, however, they came to appreciate the meaning dry latrines have for communal autonomy. Freely, they chose not to fall victim to the WC.

We hope that our readers among the "social minorities" will not read these stories of dry latrines or *comida* as catechisms for global conversion.[11] The idea of disseminating yet another global religion about eating or defecating is not only distasteful; it is counterproductive. The lessons we are learning from "the people" at the grassroots reveal that their successes remain the results of their practices, devoid of any attempt to preach, promote or advertise "the best way" to live for the whole globe.

It is folly to displace or globalize *comida*; to try to argue for the generalization of doña Refugio's fire; or to present the dry latrines of Oaxaca as the technical and social "solution" for the predicaments of the world's polluted cities. To attempt to do so would be to mimic the errors repeatedly made by social planners or engineers. Besides, we are aware that, even with the expanding body of published literature on the damaging impact of the WC, city planners and residents still fail to entertain alternatives to the WC and modern sewerage. Very few of our friends among the "social minorities" would even consider the possibility of renouncing the privacy and convenience of their toilets. For them, communal defecation will remain an aberration – one "social indicator" or even the expression of primitivism and underdevelopment. Even those who view it as the social "solution" for the "social majorities" (given "scarce global resources" or "the population explosion"), refuse it as a solution for their own lives.

Many of these friends explicitly resent the loneliness of modern life in general, and their own lives in particular. Some, visiting from Germany, tell us that more than half of the people in their country live alone in flats or houses – accepting loneliness as the price they must pay for the privacy they "need" as respite from their daily tensions and turmoils as commuters, workers, employees, drivers, passengers, consumers … Some have told us of the "community service" they participate in only during the week, in order to escape to their empty flats for the weekend; given that long stretches of communal living is unfamiliar, and, therefore, unbearable. Even after seeing the misery that comes with trying to be an individual self, many still prefer to behave like one, avoiding any long-term immersion in communal settings. Suffering the traumas of isolation and disconnectedness, they opt for therapists, shrinks or "support groups." They have created an impressive publishing industry for transpersonal healing; for inter-connectedness or "cosmic consciouness": the "no-boundary" self, reunited with the Other, now and in the afterlife.

HOSPITALITY ABUSED;
DEMARCATING POST-MODERN LIMITS

Social engineers manufacture the modern "we" with flags, constitutions and national anthems; or national highways and boundaries symbolized by Los Pinos, Rashtrapati Bhavan or the White House and other symbols; or with e-mail and the Internet. So constructed, that "we" remains as abstract as "the people" of modern nation-states.

From "common people," in the flesh, sensual and carnal, we are learning how to join and rejoin in the "we" of *comida*; in the "we" created when communities keep and look after their own "shit" (metaphorical or real) instead of transporting it far away; through shared stories that constitute communal memory, and their traditions of hospitality. These knit "the people" into the knots of nets, constituting their diverse "we's."[12]

From the "social minorities," we have learned much about industrial efficiency; about "productivity" of industrial outputs: "fast food,"[13] *alimentos*, computers and other "gizmos" essential for storing vast quantitities of industrial memory. We have learned the privacy that circumvents, erodes or undercuts the possibility of hospitality to the Other. We have acquired the privacy of the flush toilet, personal automobile and Internet. In the process of doing so, we have experienced the dismemberment that attends the socialization of the "social minorities." At the same time, we sense the difficulties of abandoning the triumphs and victories of being the individual self, achieved after phenomenal productivity and lonely effort; to start recognizing them as the sources of modern misery; as the pain of dis-memberment. We are not alone. There are others similarly embarked on journeys of communal rememberance. Just as there are individuals who refuse to even entertain the possibilities opened to us at the grassroots. We are loath to promote or sell our own journeys and adventures to the latter. We fully accept them; the "Other" promoting the "Global Project." We do not merely tolerate them. We wish to be hospitable; to accept their existence, their place in their world. We hope for a world that will be many worlds.

Yet, with grassroots hindsight, we recognize the folly of traditional hospitality. To survive, the traditions of the "social majorities" are continually revamping their open, uncritical hospitality and naive acceptance. After five hundred years of hospitality abused, ranging all the way from the case of Montezuma to the Nestlé syndrome,[14] "the people" are learning how uncritical openness to the harbingers of "progress" means the dis-memberment, death or disappearance of their "we." To escape their dark modern fate, they are creating post-modern limits, safeguarding their traditional ideals of hospitality.

This post-modern revamping is epitomized in movements like those of "the people" of Tepoztlán, a small town of Indian origin. Founded by the Tepoztec people hundreds of years ago, it is located in the state of Morelos, only 60 kilometers from Mexico City. In 1992, a few days after we arrived in Tepoztlán with the hope of staying for several months, acquaintances we made only some hours before invited us to accompany them to *comida*, celebrating the fifteenth birthday of their friends' daughter. Ten members of our family were invited to a very special event. Our acquaintances did not see anything remarkable about the fact that we were complete strangers for the family who, still unbeknownst to them, would be hosting us.

Because we were strangers, we did not know two important aspects of Tepoztlán's traditions of hosting and hospitality, still maintained by the people who have lived for several generations in what was, prior to the four Development Decades, a small traditional village, a little jewel nestled at the foot of the sacred Tepozteco peak. The first is that the fifteenth birthday still remains a community affair here; and second, their concept of hospitality includes generosity towards complete strangers, as we were at that time. For the Tepoztecos take the myth of their King very seriously, abiding by it.

The Tepozteco, we were told, was the ancient king who once returned to his village after a long and difficult journey. Dirty, his clothes shredded into rags, he was unrecognizable to his people, who threw him out of the feast they were celebrating at the time of his arrival. Enraged and saddened by the treatment meted to him by his own people, he went to his palace and, putting on his royal finery, returned to the feast. Now recognizable, he was immediately honored with the the best food available. The Tepozteco took this food and splattered his clothes with it, saying: "You are hosting the clothes, not the person inside them. Let these clothes, then, have your food; it has not been cooked for real men and women." Immediately, he returned to his mountain. Since that day, the doors of the houses of every Tepoztec remain open at all their many feasts and *barrio* celebrations. Strangers are now customarily invited to join, and enjoy, as we did, communal hospitality at feasts for hundreds with the convivial preparation of neighbors.

Because of their hospitality and other riches of their place and culture, more and more commuters want to live here, seeking to reduce this beautiful old pueblo into a "bedroom community" for the "social minorities" of Mexico City or Cuernavaca. They desire to possess "the best of both worlds": the "services" of the modern city as well as all the "old world charm" and amenities of Tepoztlán – tortillas grown, ground and shaped by hand; homes of adobe or stone lining lovely cobbled streets, where the milkman still rides from house to house on a horse on its *avenidas*, winding up to the sacred Tepozteco at dawn, heralded in every morning of the year by the symphony of several thousand cocks crowing in unison; festive markets three days a week, bringing in artisans with their fabulous hand weavings and pottery from all the neighboring provinces. Because of the urban rush into their place, Tepoztecos now differentiate among three groups of people living in their village-transformed-into-a-town: the Tepoztecos themselves: born within their indigenous cultural group; the Tepoztizos (those "added to Tepoztlán"): outsiders who feel a profound commitment to Tepoztlán, adopting its customs, while recognizing their own limits of being new settlers; and the extranjeros: foreigners, who mainly live in the valley, within modern developments of luxury houses, many of which are weekend retreats, surrounded by high walls, isolating them from "the people" of the village – clearly designed, physically and metaphorically, for the privacy of the individual self.

With thousands thronging to it in order to escape the grey skies of the most polluted city in the world, the traditional beauty of Tepoztlán has been ravaged with plastic, weekend rioters, mounting garbage, and other gifts of progress, far more so than doña Refugio's San Andrés Chicahuaxtla. All the aquifers of Morelos, for example, are now polluted. One of the biological treasures of the neighboring valley of Cuernavaca, the *maíz morado* (a violet corn), has already disappeared.

This poverty of progress as well as the richness of their traditions of hospitality and *comida* were both present at the celebration where we were graciously received. While *comida* was served on disposable paper plates accompanied by Coke right out of the bottle with a plastic straw stuck inside, it was clear that the traditional festive food, at the centre of which is Tepoztlán's famous *mole*, was not "catered" or cooked following a recipe book. Its fabulous *sabor* or flavor could only come from hours of loving labor put in by human hands. While only the matriarch of the family had the authority and privilege of filling and stirring the enormous earthen pot in which the mole is prepared, she was assisted by an impressive congregation of community women, who for several days ground, chopped and peeled all the ingredients and "secret" spices that went into this family recipe. With hospitality impossible for "the stranger" to even imagine, let alone enjoy in the world of the "social minorities," our extended family of ten joined hundreds of other guests, served food into the late hours of the star-lit night. Suddenly, its startling beauty and conviviality was blighted by the vulgar display of industrial firecrackers – one among many other modern additions to the ritual and rich *comida* of Tepoztlán's traditional hospitality.

Because their traditions are still alive, the Tepoztecs are capable of forcefully saying "*Basta*" ("Enough") to many modern intrusions. A few years ago, they succeeded in stopping the project designed by developers to rapidly transport millions of tourists to their sacred mountain from Mexico City, in twenty minutes or less. They were denounced as foolish for losing the train that could have fully "incorporated" them into one of the most modern cities of the world.

In 1995, the Tepoztecs confronted a harder challenge. A new governor, with the legal backing of the state and the financial backing of Mexico's modern entrepreneurial tzars, promoted and coordinated a multi-billion dollar investment of national and transnational companies, to create a "technological paradise," a high-tech belt – the analogue to Silicon Valley – around Mexico City, with the first phase of this development starting in Tepoztlán. The land was purchased for a first-class

golf course, luxury residences and clubs, so that the managers of national and transnational companies could communicate with the world
through interactive television and other ultramodern technologies without having to suffer the daily commute to polluted Mexico City. GTE
was involved in the project and particularly interested in demonstrating
its lucrative possibilities, in order to reformulate both urban environments and corporate management all over the world.

The Tepoztecs defeated the plan, following a long, complicated
and ugly political battle. Their victory demanded the strong unison
forged through the creation of the *Comité de la Unidad Tepozteca* (the
Committee for Tepoztec Unity) to face and overcome the united forces
of the state and the global market. They had to force out the town's
Presidente Municipal who authorized the project. Challenging not only
state and federal authorities but a hostile press and the "social minorities" promoting all the marvels of the "Global Project," a few thousand
Tepoztecos aroused the fear of "the economic centers of power," eager
for free-trade zones to draw in foreign investment, while anxious that
Tepoztlán's stance against neoliberalism could be dangerously contagious.

We cannot tell here their complex saga of struggle – with many
ups and downs, murders and massive mobilizations of global solidarity,
including that of the Zapatistas. Environmentalists circulated this local
tale of liberation and oppression on the Internet. Two aspects of this ongoing struggle are particularly pertinent for the saga of grassroots post-
modernism. First, we are learning from their dignified "No, thanks"
to the "Global Project," proffering all the benefits of neoliberalism:
supposedly "permanent," well-paid jobs for everyone; environmental
improvements, regenerating all the areas damaged by previous developments; taxes for the municipality complemented with special allocations
of public resources by the state government in order to "solve" all of
the "social problems" of Tepoztlán, including potable water, sewerage,
shortage of other municipal services ... you name it. Second, this "case"
of local resistance by "the people," circulated far and wide, is teaching
us about ways of creating extended solidarities in the quest for survival
from the "Global Project."

The battle of Tepoztlán, like all other local struggles of resistance and
liberation from the global economy, brings some fundamental questions
into the public arena for the deliberations of the "civil society." Can we,
"the people," still determine what to do in our homes and communities,
within our own territory, free of the jurisdiction of provincial or state
authorities? Can "the people" define their lives in the terms of their
own cultures and traditions, autonomous of the dictates of the state?
The battle of Tepoztlán was not, as the authorities caricatured it, an

obvious conflict between the past and the future; conceived by a small group of ill-informed activists seeking to pit tradition against progress. Obviously, the project did have the support of a small minority in Tepoztlán: from those who sold their land for quick money; as well as those who share the promoters' dreams of modernization. But the majority of Tepoztecs opposed the project (80 percent, according to one count). They had all the information they needed for their decision, neither attributable to ignorance nor conservatism, as the different authorities, local and national, alleged. The Tepoztecs' town shows ample evidence not only of hospitality to strangers but to social change as well. They have their share of sufferings imposed by the Global Project; as also they have living and vital traditions for enriching and transforming their small town. They want to overcome their acute suffering from both the social and environmental horrors that have come with their economic development. And they want to do so in their own ways, their decisions reflecting their contemporary cultural understandings. Clearly, the government and the entrepreneurs represent an obsolete past: that which seeks to suppress and co-opt democratic will by market despotism.

Of its critics, rejecting the project for only serving the rich, the Governor of Morelos demanded: "Who works for the poor?" And, he continued: "Forced to render services, who renders them to the poor?" For all his political acumen regarding the functionings of personal or market motivations, he was obviously too naive to know that the economically impoverished of Tepoztlán prefer their financial difficulties and uncertainties to the loss of dignity and autonomy implied in "being forced to render services to the rich"; to become well-paid servants and employees of transnational corporate structures. He, like the other developers still suffering from the illusion of progress, cannot begin to fathom that the so-called "poor" are able and willing to subordinate their economic temptations – of "jobs" etc. – to ways of life that they find satisfactory and comfortable, without sacrificing freedom and dignity. True, there are many people all over the world, including Tepoztlán, who have no option but to become the employees of affluent employers. But the majority, following their hard experiences with the failed promises of employment, are now renouncing those false prospects far faster than the "social minorities." And the Tepoztecs, while still honoring their King's ideals of hospitality, are drawing upon their own "tradition for changing their tradition" by refusing to open their doors to the enclosures of the market being imposed upon them by the state and federal governments.

For several months now, the Tepoztecs have governed themselves autonomously, without the help of any public moneys from the government. They have found ways of reconstituting their political bodies in order to rule over their own lives. This has called for the ingenious combination of traditional and contemporary experiences for stretching old restrictions – water, land, tools – to solve new predicaments: garbage, sewerage, drug addiction and violence among the young people, urban traffic and insecurity, and every other aspect accompanying the economic invasion of their lives. They are recovering and regaining their traditional responsibilities, abandoning the illusion that the government is taking care of them, for the price of their taxes.

On the *avenida* which goes up to the Tepozteco mountain, there often sits a dignified elder, her beautiful grey hair tied back and covered by a simple *rebozo*. By the sidewalk, she daily tends her little stall: a few bananas, some *nísperos*, potted plants, at times a box of chiclets and a few candies. After a few hours of sitting, quietly gazing at those who go by or selling under the sun, she carries back this humble stall to her house around the corner. It is a beautiful residence of stone and adobe, with a great garden full of fruits, some of which she exchanges in her stall for a little daily cash. Given the real-estate speculation that progress brought to Tepoztlán in the last years, she is regularly offered a fortune for her land – enough to make her instantly wealthy. Following the sale, she would obviously have no reason left to set up her stall on the *avenida* – as she has done for decades. But to the frustration of speculators who have plans to develop her land, doña Concha refuses to sell out.

She is not alone. From many others in her community, we hear this story. It is clear that most Tepoztecs want to continue defining what to do with their home, their lands, and their time. They are not willing to sell, as the saying goes, their *primogenitura* for some lentil soup. Their resistance, which they now link to that of others, like the Zapatistas, is an old one. As are their many frustrations. Along with various tales of their recent difficulties, they are also circulating, telling and retelling, thousands of new stories about how they are overcoming problems that in recent years they had passively signed over to "the government authorities."

As their epic unfolds, "the people" are forced to keep abreast of the "social minorities"; their latest systems of intrusion and oppression: moving beyond colonialism into the neo-colonialism of the global economy. The challenge of grassroots post-modernism is how to "catch up" with the latest mutations of the economy; "updating" ancient traditions of hospitality; protecting and cherishing them while simultaneously preventing their annihilation in the hands of "the technological bluff": its state-of-the-art marvels hiding and carrying the virus of "the individual self," the formidable killer of communities.

Decolonizing our minds means, among other things, resisting global pressures to think and act as individual selves: each separate from the other; each an industrial eater who has little or no connection with the soil on which s/he stands; each the owner of a mind which is either text or screen; each the owner of a body that "commutes"; each a "global citizen" who can be "transported" long distances; each with reproductive systems at least as private as their mailbox; each with identities that can be summarized statistically into business cards and curriculum vitae; each with memories constituted of binary bits of information. By trying to escape the world of "industrial eaters" and "ethnic" or "lean cuisine," by entering worlds of *comida* or dry latrines, we are regenerating ourselves, not our selves.

To express having hope, in Spanish, one can say: "*Abrigo esperanzas.*" Abrigar is to shelter, to protect, to keep warm, to entertain, to cherish, to nurse. People at the grassroots have few expectations, if any. But they are continually nourishing their hopes, protecting them, keeping them warm to avoid their freezing in heartless, hostile environments. They abide by their words and support themselves in the dignity of their reclaimed and regenerated commons.

NOTES

1. *Barrio* and *vecindad* have no direct translations. A *barrio* is more than a neighborhood. It is a collection of neighborhoods, like the developments of a modern city, but it is not a development. It is more in the tradition of the French quartier, in which the common traits defining the place and distinguishing it from others come from the inside, from the soul of the *barrio*, and not from the frontiers established by developers or officials. *Vecindad* is a kind of neighborhood, defined not by the mere vicinity of the houses, but by conviviality existing among neighbors.

2. Quoted by Jorge Castañeda, "Ruiz Massieu o de la ineptitud," in *Proceso*, no. 1010, March 11, 1996.

3. Illich adds: "Further, the use of role as a category of the social sciences precludes the possibility of introducing gender into the discussion. Gender relates two persons to each other who are more profoundly other than role-playing individuals ever could be. Sociology has borrowed the concept of role from the theater, where it first appeared as a technical term when European actors began to perform on an elevated stage that made scenes a sequence of 'entrance,' 'performance,' and 'exit,' on a 'set.' Thus, as a concept, role was as new to the sixteenth-century theater as it is to twentieth-century sociology" (Illich, 1982, p. 80).

4. "Is not Francisco's story a typical example of globalization?" a friend questioned us. "New York becomes a key element of his current life in Las Juntas. You are contradicting yourselves in presenting his case as an example of localization." In response, it is important for us to clarify that localization has no connection with isolation. We are not describing a fantasy world. We are telling stories about real men and women, fully immersed in "the world as it is," with the dominant interconnection, interpenetration, interaction, among different people. Localization implies mutations of the ways that people center their lives. It means moving beyond

a world of centralized structures, where the market or the state presides over the lives and decisions of everyone, hidden behind the illusion of "freedom of option," a world continually marginalizing the "social majorities," to a world in which real men and women may in fact be a direct part of the decisions affecting their lives, in the specific physical and social places to which they belong and that belong to them, and keeping at their margin the "global forces" marginalizing them. True, places like Las Juntas are seen as in the margins of society and people like Francisco are seen as marginal. By abandoning the modern social sciences, we are able to see and describe processes through which those "marginal places" become effective centers for the people reclaiming and regenerating them. In doing so, these pioneers are leading the way in making transitions to a post-modern world, relying on their traditions, as have their elders, to make their escapes.

5. Those institutions are typically western. They seem to have no historical and cultural precedents outside western culture, imposing them upon others through colonial or neo-colonial global expansions.

6. After Pisander abused it, Menelao pronounced his prophecy over Troy: "Cowardly she-wolves that you are, you feared not the anger of dreadful Jove. He is the avenger of abused hospitality who will one day destroy your city. While you were my guests, you stole my wedded wife and wickedly carried off my treasures." The victory over Troy, Illich continues, "was the judgment of divine vengeance on abused hospitality" (Illich, 1987b).

7. The history of hospitality offers illuminating clues for understanding this process. The radical estrangement of the Jews, defining a relation with the gerim entirely different to any other tradition of hospitality, took hold in western societies, through Christians and Muslims. It found fertile soil in the social context of the Graeco-Roman tradition. Since the time of Solon, a legal status was created for a growing number of residents of the city who were no longer strangers, but not yet citizens: the par-oikos, co-dweller, who does not participate in the ecclesia, the citizen assembly, but does participate in the Olympiad. The first person plural was thus redefined, after accepting groups to be addressed in the second person plural, while the outsider, the "third person," was increasingly excluded. "The primitive clarity of the opposition between the two kinds of persons, the welcome stranger and the at best tolerated barbarian was obscured" (Illich, 1987b). Since the very beginning, among the Greeks, the western tradition of hospitality was exclusive – extended only to people of the same kind – excluding others, the babblers, those not speaking a Hellenic tongue.

The fourth century created the institution which can be seen as the remote model for those of the modern welfare state: "Under episcopal leadership, Christian communities organize xenodocheia, separate houses offering hospitality in the name of the community at large. Thus the fourth-century church disembeds hospitality from the household. It became a specialized practice ordinarily and normatively exercised through an agency acting in the name of the faithful" (Illich, 1987b). In the same operation in which specific classes of people were "cared for" by different institutions, beyond any sense of hospitality, the "we" originally constituting the host – from the householder to the clan, the place, the tribe, the community of faithful – was radically transmogrified into a collective "we," no longer formed through concrete relations among men and women who belong to a place that belongs to them. It is re-constituted by an abstract, statistical aggregation of individual, genderless selves. They are strangers for each other; tied only by their abstract rights. There is no longer room for hospitality among them. The "we" implicit in *xenodocheia*, where hospitality is offered in the name of the community of the faithful, has some resemblance to the "we" of Emmaeus, the swineherd, who hosted Ulysses, following beliefs and traditions he shared with others. The "we" implicit in the social security number of an individual self, through which s/he claims his or her welfare rights for medical services or shelter for old age (pension plans) belongs to an entirely different kind. That "we" is radically dissociated from any meaning of hospitality.

8. There is, of course, a "demographic problem," mainly caused by the disruption of traditional ways for dealing (or not dealing) with the "equilibrium" between the people and their habitat. If the "demographic problem" is defined in terms of the future, for reasons of sustainability, and translated into "population control," the focus of public concern is on the Two-thirds World – which has a higher rate of demographic increase than the One-third World. But the basic "problem" for sustainability, in terms of natural resources and the environment, is created by the "social minorities," who are consuming four-fifths of the world's resources. If the issue is discussed in such terms (something we consider inappropriate), the "solution" for such a "problem" is obvious: no births should be allowed among the "social minorities," until they reduce to a fifth or less their current patterns of consumption – a goal that no environmentalist considers feasible.

9. Since the early eighties, Jean Robert has conducted extensive theoretical and practical research on human waste. He is part of an informal network of people working at the grassroots to prevent faeces from being transformed into "human waste." With César Añorve, he has created a technological variant of the Vietnamese latrine. He has written several essays on the history of the water closet, as well as on the theoretical issues involved and the technological alternatives available. In 1985, his experiences and those of many grassroots communities contributed towards addressing the special predicament of massive "shit disposal" which appeared in Mexico City after the earthquake.

These experiences stimulated lively public debates in Mexico. In association with groups from Guatemala, Colombia and other countries, two "world seminars" were held in the late eighties: the first in Medellín, Colombia, and the second in Mexico City. The organizers were at first surprised by the kind of response they got to an informal, open invitation. The presentations of "experts" from a dozen countries revealed advanced "scientific" alternatives for addressing the modern production of "human waste." They have created the Latin American Network for Alternative Technology (RETA, after its name in Spanish: *Red Latinoamericana de Tecnología Alternativa*). Several books and extensive materials documenting experiences all over the world and describing the most recent advances have been published. The documentation of this research is available from Jean Robert, Opción, S.C., Cordobanes 24, San José Insurgentes, México, D.F. C.P. 3900.

10. Among the fascinating array of creative local practices that avoid the production or invention of "waste" are those of the people of Parra, Goa, who receive mutual help from the town's pigs. For the "science" of this indigenous technology, workshops with Claude Alvares and The Other India Bookstore are recommended.

11. In the times of Punta del Este, when the Big and the Powerful were concerned with the impact of the Cuban Revolution, the World Bank formula for development of the "underdeveloped" included massive latrinization. On that occasion, Che

Guevara denounced the "solution" as the modernization of poverty; giving poor solutions for poor people, instead of struggling against poverty itself. The latrines promoted by the World Bank, and many other governmental and non-governmental organizations since then, are not only very ugly and uncomfortable – full of flies, odors and disease – and smells – they are also polluting the aquifers. Post-modern alternatives rejects those latrines, as they do the WC.

12. For one account of the way in which the not-yet-born are woven into the very fabric, the net of "we's," of the Quiche Indians, see Rigoberta Menchú's accounts of pregnancy and childbearing in *I, Rigoberta Menchú* (1984).

13. The garish architecture of "fast-food" and other industrial eateries forces hasty entrance and undigested exit. Hostile and not hospitable, they are good sites for studying the modern transmogrification of the traditional communion of breaking bread into the contemporary breaking off into the atom of the individual self.

14. Nestlé offered salvation to the infants of the "social majorities." It came in the form of death that follows the drying up of their mothers' milk, while updating human breasts, rendered obsolescent for doing what they have done "naturally" for centuries.

FOUR

HUMAN RIGHTS:
THE TROJAN HORSE OF
RECOLONIZATION?

We need to be aware that the very notion of right and law is a western notion ... It is but a window among others on the world, an instrument of communication and a language among others. The word not only is non-existent among the indigenous traditional cultures, but it will never come to their minds that human beings can have rights ... For them, it is difficult to understand that rights or entitlements could be homocentrically defined by a human being. That they, furthermore, could be defined by a sovereign state, that is, by a collection of sovereign individuals, is almost ridiculous. (Robert Vachon, 1990, p. 165)

The most destructive effect of development is its tendency to distract my eye from your face with the phantom, humanity, that I ought to love. (Ivan Illich, conversation with Majid Rahnema, Bremen, December 13, 1994)

I can no longer do what is fair. Every time I try to bring justice to our community, applying our traditional practices to amend wrongdoings, a human rights activist comes to stop me. (Rómulo Santiago, municipal president in Huayapam, Oaxaca, in conversation with the authors, 1995)

HUMAN RIGHTS UNIVERSALIZED:
LIBERATION OR ABUSE?

Like indigenous peoples across the globe, the Indian peoples of Oaxaca have suffered different forms of abuses and interventions from Outsiders. For many centuries, they have been exposed to every variety of foreign imposition upon their lives and beliefs, including attempted "melt-down" into their oppressors' national identity. All sorts of colonizers and developers have tried to dissolve their cultures and to cancel their traditions; to transform them into folklore and reminiscences of social orders imposed by successive dominant groups.

Unlike indigenous peoples across the globe who have disappeared, died off or been dissolved into the oblivion of the so-called national "melting pot," the sixteen Indian peoples of Oaxaca, a province in the south of Mexico neighboring Chiapas, have successfully kept alive their rich diversity of language and culture, while coexisting with their colonizers. The latter have ranged from the Aztecs (in the pre-Hispanic world) to the Spaniards; and, in contemporary times, from local or national elites to transnational corporations.

The pluriverse of Oaxaca's indians has resisted all those imposing their universe; their universalizable truths. Their evolving modes of cultural coexistence protect their pluriverse; adapting to each new condition of oppression and domination without losing their historical continuity. In recent years, they seem to be transforming their struggle of resistance into a struggle of liberation.

In four out of every five municipalities in the pluriverse of Oaxaca, differentiated moral and political traditions prevail, enriched through the intense interactions which these peoples have maintained over centuries with other cultures, whether dominant or dominated. They express neither the need nor desire for formal codes to give official definition to their traditions – well known and embraced by every member of the community. Their system of justice seeks neither the abstract impersonality nor the neutrality that defines the modern judicial system being exported world-wide from the West.

"Westerners," recently remarked Marcos Sandoval of the Triqui people of Oaxaca, "represent justice with a blindfolded woman. We want her with her eyes well open, to fully appreciate what is happening. Instead of neutrality or impartiality, we want compassion. The person committing a crime needs to be understood, rather than submitted to a trial."

These open eyes of their justice do not, for example, look for punishment when a person violates a shared custom. He or she is perceived as someone in trouble, who needs understanding and help; including the opportunity to offer compensations to the victim of his or her misdemeanor. If inadvertently, unintentionally, or because of a lack of prudence, someone burns a part of the forest, he or she must reforest it. If a man kills another, he must assume full responsibility for the welfare of the dead person's family for the rest of their lives. Rather than confine wrongdoers in jail, many of these communities tie them to trees or confine them to places for a few hours or days with the expressed hope of allowing their passions to calm down; or for a safe return from their delirious condition. These practices are not conceived as forms of punishment. Instead, they offer communal support: according opportunities for the soul to heed the wisdom and advice of elders, when they come to converse and reflect with those who have wronged others. Among peoples where these regimes of communal justice fully prevail, the incidence of all sorts of "crimes" or wrongdoings is demonstrated to be far lower than among the abstract citizens upon whom the state inflicts its legal regime, proclaiming the equality and impartiality of fair trials – one type of human right prized among many as parts of human "progress" (Esteva, 1992a).

The Indian peoples of Oaxaca were able to protect their indigenous regimes of justice against the threats of the Spanish Inquisition; later, from the ferocity of the dictatorship established in Mexico at the end of the nineteenth century; next, from the changing impulses of the revolutionary governments in the first part of this century; and then again, from the modernizing fever of private and public developers who have fallen upon them during the last fifty years. In all these centuries of cultural resistance to "the Other," they relied upon their own traditions; including the tradition of changing their tradition. This has helped Oaxaca Indians to adjust and enrich their regimes of justice, adapting them to every new condition. At the same time, it has helped them to hold on to their unique cultural leitmotivs: themes that have kept them as peoples within their own original and unique cultural pluriverse.

Currently, however, all these differentiated cultural groups and small communities are confronting a threat for which they are not prepared. Governmental and non-governmental activists are proselytizing another global morality: that implicit in the Universal Declaration of Human Rights. They persist in invading all communities with this "secular" religion. "I can no longer do what is fair," reflects Rómulo Santiago, municipal president of Huayapam, near Oaxaca city (see opening epigraph). "Every time I try to bring justice to our community, applying our traditional practices to amend wrongdoings, a human rights activist comes to stop me."

This contemporary threat has many faces. Sometimes it comes in the form of "social rights." To those struggling hard to maintain the autonomy of their subsistence economy, human rights activists or agents of the government explain that all Mexicans have the right to education, health, employment, modern medicine, sewerage, roads and other social services. They are urged to present their claims before the pertinent state authorities for obtaining whatever they "need." Fortunately, it is becoming increasingly difficult to convince the "social majorities" of most "underdeveloped" nations to believe in these promises and prospects of national or international agencies. Time and time again over these last five Development Decades, they have been disappointed by the promises made by professionals, politicians and activists of all sorts.

But the latest breed of developers and globalizers – new promoters of human rights – are resorting to other strategies for capturing the interests of some people. These include convincing persons suffering a communal "penalty" imposed by their own people that they have the right to a "fair trial" in an "official" court of law, as defined by the Mexican Constitution. Indigenous communities are "educated" that this constitution establishes the dissolution of exclusive communal courts with autonomy in their own jurisdictions – such as the ones that have operated within and held together these communities for centuries. That task of persuasion is difficult or even impossible for indigenous communities who know quite well the reality of the official state courts: ruled by codes that most people either ignore, consider immoral or distrust due to their corruption by the professional and the powerful, inside and outside the governmental hierarchy.

Too often, however, human rights activists add to this existing corruption by offering indigenous communities their own guarantees of intervention; of trials as "fair" as those which currently only the rich and those with government "contacts" or "strings" can obtain. People who disagree with the "penalty" imposed upon them by their communities, or find it unbearable, are thus lured and tempted by outsiders to challenge their local authorities. They are aided and abetted by do-gooders in destroying traditional local authorities. They are "educated" to appeal to an official court of law.

Through their contacts among human rights activists, at times they do succeed in winning trials against their own communities and neighbors. Ironically, among those who do succeed in having their claims fulfilled, many actually suffer more than those who fail. For their success leaves them exposed to modern frustrations, new to them. Bereft, "orphaned" from their communal support networks and centuries-old traditions for maintaining neighborliness and friendship, they fall into modern ruts: addictive dependencies upon "social services" that fail to genuinely satisfy or be "social." "Developed" more and more into assuming the shape of the modern "individual self," delinked even further from their communities, trapped and isolated in such modern ruts, they lose recourse to their customary ways. These taught them autonomy – the communal capacity to take care of their own cultural "needs," with capacities which protect them from the "service agencies" of the state.

It is no secret to "the masses" that they cannot depend upon the latter; with their promises of modern security: of jobs, pensions or health plans. The "lucky" few who wangle their way into acquiring these, even in the best of times, form crippling dependencies upon salaries that come and go with the vagaries of international currency markets – totally outside their own communal control. Along the same lines, after becoming addicted to schools, under the illusion of escalating to the upper echelons of the educational pyramid, they end up losing real opportunities for learning all the knowledge and skills they need to flourish and endure in their communities. Left bereft of their communities, necessary for children's cultural initiation, they strive harder and harder for diplomas: requisites for access to salaried jobs, yet with rapidly diminishing value in guaranteeing that the latter are available or accessible. The damage done to them by state law and education is replicated in every other facet of their lives, including their problems of healing and health. Left without the traditional herbal and other remedies of their communal healers, they must accept the dregs in modern hospitals and related medical services available to "the masses."

So it comes to pass, more and more, that under the benign banner of human rights, indigenous and other non-modern communities suffer unprecedented forms of oppression, of suffering and power abuses.

GANDHI: LIBERATION WITHOUT MODERN STATES OR HUMAN RIGHTS

The birth of universal human rights is inextricably bound up with the global manufacture of the independent western nation-state. Following five centuries of colonialism, the post-World War II universalization of this western institution continues to deal severe blows to all other political organizations; most particularly the commons cared for or "administered" through village self-governance. The evils and injustices of traditional village governance, masterfully documented by Achebe (1961, 1969) and others, are minuscule in scale or severity when compared with those of national governments; or of their contemporary descendants: the transborder corporate superstructures constituting the "Global Project," being legitimized by its gospel of human rights.

For villages or cities across the globe, the moral currency of universalizable human rights is being newly minted, promising even to contain the immoralities of state governments (national or local) as well as international development agencies.[1] This moral currency, conceived and created for abstract "citizens," follows Hobbes in containing their meanness, brutality, greed and envy; while enjoining duties, obligations and responsibilities towards fellow-citizens and flags. It replaces the traditional communal morality of peoples not reduced to modern individualism,[2] either old or new (Dewey, 1962). Functioning like the British pound, the American dollar and other "hard" currencies, this equally "hard" moral coinage of human rights enjoys the same international status of preeminence as do the other coins of the economically "developed." Both monetary and moral currencies of the "developed" destroy and devalue the "soft" currencies of communities and peoples considered not only economically but also morally "underdeveloped." Following the colonial path of Christian missionaries (who saved primitive souls from pagan gods), their descendants, the delegates of human rights agencies, offer secular salvation: the moral or economic development of underdeveloped cultures. "One man one vote"-style democracy with parliaments or senates, a national economy that manufactures classrooms, courts, patients' wards, sewerage, telephones, jobs and flush toilets, are only some among the liberty and welfare rights promised by independent modern states.

This style of "national independence" is incompatible with cultural autonomy. It is "similar to what the Canadians and the South Africans have"; it is nothing more than "English rule without the Englishman...; the tiger's nature, without the tiger" (Gandhi, 1946, p. 21).[3] Reliance on Outsiders' morality to claim liberation from them (the colonizing imperialists) demonstrates the political genius of "freedom fighters" like Gandhi. While drawing upon the colonizers' morality to demand political independence or national sovereignty from their (mis)government, Gandhi celebrates and affirms with the Insiders (his people) their own culture and customs: *Hind Swaraj* or Indian Home Rule; going beyond the western morality of the modern nation-state. Extolled only with Insiders are the virtues of *Hind Swaraj* and *dharma*: the *dharma* of voluntary simplicity, humility, non-violence, courage and justice; of "bread labor," defining and distinguishing the best of their own particular variety of "soil (agri)culture"; of indigenous village autonomy and self-governance. Their Insiders' morality is worlds apart from the Outsiders', inextricably shaped by ideals of economic growth or "progress."

This Insider/Outsider dichotomy, the moral differentiation between *Hind Swaraj* and "national independence," is lost upon "the intimate enemy": modern citizens, individual selves who "belong" to abstract political structures. Cut off from their indigenous roots, their soil cultures, citizens of newly independent states are "educated" to desire and function with the Outsiders' moral currency: human rights guaranteed by national and international agencies. The loss entailed in the moral breakdown of the Insider/Outsider dichotomy is mourned only by those still able to remember and re-member; to regenerate communitarian traditions, being attacked world-wide by the modern state; to resist the morality of abstract rights, taking over all communal matters, including sex and marriage. These are depersonalized for the abstract arena of state, national and international courts; even as the language of morality, spoken only with Insiders, is taken over by the Outsiders' language of morality. The result is tragic: breaking bonds of neighborhood and village, of affection and friendship defined by customs, community and commons.[4]

Every pluriverse is defined by the coexistence of a rich multiplicity of moral languages, concepts and discourses; distinguishing right conduct with Outsiders from customs that relate Insiders to each other. Every pluriverse has its own well-specified customs for either tolerating or being hospitable to the otherness of the Other, the Outsider. Analogously, each pluriverse is distinguished from others by the ways in which it secures the bonds of solidarity, friendship, love and neighborliness among the Insiders: those who belong to each other.

Proponents for universal human rights disregard the Insider/Outsider boundaries that define every pluriverse, condemning them as "provincial" or "parochial." Essential for the existence of a pluriverse, these boundaries disappear when national or international laws and juridical norms – of universalizable human rights, among others – enter, dominate and destroy local, communal, cultural spaces.

Cherishing and protecting such spaces, Gandhi exemplifed the mastery of two distinct moral languages: Outsiders' and Insiders'. To eject the colonizers, applying British norms, Gandhians demanded the right of Indians to national independence. To regenerate their shared morality, Gandhi celebrated *Hind Swaraj* or Indian Home Rule with compatriots only. He had no aspirations to convert the British to the morality of *dharma* or *Hind Swaraj*. Even if politically feasible, doing so would have been tantamount to reverse cultural imperialism; or perhaps the folly of casting the pearls of community before people who no longer had a taste or yearning for the commons that they had smashed to install the pre-eminent industrial state in its day – ahead of all the rest in its global takeover of Others' lands.

It would be folly to doubt the depth and completeness of Gandhi's thought and writings about his own culture. In the index of subjects of *The Collected Works of Mahatma Gandhi* (which now run to ninety volumes), there is not a single reference to "rights" or to "human rights." But there are almost three dozen direct references to *dharma*, and the indirect references to it (for example, as in "Religion and *dharma*" or "Ramayan and *dharma*") are too many to be easily tracked down. It is clear that for Gandhi, *qua* hindu, *dharma* lies at the moral core of "the good life," of "human flourishing" or of "human freedom" (Vora, 1993). Fifty years after his death, Gandhi continues to offer "nuisance value" to the modern state. At the grassroots, leading different movements, not one but several Gandhis are alive (Nandy, 1996), challenging the state with *Hind Swaraj*, defined by the *dharma* of indigenous moralities.

Wherever *communitas* or *Gesellschaft* is severely eroded by the domination of the state's juridical norms, the language of human rights displaces those that center upon communal obligations. Indigenous moralities,

extolling *dharma* and other virtues, are replaced by state systems, supposedly secular, impartial and blind – as blind to Triqui traditions as it
is to that of the Hindus, or to those Others constituting the pluriverse
of the "social majorities."

FROM BEIJING: GLOBAL PLATFORMS AND UNIVERSAL RIGHTS

In the era of the "Global Project," not even the Great Wall of China
poses an obstacle to the universalization of human rights. Thousands
of determined participants flew over the Wall into Beijing to attend
the Fourth UN Conference on Human/Women's Rights, intent upon
their universalization, spreading them to every corner of the globe.[5]
Grander and more global than all the other conferences now regularly
held from Malaysia to Mexico to promote human rights, its participants
sought to liberate and bring justice to all the oppressed peoples of earth,
and especially those whom they deem the worst off: the impoverished
woman and girl in the Third World, bought and sold, beaten and raped,
a veritable slave of husband, in-laws or employer; to the 100 million
missing women of Asia – the girls who do not survive their conception
long enough to get out of the womb and into the cradle, "culled out" as
they are after the ultrasound gender scan conducted early in pregnancy;
as well as all other persons of the human race who do not seem to them
to have even the semblance of a humane existence.

Forty thousand determined delegates flew back to their nation-states
from Beijing with a 12-Point Platform for global action. Of Herculean
dimensions, this Platform proposed bringing the unschooled, unclothed,
homeless, unfed, abused, tortured and unfairly imprisoned under one
humane universal umbrella of human rights. Post-conference workshops were organized for its implementation. Asked to speak at such
workshops, we expressed our grave doubts not only about the specific
12 Points of the Platform (each of which signifies cultural imperialism),
but more broadly about the entire human rights enterprise under way.

Our doubts and misgivings about the Trojan horse of human rights
generated shock and horror: "What are you saying! Don't you believe
in human rights or the rights of women?" This question challenged
us to reflect on the contrast with another question, asked of "fallen"
Hindus: those, for example, who have broken the Hindu taboo against
eating beef: "What are you saying! Don't you believe in the sacredness
of the cow, our mother?"

For all the similarities between these two questions, there is a radical difference that deserves to be underscored: a tolerant, non-violent

Hindu would not ask that question of a Muslim, a Catholic, a Protestant, or a person of another faith and culture, knowing that to do so would be totally inappropriate: a sign not only of ignorance regarding the Other's culture, but, much worse, of cultural insensitivity and intolerance; of cultural inhospitality to the Otherness of the Other. It is, in other words, only within a very well-defined shared cultural and religious context that it is appropriate to ask of another Hindu: "Don't you believe in the sacredness of the cow, our mother?"

Yet, for those proslytezing the "secular morality" of human rights, it is not considered dogmatic to ask of anyone, regardless of religion, race, color or culture: "Don't you believe in human rights [the modern "sacred cow"] for all men, children and women? They fail to see that their faith is as threatening to all the diverse cultures of the world as the Trojan horse was for the people of Troy.

We come from cultures and traditions for which the concept of human rights is not only alien, but, furthermore, is actually incommensurable with the central cultural ideals or virtues. Consequently, we find this modern (secular?) faith to be as dangerous to our cultures as those that sought to convince us that our peoples were pagans; that we did not have the right Gods or the One True God; that we were strange, and primitive and uncouth for praying to monkeys, elephants or the phallus of Shiv. Resisting the monoculture of any one true global God or religion, we celebrate grassroots groups that do not fall victims to this Trojan horse of recolonization.

There is, we realize, enormous violence, abuse and suffering everywhere CNN turns its global "eyes" – from Bosnia and Berlin to Beijing. Even as we mourn this tragic reality, hoping for its amelioration, we recognize that our own cultures are neither superior nor unique in possessing moral concepts for correcting our inhumanities; including, for example, India's "dowry deaths," which receive international attention and attack from human rights activists. Intent on exporting "human rights" to Hindus, these activists fail to take note of *aadar, sammaan, shradha, izzat, hak, dharma, ahimsa*, among other moral concepts that enjoin human decency as well as condemn violence against women and animals. Many of these words are not easily translated; they lack English equivalents.[6] They offer important clues about Hindu morality, its *dharma* and virtue, totally disregarded by all those who burn young brides for the procurement of a Toyota or a General Electric refrigerator.

Yet, Hindu *dharma* (for appropriate and respectful treatment of women and others) did not receive the attention and importance given to the concept of "women's rights" in Beijing. Why? In the international media coverage of the event, we never learned the words Chinese women use to describe their conceptions of a good life; or the vast variety of ways respect is shown for women in the East or in the South. Why? Neither did we learn the moral vocabularies and concepts of the bushwomen of the Kalahari or Australian deserts. Why? Why did this conference focus on (women's) rights? Why not a conference that explores *ahimsa* towards women, or *shradha* or *aadar*? The traditional women of countries like China and India are "educated" by their liberated sisters to believe that they have rights over their reproductive organs, owned by their (individual) selves. They are also similarly "educated" to claim the use of sonograms and other modern medical technologies as their rights. Since their liberators do not stay long enough to change the entire social context of the sisters being "conscientized," traditional Indian and Chinese women are practicing their modern morality of rights to abort their unborn daughters. Defenders of women's rights are outraged by the 100 million missing women culled out of the uterus before birth. Why do they pass off the deaths of these unborn girls to the feudal minds of males in these cultures? Why do they fail to perceive close connections between the 100 million missing women and the introduction of foreign technologies and alien concepts of rights and freedoms in non-modern cultures?

Anwers to these questions emerge in critical studies of global development (Sachs, 1992), revealing how and why the 12-Point Platform for Action (like the Universal Declaration of Human Rights and other globalisms) continues the cultural imperialism of colonialism; operationalizing the belief that "underdeveloped" cultures are too poor or primitive to promote the "good" of their people, while imposing dominant cultures' notions of human well-being.

Grassroots initiatives seeking their liberation from the "Global Project," however, open our eyes and "gaze," open our hearts and minds to the diverse cultural ways of thinking about the "good life"; to the radical pluralism with which the well-being of women, men and animals is understood and promoted in different local spaces of this world. Cultural diversity means not giving one culture's moral concept – that of human/women's rights – pre-eminence over others; bringing "human rights" down from its pedestal; placing it amidst other significant cultural concepts which define "the good life" in a pluriverse.

MORAL PROGRESS OR ABERRATIONS?

Human rights are only two hundred years old. The ideology and the institutional arrangements of human rights were born after unprecedented forms of social and personal deprivation took root among the "developed" peoples and places of this planet. The regime of the nation-state, fusing nationalism and statehood, was constructed at this same time, to keep the social order in a society exposed to the forces of the modern market, reducing the human condition to that of *Homo oeconomicus*.

Dharma and other cultural ideals are quite obviously irrelevant, ineffective or even counterproductive for societies designed for or directed towards economic development or "progress" (Sbert, 1992). The "social majorities" now trying to resist the economization of their lives are employing the types of strategies Gandhi finessed, defending themselves by using the state's language of "rights" to curb its intrusions. While still using it to struggle against power abuses of the state, they are drawing upon their own cultural roots for moral insights needed to overcome their contemporary ills, regenerating their commons.

Human rights proselytizers, however, continue to offer complex philosophical elaborations to demonstrate that they are inherent to "human nature" and universalizable. The mindset of human rights claimants is dominated by the dogma that their universalizability has not been recognized until the modern era either due to human ignorance (past as well as present) or to the peculiar aberrations of human history. Elaborating on these forms of aberrations or ignorance, human rights promoters present their current status as the result of a long history of peoples' struggles. After a prolonged succession of despotic regimes denying them their rights for centuries, peoples all over the earth are finally seeing the light at the end of the tunnel: "Whereas recognition of the inherent dignity and of the equal and inalienable rights of all members of the human family is the foundation of freedom, justice and peace in the world," established the Universal Declaration of Human Rights in 1948; "whereas disregard and contempt for human rights have resulted in barbarous acts which have outraged the conscience of mankind, and the advent of a world in which human beings shall enjoy freedom of speech and belief and freedom from fear and want has been proclaimed as the highest aspiration of the common people." Their promoters seek success in getting the global recognition and enforcement of human rights as established principles of social organization, through the creation of the state of law; signifying the Great March of History.

Several declarations are part of this Great March for humanity: "We hold these truths to be self-evident, that all men are created equal, that they are endowed by their Creator with certain inalienable Rights, that among these are life, liberty and the pursuit of happiness" (Declaration of Independence by the 13 American Colonies, July 4, 1776), for example; or "Men are born and remain free and equal in rights ... The aim of every political association is the preservation of the natural and imprescriptible rights of man," that is, the rights of "Liberty, Property, Safety and Resistance to Oppression" (Declaration of the Rights of Man and the Citizen, August 26, 1789).

In the course of the hundred years following such Declarations, the "self-evident truth" of "natural law" as the foundation of human rights (so cherished for Thomas Jefferson and his friend the Marquis de Lafayette) became untenable. In the twentieth century, it was no longer possible to seriously defend the "rights of Man" along the lines of natural law. Yet, precisely in this century, it came to be assumed that truth can only be established by verifiable experience – the reign of the logos; and that law comes only from the sovereign power – the reign of the nation-state. Why does the ideology of the universality of some fundamental rights for the individual self flourish today, more than ever before? How can rights be universal if their accepted source is a covenant based on reason (vs natural or divine law), and most people on earth neither share that reason nor are part of the covenant?

It was clear to Jefferson that the "divine rights of the sovereign" did not belong to him; that rights were derived from the laws of nature ("and not as a gift of the Chief Magistrate"). True, absolutism prompted men to claim (human, or natural) rights precisely because it denied them (Cranston, 1973). The popular belief of those times implies that human beings never renounced their inalienable rights when they "contracted" their entrance into the "social order;" nor were those rights diminished by "the divine rights of kings." But how did the very idea of "having" those rights emerge? The "natural law" doctrine itself possibly came from Greek Stoicism. In Graeco-Roman and medieval times, however, "natural law" imposed duties, rather than rights. How, then, could the latter became "self-evident truths"? What change in the human condition occurred for the very idea of human rights to replace the centrality of moral obligations or duties?

By the late eighteenth century, there surfaced strong objections to the idea of "natural rights." Both the political right and left exposed powerful philosophical objections. Throughout the nineteenth century, this intellectual assault continued. At the beginning of the present century, it was hard to find theorists seriously and rigorously defending the idea of "natural rights." Its successor came in the form of human rights.

Human rights are, in fact, social constructions. They are cultural inventions, and not natural discoveries. Human rights are but the formal, juridical expression of a specific mode of being and living. It is defined by the kind of man, woman and child who has appeared on earth only very recently: *Homo oeconomicus*, the possessive individual. First born and brought up in the West, this modern "person" – the individual self – is now threatening the whole world with the plague of endless needs, legitimized under the moral mask of human rights.[7]

The processes that created *Homo oeconomicus* (the possessor of human rights), as we saw in Chapter 3, disembedded the economy from commons, community and culture, while constituting it as an autonomous sphere. These processes "evolved" and mutated over almost a thousand years (Polanyi, 1975). After the enclosure of the commons, there occurred a radical rupture with the traditional past. Some describe this rupture as the transition to the capitalist mode of production (Marx); others as the transition from the aegis of gender to the regime of sex (Illich, 1982); and still others as the birth of the modern age. Economic wo/man was born after this rupture. The individual self had already been created, apparently with the invention of the text (Illich, 1987a, 1993), but s/he was still immersed in a religious cosmology (Cougar, 1973). The economic individual, a new genderless being, mobilized principally by self-interest, and dedicated to optimizing his/her behavior (the rational use of scarce means for unlimited ends), could only acquire his/her place in history when the idea of equality had become a popular prejudice (Marx), and when the assumption of scarcity, which the patron saints of economics transformed into a social law (Esteva, 1992b), had been established as a governing principle of society.

This "evolution" has transmogrified peoples and cultures so profoundly that previous virtues are now reduced to vices, and traditional vices have been elevated to virtues. Hopes have been transformed into expectations; the richness of tradition into a burden; wisdom into backwardness; awareness of self-limitation into apathy or lack of initiative; frugality into the inability to compete for the maximization of utility; envy into the motivation that heralds progress and economic growth (Dumont, 1977; Esteva, 1992a, 1992b; MacIntyre, 1981; Orr, 1992). Vitality, the daily expression of the condition of being alive in and through being entwined or intertwined with others and the world, has been transformed into mimetic desire (Girard, 1978) to "catch up" and compete. Desires have been transformed into needs, and needs into rights.

The nation-state, as a political regime constructed to put order in the operation of the national economy, was constituted as a social pact among individuals, to whom it attributed, for the simple fact of being members of the state, the right or the entitlement (Sen, 1981) to the satisfaction of their needs by the market or the state. Looking for the modern definition of human nature, we discover *needy wo/man*: dependent on economic goods and services – the objects that satisfy his or her needs for survival and flourishing. The tautology of the modern definition of human beings is their subordination to the laws of scarcity.

Economists claim that the economy has existed since the beginning of time; that it is an unavoidable condition of human society; and that its natural evolution is the modern national, international or global economy. This contention has been dismantled during recent decades, revealing that "economic laws" are but relatively recent deductive inventions supporting modern political projects. For the purpose of colonizing the present and future, they have also colonized the past (Dumont, 1977; Dumouchel and Dupuy, 1979; Polanyi, 1947; Sahlins, 1972).

Economists did not invent the new patterns of behavior emerging with economic societies, creations of the modern market. But the founding fathers of this discipline were able to codify their observations in a form that fitted well with the ambitions of the emerging interests, offering them "scientific foundations." When that form was "received" as Truth by the public and absorbed into common language, it was able to transform popular perceptions from within by changing the meaning of previously existing words and assumptions.

The founding fathers of economics saw in scarcity the keystone for their theoretical constructions. They postulated it as a universal condition of human society, with axiomatic value. Economists have even been able to transform their finding into a popular prejudice, a self-evident truism for everyone. "Common sense" is now so immersed in the notions of economic "rationality" that it is very difficult to recognize the economists' premise of "scarcity" or "rationality" as mere leftovers of modern science; words which, like others, fell into ordinary language and perception, and colonized them.

Scarcity connotes shortage, rarity, restriction, want, insufficiency, even frugality. Since all these connotations (alluding to conditions appearing everywhere and at all times) are now mixed up with the economic denotations of the word, the popular prejudice about the universality of economics, with its premise of scarcity, is constantly reinforced. However, the "law of scarcity" formulated by economists does not allude to those situations. The sudden shortage of fresh air during a fire is not scarcity of air in the economic sense. Neither is the self-imposed frugality of a monk, the insufficiency of stamina in a boxer, the rarity of a flower, or the last reserves of wheat mentioned by the Pharaoh in what is the first known historical reference to hunger. The "law of scarcity" was constructed by economists to denote the technical assumption that human wants are great, not to say infinite, whereas human means are limited, though improvable. The assumption implies choices over the allocation of means (resources). This "fact" defines the "economic problem" *par excellence*, whose "solution" is proposed by economists through the market or the plan. Such a "solution" implies

in fact the creation of scarcity to a point at which people, by the millions, are deprived of their own capacities, centuries old, to satisfy even
their more basic "needs." People's reaction to this condition, dooming
many of them to extinction and most of them to the most undignified
existence, paved the way to the welfare state, where every "need" was
transformed into a "right."

"The world," says Milan Kundera,

> has become man's right and everything in it has become a right: the desire
> for love the right to love; the desire for rest the right to rest; the desire for
> friendship the right to friendship; the desire to exceed the speed limit the
> right to exceed the speed limit; the desire for happiness the right to happiness;
> the desire to publish a book the right to publish a book; the desire to shout
> in the street in the middle of the night the right to shout in the street in the
> middle of the night. (Kundera, 1991, p. 153)

Bandied for all struggles, the universal moral flag of human rights
brought with it the loss of their content. It transformed them into a ge-
neric attitude of all towards all, through the kind of alchemy that mutates
human desires into rights. Today, the army of fighters for human rights
includes those struggling against torture by the Mexican police, against
the crimes in Bosnia or against the Castro regime in Cuba; as well as those
claiming their rights to own/buy guns, to disseminate pornographic
materials through the Internet, or to kiss in public people of any sex.

The formal codification of all those rights, the first collective step
claimed by human rights fighters in order to give legal coverage to their
struggle, has rapidly advanced to all the spheres of daily life. Wherever
the law of scarcity is already enforced as the necessary accompaniment
of economic principles, a social space is created for demanding the
enforcement of some variety of human rights. But the demand for the
universalization of these rights is also advancing through contagion into
spheres where they still express the protection of freedoms. Once the
scarcity of schools and teachers is established through the redefinition
of education, the right to compulsory schooling is enforced. The recent
scarcity of human organs (for transplants) or genes (for genetic engineering) has already created the debate about the corresponding rights,
which are starting to be included in national and international codes.
Freedoms like those associated with cultural practices (in birth, marriage
or death, for example) are increasingly formulated in terms of rights.

The final step in the global takeover by the monoculture of human
rights is now the object of an international debate. Powerful voices are
currently claiming that the "community of nations," the United Nations,
should be endowed with powers and resources to apply a global right
of intervention anywhere on earth "for humanitarian purposes": that is,

with the explicit aim of protecting human rights. The codification of that new right formally breaks one of this century's international rules, based on the principles of people's self-determination and protection from foreign intervention in national affairs. Highly controversial, this "right" is being recognized as one more way to legitimize colonial interventions.

This charge, by now well founded and documented, expresses the very essence of human rights as colonial tools for domination. Colonialism always implied a kind of moral and political violation, something imposed by the brute force of the physically strong, with different kinds of ideological emblems used to legitimize such violation. The Cross coming with the Sword took different shapes – like development or democracy in the postwar era. What is now under discussion would amount to the final consecration of the legal and legitimate right of colonial intervention ... in the name of human rights.

We are aware that in packing into a few paragraphs such a complex transformation of the human condition, we leave ourselves vulnerable to the charge of controversial oversimplifications and interpretations. We assume that risk in order to give the bare outlines of a sketch without which few can appreciate our concern and our hope for the end of the global encroachment sought by the regime of these rights.

Human rights are an historical fact. In the story of humans on earth, these rights have a clearly identified beginning. Therefore, they can have an end. Their end is being written into the epic of "the people" at the grassroots.

CELEBRATING THE PLURIVERSE

All those who want to bring the whole world under the umbrella of human rights insist that that is the only way to satisfy the basic needs which define people *qua* human beings. Contemporary experts influenced by the likes of Maslow now include the need for love, company, affection, in addition to the usually mentioned "material" needs in their human rights agenda. Given this universe of "basic needs," given this universality in the human condition, the universalization of human rights should be recognized; and the appropriate legal and institutional system should be created to implement and enforce these on a global scale – so goes the chant of those marching for universal human rights.

We are trying to resist this heartrending chant and the line of reasoning that underlies it. Our grassroots experiences continue to teach us that we do not live in a universe, but in a pluriverse; that the universality in the human condition claimed by human rights propagators exists only in their minority worldview. After becoming aware that we live in a pluriverse, after learning to accept the radical heterogeneity of Being (Machado), we have no desire to return to primitive tribal violence or traditional provincialism. (Neither do those who have experienced these forms of violence first hand.) Discarding modern provincialism (inherent to the global human rights march) opens doors of hospitality (pre-modern as well as post-modern) for dis-covering others.

Every culture is enriched through learning from both the positive and negative implications of embracing human rights, with its particular formulations of human well-being or suffering. But that "fact" does not give to the morality of human rights universal superiority over other cos-movisions. It is to treat it as one cosmovision – which can be enriched by others at least as much as it enriches others' cosmovisions. While rejecting the notion that we can only be better Punjabis or Zapotecs by embracing the ideal of human rights, we are not denying that we will be enriched through conversations and other experiences with reflective practitioners of human rights. Assuming the dignified position of decolonized peoples, we offer these insights with the humility that seeks mutuality.

Those who have the courage to depart from the Grand March of Human Rights have countless other cultural paths open to them. These cultural alternatives do not entail alliances with the Pinochets, the Pol Pots, the oppressors of Tibet, the Burmese military dictatorship, the propagators of Hindu dowry deaths or Islamic fundamentalism. In break-ing free from the oppressiveness of the Universal Declaration of Human Rights, we can begin to celebrate the ways cultures single themselves out, giving conceptual form to their singularity – which includes the ways in which they even classify, identify or define human invariants.

Undoubtedly, there are some invariants of human behavior: traits that characterize a species and distinguish it from others in time and space. Being men or women, we are singled out from other species in the cosmos. But do these "commonalities" entail the globalization of human needs or rights? True, all of us breathe and eat. All find in daily life reasons for joy and sorrow. All social groups speak and prefer some things to others, although we do it in different languages and move in separate directions in the quest for what we like or to avoid what we dislike. To say that all breathe and eat, or need security and educa-tion, suggests one type of selection of traits – very culturally specific in definition. In establishing these, or any other specific categories of "men and women" or "human beings," one is necessarily engaged in separation and abstraction from reality. This capacity for abstraction can be seen as a creative treasure, part and expression of the human endow-ment as species, so long as one is fully aware of what one is doing. If, as Plato wanted, one consciously keeps clear parentheses around what one has abstracted after sequestrating reality, it is possible to move with freedom inside the parentheses, without violating the complexity of the pluriverse that constitutes reality. Distortions of reality start to occur, however, the moment one attempts to suppress or forget the sequestration, concluding that one's ingenious abstractions are synonymous with reality; or that this reality now belongs to the person abstracting; or that he or she has succeeded in knowing it as it "really" is, once and forever, everywhere, for he or she finally owns the Truth.

Every abstraction, every conceptualization, every classification or codification needs to be embraced with the humility that it is only one possible act of relation. In order to keep arrogance and aggrandizement at bay, there is the need to repeatedly remind oneself of what have been designated as the different forms in the poles of that relation, following different philosophical schools: subject/object, subject/predicate, or knower/known, user/used, etc. But in no case of relating through abstracting is it possible to eliminate one of the poles of the relation. It is not possible to forget the subject. And the subject is always historical and specific: he or she cannot be abstracted out of the relation, adopting some divine view from "nowhere." The act of knowing is always performed by a subjectivity specified by locations in cultural time and space. Every time I think or speak, I become dependent on my culture (Panikkar, 1993).

"What can be "cultural" about the act of breathing?," asked a friend, expressing surprise at our argument; "all humans breathe the same." We are not examining here the different ways of breathing, so clear between a peasant of Bolivia or the Himalayas, the Inuit and the Bedouins. We do recognize the similarity or homogeneity of the biological processes involved in their breathing; all of them will drown the same way in water. We are focusing on the very notion of breathing. There are people who will die without having it, while others have differential, elaborated notions about it. The way we perceive and conceptualize breathing, abstracting it from all other acts or realities, is clearly culturally specific. We all may have the same class of "physical" eyes, so different to the eyes of a fly or a fish, but behind a concrete wall or any object we will see different colours – not to say images – depending on our training and culture. The three thousand tones identified by an expert are not his or her inventions – they exist and other experts, with the same training, will also be able to identify them. But they express a specific way of interaction between the expert and the world that cannot be but culturally specific, rooted in a particular culture.

To abstract or to classify with each other, we require common cultural backgrounds. These backgrounds constitute horizons of intelligibility of each culture. Without this horizon, any exploration will be without limits, falling headlong into a vacuum, or becoming incoherent or incomplete.[8] Common backgrounds are constituted through faith or *mythos* – as we suggested in Chapter 2. We bring this up again only to underscore the pluriverse of cultures, each with its own common background, its own horizon of intelligibility. There cannot exist cultural universals, universal cultural codes, not even that of cultural diversity – an ambiguous and problematic expression which, wrongly understood, presupposes the existence of a supra-cultural criterion for establishing the fundamental difference of cultures. Cultures are incommensurable – a condition which seems clearly uncomfortable for those accustomed to extrapolating their own perception of reality on others.

We use the word "culture" with enormous diffidence. We know that it was born as a rejection of "the otherness of the other"; of the one who is not like oneself. The original meaning of the word which, following the OED, first used only in 1867, alluded to "a language and culture which was wholly alien." It came to be used by academics in the beginning of this century to deal with "primitive cultures," adding new connotations. Such rejections were and still continue to be transformed into the desire of appropriation or suppression. Like every modern desire, it rapidly became a right. Next, those classifying peoples different to their own in the category of "cultures" assumed the right to intervene, a right that over time comes to also be adopted as an obligation. By an inscrutable intention of Divine Providence, said Rudyard Kipling, the Indian race was deposited on the shoulders of the English race. He expressed perfectly the types of alibis used as moral supports for the projects of colonizers of all stripes. We are afraid that an analogous impulse is now permeating many human rights proselytizers, warriors and activists. It is most certainly the impulse which currently legitimizes the "right of intervention" for "humanitarian purposes" in international fora. (Later, we will discuss the cases of some human rights activists, like those of Amnesty International, for whom this argument has no application.)

Each culture has its own common background, its own horizon of intelligibility. Each culture is a world, a universe. It cannot be reduced to any other culture's ways of seeing and living reality. It is another reality. Only "others" can reveal one's own myths; make them visible; eliminate their covers in order to be dis-covered and transcended. But all efforts in that direction will be useless, and the observer will not be able to see or dis-cover unless he or she is ready to love, to listen with care and affection, to identify with what is revealed. None of this entails assimilating oneself to the realities of others; or accepting these without reservations. All it demands is hospitality; the openness to be hospitable to the otherness of the other (Panikkar, 1993, p. 17).[9]

This hospitality to another culture, daring audaciously to re-cognize it in its radical difference and therefore to respect it, demands profound humility; to re-cognize one's own limits, the scope of every form of intelligibility of the world. It requires learning to see the other culture, without necessarily admiring it. One cannot really see the Other without respect. This respect must be assumed as a condition for love. Neither respect nor love implies blindness, inaction or indifference to the Other's perversions or wrongs. Quite the opposite: it calls for moving passionately to perceive it, as an expression of difference; and, perhaps, even to attempt correcting it, following the urge to shorten distances, but without sacrificing respect and love.

Intercultural hospitality is impossible without a respectful and loving dialogue, a dialogue which changes its own terms. These terms are the point of departure for the dialogue. But during the course of its realization, under the assumption of radical pluralism, they change as a result of the interaction. What do we mean here by love? What we are saying has no relation at all to guilt: that suspect sentiment which moves people to send a check to their favorite charity, after seeing hungry children on the evening news. Even less does this respect and love have any relation with sentimentality, the condition of Homo sentimentalis: not the man who feels (for all of us feel), but the man who has made a value of sentimentality, the man brilliantly unmasked by Cervantes (Kundera, 1991, pp. 218–19).

Justino Fernández, professor, historian and art critic, for years visited Coatlicue, a monumental Aztec statue. It exerted such a strong fascination over him that he found himself at times unable to resist the impulse of surreptitiously touching it. Because of its fascination for and familiarity to him, he never found it to be frightening – even though he was very aware of the fears and revulsion it created in most people – experts or laypeople, researchers or tourists – who described it as "a monstrosity," "a monstrous monolith," "horrifying," "the monstrous in monumental proportions," "terrifying." After many years of courting it, he dared to write a long book to settle accounts with his own relation to it. This book reveals how he came to recognize the limitations of facing a work of art with a critical-historical or an "impressionist" attitude. Neither the purely rational nor the purely emotional is appropriate. He thus describes the "aesthetic co-motion" which can synthesize those two attitudes, as well as the revelations which this synthesis produces, through which both its beauty, the aesthetic impact that co-moves, and its historical content or meaning are manifested. The pages which he dedicates to Coatlicue, once she has revealed herself to him, clearly show the hands of a man in love; one who succeeds in poetically sharing with others the intensity of his emotion. His success lies, among other things, in his ability to avoid the transformation of Coatlicue into a Dulcinea, and his refusal to be dominated by sentimentalism (Fernández, 1959).

The celebration of radical pluralism demands that kind of love. This love is to be found in the act of identifying oneself with the Other, surrendering to the Other's identity, trying to immerse oneself in it, without ever losing one's own identity. This pluralism cannot be equated with moral relativism. Pluralism is not the same as plural. That truth is pluralistic implies denying that it is either one or many; that it is possible to reduce it, to quantify it, to compare it, with a "superior," supra-cultural criterion (Panikkar, 1990a). Approaching the world as a pluriverse, without renouncing one's own universe, calls for the adoption of diatopic and dialogic approaches which bring us to juridical pluralism (Vachon, 1990). With this comes a radical questioning of any universalist attitude about law and rights. Cultures that probably represent the majority of the people on earth lack words or concepts equivalent to the notion of "a right." In these cultures, the western notion of rights contradicts their sensibilities and notions of responsibilities for communal or cosmic solidarity. That is why they find it incomprehensible that women, men and children can have rights or entitlements. Furthermore, that these moral elements can be declared by a nation-state or by a charter convened between the governments of nation-states is almost ridiculous for them (Vachon, 1990). Should the new living Buddha be recognized by a Tibetan monk because this is decreed by the Chinese government? How does he deal with the idea that the rights and duties of the living Buddha were established in an international treaty based on the United Nations Charter?

Cultural "lacks," "gaps" or "failures" can of course be remedied through "liberal education" or legislation, maintain their proponents. Governments and human rights activists daily attempt to compensate for the "failures" or "inadequacies" of others' cultures by following the paths prescribed by such remedies. Following our intuitions and experiences, however, we take hope from the fact that it is equally possible for those other cultures to resist this imposition; to break away from their "liberal educators'" norms by affirming their own cultural conceptions of "decency," "goodness" or "justice"; to learn that the western notion of rights is avoidable; that it is substantively individualistic; that it poses a threat to communal identity; that the force of human rights laws conveys cultural violence, nothing less than an abuse of power.

When perceived from the point of view of western anthropology, custom is a mode of behavior socially accepted by a people in a culture, often viewed as an inferior or primitive stage of human society. For customs lack universalizable moral principles or norms (Kohlberg et al., 1983). This is especially true when a norm is understood as an abstract and vertical provision. (In geometry, where the term was born, the line or plane is normal when it falls perpendicularly, from the top down.) Laws are usually identified with the juridical regime of the nation-state, perpendicular and top down. Societies and cultures in which customs or customary patterns prevail usually resist such types of laws, both because the nation-state (with its juridico-political western design) is alien to them and because they want to keep alive their own justice and juridical systems.

In the western tradition, the state of law represents the accomplishment of two conditions: the existence of norms of general effect (taking the wide sense of the word "norm" as a principle of behavior); and the will of the social body for the enforcement of those norms.[10] Paradoxically, even today, those conditions are better met in non-western cultures than in those fully assimilated to the abstract set of norms of the nation-state. And the latter is, unavoidably, a regime emerged, imposed and strengthened at the expense of custom; violating it, eliminating it or reducing it, to cover increasingly more spheres of social reality and behavior, and to submit them to mechanical and abstract arrangements (Bobbio, 1976). Given their nature, these arrangements increasingly escape human control and legitimize the monopoly of violence inside the nation-state.

Custom has been, historically, a fundamental source of moral principles (what is "right" or "wrong"), "claims" and "obligations," "entitlements," and principles regulating social life, about what should be respected or denied. Local autonomies, in all their shapes, as well as rebellion against all forms of authoritarianism, have had customs as a source of inspiration and strength and a social and political stronghold. To impose itself, every empire has had to first submit customs to centralized control; and thereafter, to promote their extinction.

The modern democratic state, as a regime of domination, has followed this authoritarian tradition (Alvares, 1992; Nandy, 1992). It has built its inherent centralism on the absorption of customs, their supression, their transformation into law. To do so, it has used processes which make the codified laws of the state the main, if not the only, source of right, thus "legalizing" the society and "statizing" the law. In all cultures there have been many sources of rights: custom, tradition, brute force, etc. Modern law still recognizes alternative sources of rights, but only when they are explicitly established as such in law (in an operation which reverses the source of legitimation). And the law itself emanates from the legislative organ of the state, which has the monopoly of legitimate violence to enforce it. The "legalization" of rights and "statization" of law advance through the mass production of norms no longer derived from communal customs that evolved before the emergence of the nation-state. As the state machinery expands, getting more strongly established and entrenched, deliberations about rights are entrusted exclusively to the legislative organ. Suppressing spontaneous bonds between people, both in the small territorial units and in the great social collectivities, state control expands by reducing and resisting all forms of local autonomy. It attempts to assure absolute fidelity of the citizens-subjects whose social and political relationships cease to have their own center, to subordinate themselves to public or private capital of the centralist state, founded on the individualization of the possessive, envious and covetous individual, the *Homo oeconomicus*, created in the West. The state attempts to homogenize all natural communities in its territory; to impose upon them the same way of thinking and behaving, the same habits, to establish what is called *el imperio de la ley* ("the Empire of the Law"). And the latter, in the real world, operates as a tool of domination. It is a norm that is general with respect to its addressees, abstract with respect to the foreseen action, and imposed as an act of deliberate will by the dominant power. That "dominant power" pretends today to ground its legitimacy in the illusion of democracy, masking the reality that a very small minority imposes its will on the people in the modern democratic state – as explored further in Chapter 5.

Faced with the fact that there still subsist wide and numerous cultures with juridical regimes different to the western law of the nation-state, it is yet not too late in the day to start respecting these "Others." To postulate the universality of human rights and to actively promote their enforcement, their quantitative and qualitative extension, is nothing less than the theoretical and practical attempt to dominate the majority of peoples on earth. It can only be achieved through moral and physical violence and power abuse. To recognize and to respect the incommensurability of cultures requires the acceptance of juridical pluralism. Rejecting the universality of any norms – regarding human or other rights – is compatible with accepting in theory and practice modes of consensus and agreement for regulating and orienting intercultural relations.

TORTURE AND VIOLENCE: THE BOTTOM LINE

Some human rights champions do recognize the validity of these observations. They have begun to acknowledge severe limits to their enterprise of universalization. They are slowly learning to perceive that it is especially counterproductive when it gets translated into the growth of bureaucracies and regulations which suffocate the freedoms earlier enjoyed by peoples and communities that they are supposedly liberating. Rights to abortion or reproduction are even more problematic when exported to the cultural contexts of "aliens." There is mounting evidence of all horrors that accompany the invasion of traditional contexts by modern "rights" and "liberties." The daily destruction of female "fetuses" in India and China is just one example of what "emancipated" women's "rights" to their "reproductive organs" do to the bodies of unborn females in these "underdeveloped" or "unliberated" cultures.

Some human rights activists are beginning to critically question concepts of universal "social rights" after learning to recognize and respect the incommensurable ideals and traits of different cultures. But even they refuse to renounce the global banner of "universal human rights" in their war against torture, slavery, unjust imprisonment, ritual injury or sacrifice, lynching or rape, and other horrors. Assuming such practices to be universally unacceptable, they assert their moral obligation to fight against them wherever they appear – applying persuasion, the imposition of impersonal national or international laws, or even force on behalf of the universal spread of human rights. Their moral outrage is not lessened by arguments that the violence or torture in question is legitimized by custom or law; or that they belong to cultural traditions different from their own.

Our arguments do not seek to paralyze or inhibit those who cannot turn their backs on horrors occurring outside their own communities. In fact, we applaud all persons whose interests go beyond the maintenance of their private lawns, or their ownership rights to guns and firearms. While lauding these larger sympathies, however, we also seek to reveal the ugly underbelly of all moral ventures into the lives of peoples whose cultures are neither known nor understood by well-intentioned interfering Samaritans. The cultural damage and counterproductivity perpetrated by the universalizing of human rights can only be appreciated once their underbellies are studied with open eyes.

Rigoberta Menchú renders naked the recolonization occuring with the contemporary Trojan Horse called "education as a human right." She notes:

> We don't celebrate Guatemalan Independence Day ... because, in fact, it isn't a celebration for us. We consider it a *ladino* celebration because, well, Independence as they call it means nothing to us. It only means more grief and greater efforts not to lose our culture. Other than that it has no meaning for us at all. It is only celebrated in the schools and the people with access to schools are above all people with money. The majority of Indians have no access to primary or secondary schools. The bourgeoisie, middle-class people, celebrate it but lower down there's none of that. When teachers come into the villages, they bring with them the ideas of capitalism and getting on in life. They try

and impose these ideas on us. I remember that in my village there were two teachers for a while and they began teaching the people, but the children told their parents everything they were being taught at school and the parents said: 'We don't want our children to become like *ladinos.' And they made the teachers leave.* What the teachers wanted was for them to celebrate the 15th of September. They had to wear school uniforms and buy shoes. *We never buy those things for children.* They told them to put on a uniform, to disguise themselves by taking off their own clothes, their costumes, and putting on clothes of all one colour. Well, the parents didn't want their children to be turned into *ladinos* and chased the teachers out. For the Indian, it is better not to study than to become like *ladinos.* (Menchú, 1984, p. 205; emphasis added)

Menchú's words re-echo the words of an Indian from another era and hemisphere:

Modern ... education makes young people unfit for any useful function in life. The vast majority of people that sent their children to the schools were agriculturists.... There is no doubt that the young people when they came back knew not a thing about agriculture, were indeed contemptuous of the calling of their fathers ... Almost from the commencement, the text-books ... never [teach students] any pride in [their] surroundings. He feels no poetry about the home life. The village scenes are all a sealed book to him. His own civilization is presented to him as imbecile, barbarous, superstitious and useless for all practical purposes. His education is calculated to wean him from his traditional culture. (Gandhi, 1953, pp. 32–5)

Studies of the Trojan horse of human rights – to education, jobs or health-care – might start with the legal arrangements of the nation-state. Too often these express themselves in laws that are tantamount to power abuses: organized and enforced as these are at the expense of customs and traditions that continue to be smashed through the use of state violence – more intense than the communal wrongs they are supposed to ameliorate. (In Chapter 5, we study how the construction of the nation-state establishes the Empire of the Law at the expense of all other social/communal arrangements; and how the statization of law is formulated and enacted by organs of the state.) Our studies also reveal the importance of struggles against *the abuse of the abuse*: the arbitrary and illegal use of torture or prison; the proliferation of abusive police and military forces legally held by the state. The work of many international activists, like Amnesty International, is concentrated upon these kinds of abuses. Their solidarities with the violated can, however, become counterproductive when these reinforce the state whose abuses they are trying to stop. To prevent this counterproductivity of their activities, their struggles might explicitly include the erosion of legal arrangements used for the centralization of state powers all over the world. The purposes of decentralization are not helped by the claims of international organizations for universal human rights. By abandoning such universals, among others, they could contribute towards creating political spaces that modify and erode modern legal arrangements through which states abuse culture and commons.

Grassroots communities appreciate the initiatives of activists who use state laws and norms to curb its instrusions; to stop its programs and projects, damaging the lives, cultures and environments of "the people." Gandhi's politics of liberation epitomized this kind of struggle: appealing to the highest moral ideals of the colonizers, while not renouncing his own culture's moral ideals, defining human well-being or "the good life." Following this vein, champions of human rights might critically question and compare different cultural conceptions of "torture." How are contemporary struggles for human rights shaped by conceptions of "torture" that are either too broad or too narrow when viewed from the sensibilities of Others' cultures? Does not the problematization of "torture" raise new reservations for the "cleanest" cases of struggles on behalf of human rights?

Peeling through the layers of cultural imperialism inherent in charges of "rights" and "torture," we remember the simple tale of the bushman who killed a goat belonging to a herd. He did so after properly asking the goat's permission – in full accord with his tribe's customs. Following these tribal customs, he could not even conceive the idea that the herd had an "owner" with "rights," as legitimized by the laws of the state. Tried in a court of the state after his capture, he unhesitatingly accepted what he did without guilt. In fact the words "guilty" and "not guilty" do not exist in his culture and customs. But the arbiters of "impartial law" could not take into account his customs, which ignore the very notion of "rights" of "private ownership." Put into jail, he was unable to understand where he was and why. What was the meaning of the law, or the legal and legitimate reasons of the sentence imposed upon him after an impeccable trial by a fair judge? "How was the trial?", asked the absent-minded white researcher. "They gave him the death sentence," answered his assistant, well acquainted with the bushman's kinship. "For killing a goat?", asked the puzzled white man. "No. Three months in jail. Same thing. He will die for sure. He has never seen a wall in his life. Now he has walls all around him. He refuses to eat or drink, for life in a cell is inconceivable to him."[11]

Prison or capital punishment are not classified as "violence," "torture" or "the violation of human rights" in many modern societies – in so far as these stem from a "legal trial." Neither are compulsory schooling, "just wars," dismemberment on highways, prolongation of the lives of the dying and the brain-dead, and other practices of "developed" or "civilized" states. For other peoples and cultures, however, classrooms and jails, like old-age homes or hospitals, are considered inhumane places, subjecting people to torment and torture. In contemporary "civilized" societies, the privileged medical profession tortures and torments to extend the lives and agonies of terminally ill patients; to prolong this new abstract entity called "life," regardless of the physical and psychological suffering of those dying or of their families. Among peoples who practice the arts of suffering, dying and voluntary simplicity, the swimming-pools, houses or other symbols of these modern "healers'" wealth are as horrifying as the physical "torture" of their treatments or the torture of social injustice which kill the hungry and homeless, while their "healers" claim their liberty rights to "eat cake." Then again, there is no violence, torture or abrogation of human rights for the administrators of modern universities who prohibit faculty and staff from bringing or nursing their new-born infants in their offices or the classrooms – asserting that a mother giving milk to her baby in public is considered to be engaged in unseemly, unprofessional or unproductive conduct. These criteria of "professional conduct" are tantamount to heartless torture for peoples and cultures where nursing young children or keeping them close to their mothers is considered "natural," and, even more so, are deemed "morally desirable" for the well-being of everyone in the community.[12] Clearly, what "civilized" peoples consider acceptable or even desirable is tantamount to torture in the cultures of the Other.

THE KITSCH OF HUMAN RIGHTS: THE LAST MORAL RESORT FOR RECOLONIZATION?

While unveiling the perfect Trojan horse for the contemporary western recolonization of the world, we underscore the fact that some of the most courageous people we know are struggling for human rights today. Close friends of ours have escaped torture or unjust imprisonment because of the interventions of human rights activists. We know men and women who have risked their social positions, even the lives of those dearest to them, in their quest to protect human rights – for persons known or even unknown. Perhaps there is no other "global cause" with better moral intentions or record of successes in decreasing mutilations, imprisonment, mis-trial or death than the struggles of human rights activists in every state.

These moral triumphs or humane intentions do not, however, allay our profound misgivings with the vanguard of women and men who marched into China to denounce human rights abuses or to universalize the moral currency of human rights. We balked at the American delegation's main aim: "making sure no ground is lost," particularly in defending the idea that women's rights are "universal."

How can the Grand March for Human Rights become kitsch, as Kundera suspects? Remember the Grand March into Cambodia in *The Unbearable Lightness of Being* (Kundera, 1984)? The best European and American intellectuals courageously join the procession of do-gooders and modern Samaritans committed to breaking the ban that prevents providing health-care to undernourished and dying Cambodian children. In spite of the actresses and other Hollywood celebrities on the make being outnumbered by the intellectuals genuinely committed to promoting the rights of all humanity, the march is nothing more than another modern press event, celluloid high drama, a show of shows which primarily produces excellent front-page coverage and memorable photo images. Like all "good shows," it cannot go on interminably. Human rights activists, their modern march completed, return to their daily lives. In Cambodia, as in Tibet, China or elsewhere, life goes on as the flashlights fade following yet another international media event on human rights.

Clearly, Kundera's "deconstructions," like those of Panikkar, Illich, Vachon and others, have not succeeded in eroding the modern myth of universalizable human rights. Even after the discreditation of natural rights that came from the philosophical debates of the last two hundred years, international human rights bazaars continue to become bigger and bigger media events. Their universalizability rests in the faith that they benefit the whole of humanity. Exploring their incommensurability with the moral sensibilities defining other cultures, we have discovered their deep roots in the specific cultures of peoples who have been driven by the sentiments of "the one best morality," "the one best educational system," or "the one best religion" for everyone. They are tainted by the same urge of salvation that all modes of cultural imperialism express to mask or legitimize their oppressiveness. Even with the best intentions of preventing power abuses, global quests to universalize human rights are counterproductive. Their counterproductivity lies in the fact that while attempting to protect people from one kind of abuse, they perpetrate another kind: a cultural domination that is unprecedented in its destruction of the human pluriverse, with its diverse interpretations and understandings of what constitutes "the good life" in communal and cultural terms.

At the risk of being accused of parochialism, cultural relativism or, worse yet, inhumane indifference to dowry deaths, clitorectomies, gay bashing and to the million other ways in which people torment and torture each other, we want to explicitly reject all contemporary attempts to globalize human rights. Their moral and philosophical foundations are increasingly suspect to us. Their negative impact cannot solely be attributed to wrong interpretations or inappropriate enforcements; the problems inherent in the Universal Declaration of Human Rights lie in the very nature of such ideals; in their core and their essence. All of us interested in struggling against injustices and power abuses will enjoy greater freedoms once we learn to extend ourselves beyond our own cultural context, enlarging our understanding of the conceptions of violence, torture and other evils that plague people in unique ways in their own cultural contexts; as well as the varieties of good they enjoy, in terms that make them singular, unique and culturally distinct.

In and through this process, we find that, among other social ills, one of the reigning contemporary evils we are struggling against is the universal enforcement of one culture's ideal of the good life. Furthermore, given our own cultural sensibilities, our own cosmovisions, our own cultural windows from which to view the world, we have other misgivings about the culture of the Other that has spawned the notion of human rights. With all the humility and tentativeness necessary for respectfully refusing to pray before the "sacred cows" of Others, we venture even further, suggesting that even within the culture where they were born and have dug their deepest roots, human rights claims are actually deepening the damage inherent in the lives of their claimants. We realize that our interpretation of human rights is not the only one possible, not even historically. We realize that the relativization of human rights is a very delicate surgical operation. This western primordial myth cannot be reduced to a concept, a definition. It is a myth that is open to many interpretations. We trust that in expressing our departure, we are perceived neither as supporting totalitarian systems of (mis)governance, nor of being totalitarian and exclusivistic. For our hope is to open doors for cross-cultural dialogues: between rights and *dharma*, for example; or between rights and *li*, etc. Doors leading to de-absolutizing human rights are currently shut by their universalizers; imposing them as a necessary reference point for assessing and judging all the diverse cultural practices and traditions of the world.

THE CURRENT THREAT

From Beijing, crossing over the Great Wall of China, the "global dreamers" dream that three generations of human rights will finally be enforced for every man and woman on earth; constituting the moral foundations for the "global village." Their plans, projections and blueprints of this village promulgate the universalization of civil and political rights,

economic, social and cultural rights and solidarity rights, associated with
the three themes of the French Revolution (*liberté, egalité, fraternité*).

Even as this myth is overtaking the moral imaginations of the "social
minorities" at the end of the Cold War, the "Global Project" is dismantling most of the institutional arrangements of the last two hundred
years, conceived and designed for protecting individuals from the power
abuses of the market or the state. The welfare state was constructed
around those normative themes, and reflected long and difficult social
struggles to protect people from the excesses of market forces, to keep
the social order and to ensure humane attention to the disabled or destitute. All those arrangements are now being rendered defunct by the
assumption that defines the very core of the "Global Project:" the self-
regulating market will take care of people's claims and needs better than
state bureaucracies and regulations or corporate arrangements. Behind
the mask of global "progress," justice and care, the transborder corporate
superstructures constituting the "Global Project" are claiming to take
over the management of job creation and other functions that national
governments increasingly lack the competence to accept or perform.
When the Clinton Administration failed to get labor and environmental
rules incorporated into GATT, the President urged US corporations to
develop a "voluntary" human rights code. Some of them have already
adopted a charter for this purpose. Recently, the human rights officer
of Reebok International proudly announced the company's acceptance
of that responsibility: "The old boundaries between public and private
sectors have been shattered at the edges with regard to business and
what we can do with this. With our human rights standards, we hope
to prevent some abuses that took place in the West during the Industrial Revolution."[13] To be sure, the companies will take good care of
the people. They are busy elaborating their own "ethic codes." Some
corporate kings have already established Human Rights Departments
for their operations "abroad," in order to avoid some of the misdoings
of the Industrial Revolution.[14]

That these basic moral posturings of the "Global Project" are farcical
is irrelevant to the myth-makers of human rights or to their converted
"true believers." Dramatic reductions are taking place in the bargaining
power of people's organizations to include complementary protection
for those rights in their job contracts. Amongst the "social minorities,"
those suffering the first and most damaging effects of the current wave
of social and economic changes are legitimately struggling to protect
what they assume to be social conquests of the modern era. In their
endeavors, they are being joined by individuals of the "social majorities" – especially those whose sufferings have been exacerbated by the

impact of the "Global Project," both in their current conditions and in their expectations. They seek support for their struggles in the Universal Declaration of Human Rights and the legal arrangements existing in all countries to protect them.

Theoretically, there is great support for these expectations. For regardless of the intensity of the differences that emerge in contemporary debates about economic, social and political theories promoting or challenging the "Global Project," the concern for the advancement of human rights appears to be clearly universal. As the Nobel laureate and political dissident Andrei Sakharov once wrote:

> The ideology of human rights is probably the only one which can be combined with such diverse ideologies as communism, social democracy, religion, technocracy and those ideologies which may be described as national and indigenous. It can also serve as a foothold for those ... who have tired of the abundance of ideologies, none of which have brought ... simple human happiness. The defense of human rights is a clear path toward the unification of people in our turbulent world, and a path toward the relief of suffering. (quoted in Burns, 1995, p. 664)

The formulation and advancement of universal human rights have precedents in ancient times, particularly for the humane treatment of foreigners. Only after the French Revolution, however, did the idea take hold in individual countries as a social need and reality. And only after World War II did the universal enforcement of human rights become a matter of effective concern in the international arena. The "faith in fundamental human rights" was explicitly established in the Charter of the United Nations in 1945. This further rendered obsolete the idea of "natural rights," which informed the Bill of Rights in England (1688) and the Declaration of the Rights of the Man and the Citizen in France (1789), whose precedents were the English Magna Carta of 1215 and the *Fuero Viejo de Castilla*, in Spain, in 1394. But the very idea that every human being is entitled, at least in theory, to some basic rights had already won wide acceptance and recognition among the "social minorities," even during the period of colonialism when they were oppressing their slaves and other indigenous peoples. It became one of the central pillars of nation-building in the postcolonial period after 1945.

Our deep admiration for human rights activists and dissidents like Sakharov notwithstanding, we cannot turn a blind eye to the oppressive underbelly of any well-intentioned unification of all peoples and cultures under the single moral banner of human rights. The moral ideals inherent in the concept of human rights open only one among diverse cultural windows conceived to promote personal and collective well-being, protecting peoples from the social and natural forces resulting in exploitation, oppression, persecution and other forms of deprivation. Learning from "common" men and women in our own cultures, we invite others to cherish different cultural landscapes, through windows that are neither circumscribed nor limited by any global agenda – including that of universalizing human rights. In doing so, we join those who are affirming their own as well as others' cultures in exploring the fundamental and far-reaching diversity of personal and collective conceptions of well-being and flourishing, or of human evils, horrors and deprivation. Opening and gazing through such windows, we seek to avoid nostalgia or sentimental reminiscing about the "good old days" of pre-modern times. Instead, our inquiry into non-modern cultures is acutely contemporary; as are the post-modern modes of Being in the world revealed to us at the grassroots. These are transforming the modern world, including its contemporary variations on the Bill of Rights.

The new liberation of women and others, in the epic now evolving at the grassroots, is occurring side by side with older varieties of liberation. Among the beneficiaries of the latter are children – enjoying the opportunities and the freedoms they had for centuries preceding the introduction of compulsory classrooms into their communities. This resumption of their children's freedoms means that whole communities, through regenerating their traditions, are once again assuming responsibility for the initiation of their young ones into their culture. They are learning to resist the state requirement to hand over their children to "experts," "professional teachers" and other varieties of agencies of Outsiders whose "education" means abandoning their communities for the cities, with the "help" of charity, handouts and human rights.

Among the "social majorities," undoubtedly some are still struggling for the enforcement of their "right to education," through more or better teachers and schools. But there are many others who have started to react to the specific horror imposed upon them in the name of the human right to an "education." This right systematically disregards the skilled and highly knowledgeable elders of their own cultures, classified as "uneducated" because they have not attended school or been conscientized. Their new awareness has been strengthened by their observation of the final results of modern education among those who they previously considered privileged. More and more, it is becoming common knowledge that investing many years of life in the educational system is too often a road that transports peoples away from their cultures and communities to the sprawl of urban ghettoes. Others escape these hells to go "nowhere": thousands of engineers or lawyers are suffering as dish-washers or taxi drivers the frustration of not getting what was promised to them when they started their "education."

They discover, day after day, that even progressive efforts involved in the "pedagogy of the oppressed" are also colonial tools to impose upon them the specific shape of the Outsiders' "conscience."[15]

BEYOND THE VIOLENCE OF HUMAN RIGHTS

Imposing universal definitions of torture or evil upon different cultures is tantamount to the abuse of power, legitimized today under the umbrella of human rights. Recognizing this, however, implies neither a descent into paralyzing relativism nor candid pacifism. Understanding the power abuses imposed by the minorities upon the world's majorities under the umbrella of human rights does not condemn any one to inaction or indifference when confronting rape, torture, humiliation or malnutrition. Among other goals, our argument renders naked the cultural biases or hypocrisy of those condemning some traditional "ritual sacrifices," while accepting the death of thousands or millions in a "fair war," or on national highways that promise speed, efficiency and excitement. It equally denounces the pharisaic cowardliness of those who, under the guise of respecting others' cultures, advise doing nothing about the latter's horrors, while tying the hands of those who are trying to rectify or ameliorate matters. We are particularly concerned with the current use of "traditions" as an argument against human rights activists on the part of the abusers: state authorities or armies trying to hide from the public their crimes courageously denounced by those activists.

Opening doors to genuine intercultural dialogues means going beyond the global morality decreed by the Universal Declaration of Human Rights. These dialogues are possible only if every culture affirms itself in what it is, while at the same time opening itself to others' cultures, in order to explore incompatible or overlapping cross-cultural notions and common conditions for their interaction. This is perfectly compatible with following one's own deep cultural impulses, which include identifying evil wherever it appears, being faithful to the terms of one's own culture, and fighting against this evil with the available means.

Instead of being converted to the morality of human rights activists, oppressed persons and communities everywhere need allies willing to co-move with them. *Conmoverse* (co-move) is a beautiful word in Spanish. It does not mean merely moving oneself with the other – as opposed to moving the other, as promoters of the alien "rights" catechism urge. In addition, it calls for joining heads as well as hearts and stomachs in the dance that brings cultural changes, interchanges and exchanges.

These new frames of reference cannot be constructed with the abstract structures of the state, without which abstractions like universal human rights lose their meaning or significance. Obviously, they lie outside the horizon of intelligibility of "primitive" or "underdeveloped" cultures, for whom the nation-state has always been an alien entity, one incompatible with realizing their own cultural ideals of self-governance. (We explore this critical point further in Chapter 5.)

TOWARDS NEW INTERCULTURAL DIALOGUES

Abdullahi Ahmed An-Na'im's *Human Rights in Cross-Cultural Perspectives* describes his long, puzzling, personal journey as a Muslim advocate of human rights. This personal situation compelled him to focus on "the obvious conflicts and tensions between international standards of human rights, on the one hand, and principles of Islamic Shari'a (the comprehensive religious, ethical, and legal norms which purport to regulate the private and public lives of Muslims), on the other" (An-Na'im, 1992, p. 427). For ten years, he tried to identify those conflicts and tensions, seeking ways of resolving them from an Islamic theoretical point of view. After discovering the limitation of a formalistic approach to the international standards of human rights, the rejection or hostility of all the major cultural traditions of the world to those rights and the importance of appreciating the concrete social, political and economic circumstances of each society, he found that his task was much more problematic than he imagined at the outset. He now believes that "universal cultural legitimacy is essential for international standards of human rights. ... [I]f, or to the extent that, the present concept and its contents are not universally valid, we must try to make them so" (An-Na'im, 1992, p. 431). But at the end of the collective volume where he attempts to present cross-cultural perspectives on human rights, he has no answer to his original question. He still thinks that it is possible to achieve that "universal cultural legitimacy" by extrapolating as much as possible international standards, to explore their revision, and by trying to bridge the gap from within each culture as well as between them and the norms and values of the other. He establishes a research agenda for that purpose, concluding that "in view of the unacceptable discrepancy between the theory and practice of human rights today, every effort should be made to understand and redress the underlying reasons for the discrepancy" (An-Na'im, 1992, p. 435).

For several decades, Robert Vachon has also been exploring those "underlying reasons." His own journey evolved from the intercultural experience of working with Indian peoples in Canada. He founded, with Jacques Langlais, the Monchanin Cross-cultural Centre, later transformed into the Intercultural Institute of Montreal, and for many years he has been the Editor of *Interculture*, the journal published by the Institute. For both the Institute and the journal, he continues to search for as well as to discover approaches that are intercultural (undertaken in light of the diverse cultural traditions of contemporary peoples, and not solely in the terms of modern culture), inter- and trans-disciplinary (calling on many 'scientific' disciplines, but also on other traditions of knowledge and wisdom (ethno-science) as well as on vernacular and popular knowledge), and dialogical (based on the non-duality between *mythos* and *logos*, *theoria* and *praxis*, science and wisdom, wisdom and love). Robert Vachon and his collaborators have been creatively elaborating upon and applying the teachings of Gandhi, Raimón Panikkar and others in their quest for cultural pluralism and new approaches towards social harmony.

One of Vachon's recent essays, "Guswenta or the Intercultural Imperative" (1995a, XVIII (2–4)), offers some fascinating clues as to the predicament described by An-Na'im, on which we have elaborated in the course of this chapter. Exploring how to re-enact a Peace Accord between the Mohawk Nation and the North American nation-states (and their peoples), Vachon finds the need to proceed "to a triple *cultural disarmament*, on the basis of a fundamental distinction between the culture of modernity, primordial Western culture and primordial Mohawk culture, the three being irreducible one to the other or to a common denominator" (XVIII (3), p. 41). He reflects on the importance of trying

> to carry out an intercultural dialogue between these three cultures, in an interculturalism of conviviality, radical relativity, non-duality and harmony in and because of our differences. We shall care that it be interpersonal, internature, interreligious, interpolitical, avoiding mere inter-ethnicity, multiculturalism, pluriculturalism, or the prostituted interculturalism of acculturation and integration which is assimilation to a system model. Hopefully, it will be a dialogue of interculturation and not an ideology of fusion and hybridization of cultures.

Finally, concludes Vachon,

> for each of the three poles or centers (modern, Western primordial, Mohawk primordial) we shall try to hold fast to their distinct and *unique cultural authenticity*, without prejudice to each one's pluralistic identity in the circle of life that – all together – we constitute (for cultural identity is not a univocal object but a horizon of intelligibility). We are aware that this calls for a mutation, on the part of each pole. This mutation cannot be imposed or even simply chosen, but is an imperative of the pluralistic, dynamic and always surprising nature of life itself. (XVIII (3), p. 41; emphasis added)

Vachon is now working on a possible method, thematically new, to accomplish that endeavor.

Vachon's *Interculture* and An-Na'im's *Human Rights in Cross-Cultural Perspectives* exemplify radically different quests. Like many human rights theoreticians and activists, An-Na'im recognizes well the tensions and conflicts between the international standards of human rights and the major cultural traditions of the world. After identifying all the weaknesses and ambiguities of the concept, agreements and practices of human rights, he joins the defenders of human rights in concluding that these signify a great human achievement; one which must be respected, while courageously working for its revision in order to bring to it "universal cultural legitimacy."

The cultural imperialism inherent in this type of human rights enterprise is revealed by Vachon. To fully embrace the very nature of the predicament now confronted by contemporary peoples means humbly accepting all the difficulties of engaging in intercultural, inter- and transdisciplinary and dialogical dialogues among all cultures on earth, rather than dismissing them as romantic, utopian and even impossible endeavors. Engaged in this quest, Raimón Panikkar observes: "Wisdom emerges when the love of knowledge and the knowledge of love coalesce."

Gandhi's search for this wisdom through his "experiments with truth" leads him to humbly caution any one inclined towards universal rights or truths for all peoples and cultures:

> [S]eeing that the human mind works through innumerable media and that the evolution of the human mind is not the same for all, it follows that what may be truth for one may be untruth for another.... All that I can in true humility present to you is that truth is not to be found by anybody who has not got an abundant sense of humility. (Gandhi, 1970, p. 433)

With this humility, Gandhi's *dharma* led him to the work of peace to create a "paradise on earth." He cautioned that this work of peace "can only be done by local men in their own localities" (p. 434). Not the credo of universal human rights but his own Hindu *dharma* led Gandhi to struggle where he stood for a place in which

> there will be neither paupers nor beggars, nor high nor low, neither millionaire employers nor half-starved employees, nor intoxicating drinks or drugs. There will be the same respect for women as vouchsafed to men and the chastity and purity of men and women will be jealously guarded. Where every woman except one's wife will be treated by men of all religions, as mother, sister or daughter according to her age. Where there will be no untouchability and where there will be equal respect for all faiths. They will all be proudly, joyously and voluntarily bread labourers. (p. 240)

There are clear overlaps of Gandhi's *dharma* with the ideals of human rights. Equally clear, however, is the radical departure of *dharma* from the welfare state, including the national economy needed for its existence. Clearly, the *dharma* of "bread labor" is incompatible with the political economy or the moral worldview in which "welfare rights" or "liberty rights" are firmly rooted. The welfare state or the neoliberal global economy are marginalized by "home economics" (Berry, 1987) or the economy of communal commons in which the *dharma* of bread labor flourishes. Furthermore, unlike the supposedly secular morality of human rights, the ethics of bread labor creates open spaces for the flourishing of other cultural and religious ideals.

The skills of being "bread laborers" are fast vanishing in the world inhabited by "the social minorities." The welfare state as much as global neoliberalism, aggressively holding out the promise of finally realizing universal human rights, are making it more and more difficult for the world's "social majorities" to practice these skills proudly, joyously and voluntarily in their own cultural spaces. Their courageous struggle to do so, against all odds, make their current initiatives into a post-modern epic.

NOTES

1. There are at least four distinct contexts in which claims are being made today on behalf of human rights:

Violations by state authorities. Human rights claims are being made against two kinds of power abuses: against people's liberties and against people's livelihoods. The loss of the latter are often associated with activities and decisions of the state, the World Bank and other international agencies promoting economic growth, "sustainable green progress" or "eco-development." The loss of the former are associated with power abuses that range from the Tiananmen Square massacre to the destruction of the homes and villages of millions of citizens (for the construction of dams being built to meet the growing demand for energy, the mining of uranium, the building of nuclear power plants or the dumping of toxic waste); to the ruination of their natural spaces through "benign" quarry mines dug where people currently get their drinking water and fish; or forced abortions and vasectomies for the purpose of population control. In all these cases, individuals or communities resort to human rights for claiming respect for their homes or villages; protection for the ecological health of their communal spaces (including forests and farmlands); or protection for their own health, threatened by the emission or production of carcinogens, the ruination of soil by pesticide spraying, or increases in malaria and other diseases caused through river damming and other projects for industrialization and the growth of the national and global economy. Making human rights claims in these contexts, individuals and communities seek to limit, curb or curtail interventions and interferences of national and international institutions into the lives of ordinary citizens, particularly those already politically and economically marginalized.

In some cases, such power abuses by the state authorities represent a violation of the law: raping of women by troops, looting by officers or the police, etc. When brought to court, state authorities all too often try to wash their hands of the matter, attributing responsibility for the wrongdoing to "unofficial" members of the public forces who commited the crimes. For example, after a recent massacre of seventeen unarmed peasants in Guerrero, Mexico, the special prosecutor designated for the case exonerated state authorities by accusing a group of policemen, attributing the incident to their "lack of appropriate training." Only the pressure of opposition parties and human rights agencies and activitists, and the public reaction elicited by the presentation on the main TV network of a video showing the killings, forced the resignation of the Governor and the intervention of the Supreme Court. Most cases of abuses by state troops can be exposed to punishment by the military authorities. "The link between human rights and military honor is so close in democratic armies, that, in fact, any violation of human rights is considered as a severe offense to military honor" (García, 1994, p. 67). This very fact determines that in many cases the military authorities try to hide the crimes committed by the troops, making it extremely difficult for human rights activists to bring and win their cases in court.

One variant of these claims is defined by cases where the rights violated are not recognized as such by the state, or in which the state refuses to recognize what it has done against some individuals or groups as a violation. In these cases, state authorities apply legal procedures against the liberties or livelihoods of some people, claiming reasons of "national security" or "welfare rights" for all citizens. They justify the short-term suffering or deprivation of a minority (those, for example, whose homes and lands are drowned by dams or mines), claiming that these promote the well-being of the majority (whether citizens of the state or of the "global village"). Most acts of violent repression or imprisonment (like in Tiananmen) are explicitly committed by governments in the name of the common good: to protect the society as a whole against the "subversive behavior" of some individuals or groups. In these cases, human rights activists encourage public and political pressures, rather than legal trials, in seeking to amend the wrongdoings of the state. In the case of "prisoners of conscience" – persons or groups imprisoned either without a fair trial or court proceedings that are tantamount to a mistrial – human right groups, like Amnesty International, either seek the release of the prisoners, or demand a fair trial and a punishment that is commensurable with the crime.

Violations by people. Human rights are being currently claimed to curb, curtail, restrain or end the power abuses of families or small communities oppressing particular individuals or groups. Their power abuses or the crimes of cultural practices are very diverse in span: ranging all the way from the "dowry deaths" of the young brides in India to the sale of young girls and boys for sex, or of babies for adoption; clitorectomies or forced vasectomies; the harassment, molestation, rape and murder of gays, lesbians and all other "minorities" who "choose" to depart from the majority of their tribe/clan/community in terms of religious practices, sexual preferences, resistance to compulsory schooling, among others. In all these cases, human rights activists or human rights agencies demand interventions from the state. In making human rights claims, they point to the state's negligence in curbing the inhumanities perpetrated by some citizens against others. Seeking to end this negligence, state police or the judiciary are urged to take action: imprisoning or bringing to a legal trial those particular families, communities or institutions hurting either their own members or others who do not comply with the particular customs of local or regional groups.

In all these cases, it is important to keep in mind that demands for the observation of human rights are always claims presented to and against the state government, judiciary or some legal national or international authority. Human rights commissions usually reject all those grievances presented to them where supposedly no authority was involved. And human rights activists are most challenged in dealing with cases of particular individuals, families or communities committing crimes that disregard the human rights of other individuals. Here the challenge lies in discovering to whom these claims must be presented. In many of these cases, they accuse the state authorities for their failure to fulfil their responsibilities in not preventing heinous cultural practices. In these cases, on behalf of families affected by such practices, they may attempt to bring them to the attention of court officials who failed to protect them against collective behaviors violating their human rights.

Claims by a state.   Human rights claims are also made by one state on behalf of the citizens of another state. The US government, for example, has persistently accused Cuba of human rights violations, seeking the cover of international legitimacy for its own political offenses against the island.

The most prominent human rights cases seem to involve the denunciation of wrongdoings of some state authority against innocents (allegedly to promote the interests of a ruling local or national group), or of omissions: the failure of a state authority to do what it was morally obliged to do in protecting the human rights of people.

Claims for the lack of enforcement of rights.   Claims are presented about rights to something, arguing for the universal entitlement to it. These include the right to practice a specific freedom, like freedom of expression repressed through a blockade or censorship; or to receive the welfare of services like education, health, roads, sewerage and the other paraphernalia of "the developed"; or to be respected (through a fair trial, among other processes).

Contemporary human rights struggles seek to win the legal recognition of some claim to something for specific groups. They seek the enforcement of those claims through the establishment of laws. Such struggles center their attention or demands upon the omissions of the state. These are not usually the concern of human rights agencies and activists that focus basically on pointing out power abuses of the authorities, highlighting violations of existing laws or of international charters.

The four categories identified by us offer a rough sketch for classifying contemporary claims made for human rights. Sadly absent in all these debates and struggles, both to stop power abuses or to induce state action, is a critical reflection of the ways in which the discourse of human rights has come to dominate; has become in itself an expression of a power abuse: yet one more variety of cultural imperialism that has taken on global proportions. Our concerns, shaped by our grassroots journeys, stem from the realization that the reigning human rights discourse shows little respect for differences in culture; or little appreciation for the scale, the *ethnos*, the *hexis*, the horizon, the context necessary for talking meaningfully about protecting "the good" of persons or places.

2.   For the moral virtues that govern villages, see, for example, the "Testimonies by Eminent Men" included at the end of the publication of Gandhi's *Hind Swaraj*. Here, Sir William Wedderburn writes: "The Indian village has thus for centuries remained a bulwark against political disorder, and the home of the simple domestic and social virtues. No wonder, therefore, that philosophers and historians have always

dwelt lovingly on this ancient institution which is the natural social unit and the best type of rural life; self-contained, industrious, peace-loving, conservative in the best sense of the word" (Gandhi, 1946, p. 80).

In the same vein, writes J. Seymour Keay, MP, "It cannot be too well understood that our position in India has never been in any degree that of civilians bringing civilization to savage races. When we landed in India we found there a ... civilization ... not perfunctory, but universal and all-pervading – furnishing the country not only with political systems, but with social and domestic institutions of the most ramified description. The beneficent nature of these institutions as a whole may be judged from their effects on the character of the Hindu race. Perhaps there are no people in the world who show so much in their characters the advantageous effects of their own civilization: they are shrewd in business, acute in reasoning, thrifty, religious, sober, charitable, obedient to parents, reverential to old age, amiable, law abiding, compassionate towards the helpless and patient under suffering" (Gandhi, 1946, pp. 77–8).

3. The profound betrayal to their own cultures inherent in this fashion of national independence compelled Gandhi to write *Hind Swaraj or Indian Home Rule*. Pointing to the unbridgeable cultural chasm separating *Hind Swaraj* from western-style "national independence," Gandhi clarified for his own people that in the latter "brown sahibs" merely take over the management of colonizing institutions from the "white sahibs." These include not only their schools and factories, but also their laws, courts and parliament: "The condition of England ... is pitiable. (Their) Parliament is like a sterile woman and a prostitute. ... That Parliament has not yet, of its own accord, done a single good thing. Hence I have compared it to a sterile woman. ... The members ... are hypocritical and selfish. Each thinks of his own little interest. It is fear that is the guiding motive. ... Now thousands of workmen meet together and for the sake of maintenance work in factories or mines. Their condition is worse than that of beasts. They are obliged to work, at the risk of their lives, at most dangerous occupations, for the sake of millionaires. Formerly, men were made slaves under physical compulsion. Now they are enslaved by temptation of money and of the luxuries that money can buy. ... This civilization takes note neither of morality nor of religion. (It) is irreligion, and it has taken such a hold on the people in Europe that those who are in it appear to be half mad.... This civilization is such that one has only to be patient and it will be self-destroyed.... Civilization is not an incurable disease" (Gandhi, 1946, pp. 25–7).

4. Reflecting upon the way in which the Anita Hill/Clarence Thomas hearings render naked this breakdown in American society, Wendell Berry explains how and why the era of rights brings about the demise of communal virtues. With the death of these virtues, juridical inflation occurs. See Wendell Berry, *Sex, Economy, Freedom and Community* (1992).

5. See, for example, Tony Emerson, "The Rights of Women," in Newsweek, August 28, 1995, p. 11. Reporting on the UN conference in Beijing, this article predicted that women's rights in general and human rights in China were likely to dominate in Beijing.

Also see the "Platform for Action," which emerged out of the UN Fourth World Conference. Concerned about the lack of awareness of, and commitment to, internationally and nationally recognized women's rights, the 12-Point Platform for Action starts with the persistent and increasing burden of poverty on women and their unequal access to and inadequate educational opportunities. It ends with the lack of adequate recognition of and support for women's contributions to managing natural resources and safeguarding the environment. Each statement of the 12-Point Platform for Action is either an expression of concern regarding the violence against women, or a demand for universalizing the rights enjoyed by the economically privileged in the "developed" world.

6. The Indian word *hak* refers to claims people make upon each other. These are fundamentally inter-personal and communal. Unlike rights, these claims or *haks* are not universalizable; nor are they demanded of nation-states or international organizations. Within each community, within each of its cultures or sub-cultures, we discover very specific and well defined *haks*. Pulled out of their specific localized contexts, they lack any meaning. Furthermore, any attempt to universalize them will create the same problems being caused across the globe by human/ women's rights today. Just as the Hindi word *shanti* (with its roots in Sanskrit) cannot be rendered simply equivalent to "*shalom*," "peace" or "*paz*" (Illich, 1992), similarly there are difficulties in translating into English or any other language our well-localized Hindu meanings of *ahimsa, aadar, sammaan, shradha*, and others used to teach men and women how to engage in virtuous conduct with each other. Each of these terms for describing virtuous or laudable conduct calls for a patient, diligent, open-minded journey into the depths of Hindu culture. Rendering any of this equivalent to English does neither language justice. It also serves to remind us not to be cavalier in taking moral concepts, like "rights" or "*ahimsa*," from one cultural cosmovision into another.

7. On the history of individualism and *Homo oeconomicus*, see Louis Dumont (1977). For a penetrating critique of the monoculturalism inherent in the notion of human rights, and a defense of radical pluralism, see Raimón Panikkar, especially 1995, pp. 109–33.

8. For a particularly charming account of foundational myths, see Claude Alvares (1995).

9. "Hidden forces" are still an "explanation" for phenomena occurring in the daily life of many people. A "scientific mind" may "explain" to them that this specific death was caused by a specific event: an accident, a disease. But this "explanation" will do nothing to change the belief in the "hidden forces" producing that accident or disease. The "scientific mind" has no explanation for the event itself (why it happened to this man in this moment), unless it recurs to the belief in the theoretical possibility of identifying an unending series of specific causes that will rapidly vanish in the unknown past. The disqualification of beliefs in "hidden forces" as "primitive" simultaneously dismisses the humility that underlies the mysteries of real life – which by their very nature will remain as such, as mysteries, for common men and women. In pretending to know, the "scientific mind" hides its own arrogance from itself.

10. There is no state of law if there are no norms, if those that exist have no general effect, or if those in general effect are imposed (like in a colony).

11. From the film *The Gods Must be Crazy* (written and produced by Jamie Uys, CAT Films, 1980; a Twentieth Century Fox release).

12. We are fully aware that the international norm about torture refers to physical and psychological damage caused by an authority to produce a confession. We celebrate the struggle to prevent such abuse of the abuse. At the same time, we

cannot but observe that such a definition of torture can be applied to the methods of any modern school, spoiling children's lives to force them to "confess" in their exam.

13. Quoted in *Newsweek* (Latin American edition), June 26, 1995, p. 48.

14. See, for example, Michael Hirsh, "Let's Get Out of Here?," in Newsweek, June 26, 1995, pp. 45–9. In the meantime, the leaders of such organizations are being called "corporate killers" and "hit men." While it "used to be a mark of shame to fire workers en masse," the new corporate "ethic" of Wall Street of "greedheads" loves it. See Allan Sloan, "The Hit Men," Newsweek, February 26, 1996, pp. 10–14.

15. See Ivan Illich, *Deschooling Society* (1970b). Later, arguing "in lieu of education," Illich reveals "fundamental alternatives" to education, reminding us that we "often forget that the word 'education' is of recent coinage"; that it has come to mean "an intangible commodity that had to be produced for the benefit of all, and imparted to them in the manner in which the visible Church formerly imparted invisible grace. Justification in the sight of society became the first necessity for a man born in original stupidity, analogous to original sin.... Schooling and education are related to each other like Church and religion, or in more general terms, like ritual and myth. The ritual creates and sustains the myth; it is mythopoeic, and the myth generates the curriculum through which it is perpetuated. 'Education' as the designation for an all-embracing category of social justification is an idea for which we cannot find (outside Christian theology) a specific analogue in other cultures. And the production of education through the process of schooling sets schools apart from other institutions for learning that existed in other epochs" (Illich, 1977, p. 76).

FIVE

PEOPLE'S POWER:
RADICAL DEMOCRACY FOR THE
AUTONOMY OF THEIR COMMONS

Keeping citizens apart has become the first maxim of modern politics. (Rousseau, quoted by Ignatieff, 1985, p. 106)

We need to force those petrified relations to dance, singing to them their own melody! (Karl Marx, epigraph in Johannes Agnoli and Peter Bruckner 1971).

[D]emocracy depends on localism: the local areas are where the people live. Democracy doesn't mean putting power some place other than where the people are. (Douglas Lummis, 1996, p. 18)

To these preoccupations and perplexities, this book does not offer an answer. Such answers are given every day, and they are matters of practical politics, subject to the agreement of many; they can never lie in theoretical considerations or the opinion of one person, as though we dealt with problems for which only one solution is possible. (Hannah Arendt, 1958, pp. 5–6)

DEMOCRACY TODAY: SUBVERSIVE OR DEAD?

Is democracy subversive? Is it challenging the "Global Project"? Or being subverted by it?

According to mainstream conventional observers, the coalition of economic interests and public policies defining the "Global Project" are being articulated in a historical period described by them as the final victory of democracy. The dismantling of Reagan's "evil empire" marked the end of World War III, euphemistically called the "Cold War." It had winners and losers. What is seen by many as the triumph of capitalism and the market in economic terms is interpreted in the political arena as the road towards the "universalization of democracy" and the end of anti-democratic regimes. The democratic face of the "Global Project," rather than its technological, economic and social promises, constitutes the core argument for it; its moral justification and grounds for legitimation. It is the main foundation for the arguments of those who proclaim "the end of history." Market forces and the free trade of democratic regimes will bring social justice, human rights and freedom of choice among diverse options to every man, woman and child on earth, eliminating all the despotic and authoritarian elements of other regimes – socialist, communist, fascist or pre-modern. If that is the case, how can democracy be subversive to the "Global Project"?

Until now, the "Global Project" seems to be fulfilling its political promises. Its disruptions are helping several democratic movements to get rid of their despotic regimes: subverting the latter, it is bringing democracy to the countries lacking it. Furthermore, within the "democratic regimes" themselves, the generalized discontent with some highly unpopular policies of the "Global Project" have fostered people's movements, leading to increased citizen participation in some public policies and decisions. Given these "proofs" that democracy prospers with the growing impact of the "Global Project," its critics are dismissed by its proponents as Umberto Eco's "apocalyptic people": those waiting for "the catastrophe"; or those fearing the renaissance of the police state.

The "catastrophe" of the "Global Project" that some foresee in the future has already occurred for the "social majorities." They are suffering many of the worst consequences of market excesses, while simultaneously harassed by state force, all too often used against them to subvert their legitimate claims. Modernity never did bring democracy to them; but damaged the democracy of their commons. The claim of individual rights against the absolute state of monarchy or colonialism supposedly liberated society, including all those local spaces and political bodies in which "the people" were able to exert their power even under the most despotic pre-modern regimes. In fact, that "liberation" has attempted to dissolve those local political bodies surviving through colonial and other repressive regimes, thereby subordinating local autonomy to the design of the centralist modern democratic state. The "Global Project" is attempting to further dissolve and destroy what still remains of those democratic commons.

Post-modern grassroots movements identify modernity with the death of democracy, not its flourishing. They reveal how the "Global Project" is preparing democracy's tomb, even if the authoritarian apocalypse is avoided. To recover and regenerate people's power, they seek autonomy from the state so that local spaces may exert and govern themselves in their own cultural terms. Radically challenging the "Global Project," they seek to subvert the foundations of modern power structures.

THE RISE AND FALL OF DEMOCRACY

Democracy is now both *the* supreme universal ideal and a frayed flag. Only the likes of the Nazis dare to openly challenge it. But to be in favor of democracy does not say much today in settings deemed paradigmatic – most particularly the setting of the modern nation-state, with its ritualized circus of votes and election years.

The dominant perception is that democracy is a form of government. For the experts, democracy is formal, or it is not democracy. The most cherished ideals or goals of society need to be subordinated to democratic forms, including the competition for votes. If you are a real democrat and also a communist or an anticommunist, you need to subordinate the second credo to the first. To return to power in Poland or Russia today, the communists recognize that they must be voted in; some of them have accommodated their ideology to the current trends; some others are required to conceive political programs through which capitalism will be suppressed by consensus. To do otherwise today implies cynicism in the tradition of a Truman who, when he recognized that Somoza was a dictator and a son of a bitch, replied that he was *his* son of a bitch; or in the tradition of Stalinists who called their authoritarian states "popular democracies."

Contemporary democratic theory studies those forms. It seeks to identify the differential traits or organizing principles characterizing societies called democratic. It confines itself to a tautology: systematizing and formalizing those aspects of the dominant or powerful "democratic" societies as models – too often the US. There is a striking similarity between theories of democracy and development. Instead of offering principles, the latter are but mere descriptions of developed countries, presented as models for the underdeveloped. In like mode, modern democratic theory remains for the most part a mere description of "advanced" states: those considered democratic almost by definition and offered as models for "undemocratic" states.

Some experts focus on procedures and formal conditions for exerting or controlling political power, following the thesis that Schumpeter made famous: "The democratic method is that institutional arrangement for arriving at political decisions in which individuals acquire the power to decide by means of a competitive struggle for the people's vote" (Schumpeter, 1975, p. 269). These are also studied as the constitutive elements of modern democracy.[1] More and more, however, such an idea of democracy has come to lack prestige or plausibility. As far back as Aristotle, taken by some to be the classical authority on the subject, such competition was recognized as leading to corrupt and undesirable forms of government. For two thousand years, a majority of reasonable people repudiated such regimes of government. At the end of the eighteenth century, Edmund Burke expressed the dominant opinion in his time, claiming that "a perfect democracy is the most shameful thing in the world" (quoted in Bishop, 1989, p. 1).

Many strong arguments continue to be made against that democracy. The government of the majority will always express the interest of a faction, a part of the society, using its power to serve its own interests, and not the common good. And the government of "the crowds" will always be unstable, given their propensity to follow demagogues. "In democracies," affirmed Aristotle, "the most potent cause of revolution is the unprincipled character of popular leaders" (quoted in Bishop, 1989, p. 11). A skilled tyrant can capture the heart of the masses, as amply demonstrated in the modern era.

Rather than arguing for democracy in the abstract, an ideal exposed to serious criticism, reflective democrats in the tradition of Aristotle argue for "democratic elements" in a society. Included in them is the elimination of requisites of ownership to be a citizen. Aristotle preferred the selection of officers by lot; he thought that elections accentuate the oligarchic trends inherent to democracy, since they benefit the wealthy who buy votes.

While some of those objections have been addressed, new problems have appeared – such as those associated with the latest technologies of communication. It is argued, for example, that there is no remedy for the forms of manipulation and control of voters through modern mass media, rendering illusory the effectiveness of suffrage. Other criticisms of contemporary democracy focus on today's regime of political parties. For many years, conservatives resisted universal suffrage out of fear for the "tyranny of the majority." But the latter never appeared, "given the extraordinary success of the party system to control democracy" (Macpherson, 1977, p. 64). Objections to the party system include not only the manipulation of voters, but the elitist control of the options available to the electorate. (To mention one recent example, when 70 percent of the American citizens supported the idea of suspending nuclear testing, they were given the choice between two candidates opposing this suspension.) The competition for votes, furthermore, forces the parties to adopt platforms that are but mirrors of each other. Thus the parties exclude popular options, for fear of reactions from the centers of power to those options – a fear with good foundation. On the other side, there is a lack of effective mechanisms for the members to control the leaders of their party: intra-party democracy is almost entirely absent (Macpherson, 1964, p. 18).

Instead of the government of the majority (repugnant to Aristotle), today's democracy is a system in which party elites and their partners – or the opposition – control the state, limiting voters' options. "Do we seriously maintain," asked Jordan Bishop,

> that any of our societies are democratic in the sense of "a system in which the majority actually controls the rulers, actually controls those who make and enforce political decisions"? ... In the United States, the self-proclaimed prototype of democracy today, the majority has simply given up; all elections are decided by a minority, and even there it is doubtful whether the electing minority actually controls policy. Incredible as it would seem ... 20 percent of the races for the seats in the United States' House of Representatives were uncontested.[2] (Bishop, 1989, p. 10)

In the "real world," the democratic model has always been elitist: ensuring the reproduction of self-elected minorities. Consequently, the elite stratas that once resisted suffrage for fear of the "tyranny of the majority" are now defending it with passion. Today, ruling parties and the media effectively prevent the government of the majority. In modern democracies, a small minority decides for the people: it is always a minority of the people, and almost always a minority of the electorate who decides which party or coalition of parties will exert the powers of government. A minimal minority promulgates the laws and makes the important decisions. Alternance in power between competing parties or "democratic counterweights" does not modify that fact. This awareness does not necessarily entail an argument against democratic governance. It does reaffirm, however, the right of the people not to be governed against their will; that is, made to believe what is unbelievable; or, as the Spaniards put it colloquially, being forced to *"comulgar con ruedas de molino."*[3]

The construction of modern democratic forms of government was no doubt a popular victory: it reclaimed for the people the sovereignty and the power previously attributed to kings. "In Monarchy the whole, the people, is subsumed under one of its particular modes of being, the political constitution. In democracy *the constitution itself* appears as *one* determination, that is, the self-determination of the people. In Monarchy, we have the people of the constitution; in democracy, the constitution of the people" (Marx, 1975, p. 29). It was clear to Jefferson that the "divine rights of the sovereign" did not belong to him; nor were they "a gift of the Chief Magistrate." The fact that absolutism denied "men's rights" prompted men to claim them. That same operation, however, created a new political mythology, now dominant. The capacity of electoral majorities to orient political action and determine its results was assumed as an uncontestable democratic principle and a reality. Such majorities are but fictitious aggregates of individuals, theoretically endowed with reason. Their supposed homogeneity derives from the myth, constructed through modern ideology and propaganda, that the vote can express the real interest of everyone, determining and orienting rational political action.

It becomes more and more evident every day that the modern nation-state, in which contemporary democratic regimes operate, is being transmogrified into a conglomerate of "anonymous" corporations, each dedicated to promote their own products and to serve their own interests. The conglomerate produces "welfare" (education, health, transportation, jobs, etc.). In time, the political parties convene the stakeholders of all corporations to elect a board. And now the dominant corporations are not only gigantic multinational companies, but also the gargantuan professional associations and workers' unions working for them or for the state, instead of offering countervailing power. Defending their own interests, they strengthen the system from which they derive their dignity and income; but which also keeps them under others' control (as the French workers' strikes aptly demonstrated).

The cynicism, corruption and decomposition of governments and parties now prevailing in the leading modern democratic societies is only matched by

> the continual injection of fear, misery and frustration among the subjects of democracies.... [This] has reached a point in which it has become necessary to reformulate the foundations of the institutions protecting the current state of things, without accepting the blackmail of the deceitful Democracy/Dictatorship dichotomy.... At the point in which democracy is affirmed as the taboo of the tribe it starts to deny itself, to institute itself as a naked form of dominance, as brute injustice with no other purpose but to perpetuate the current state of things, so unbearable for so many people.
>
> Is it not one of our special variants of contemporary fundamentalisms? Does it not take itself as the only possible way, rather than one among the possible and desirable? Does it not share with other fundamentalisms the pretension of being the definitive Truth and a conquest which we cannot renounce? Is it not animated by the same aspirations of universality and criminally expansive fervor? Does it not possess the same blindness about itself? Does not the contemporary belief in Democracy come under the same *illusion* as believing in the Koran or the divine character of the Empire?

These warnings were formulated in Spain a few years ago (González Sainz et al., 1992, pp. 9–10). They are increasingly pertinent for the current debate on democratic governance. The central questions cannot be reduced to improving the reigning institutions of representative democracy. They require thorough reconsiderations, dis-covering how and why these institutions are increasingly counterproductive: performing the opposite of what they are supposed to do.

Radical trends in contemporary theory and praxis are attempting to recover and actualize the root meaning of the concept of democracy, its very essence. They reveal that alternatives to so-called formal democracy are necessary to avoid both the authoritarian apocalypse or the violent chaos now threatening us. If these radical alternatives are not attempted, we are doomed to suffer all the implications of the pseudo-democracies that serve as the modern models of government. Alternative conceptions and practices of democracy are being reflected upon in the emerging literature which derives its inspiration, first and foremost, from popular movements at the grassroots.

RADICAL DEMOCRACY

Formal or representative democracy, operating in the modern nation-state, has not been particularly appealing for the "social majorities." This fact has been miscast by social scientists and academics as their "under-developed politicization." We needed new eyes to read the signs of their political maturity, stemming from their specific experiences of oppression under the formal democratic regimes of the "social minorities."

Government for the People? Or People's Power?

Their more recent experiences with modern centralized states have taught the "social majorities" that governments supported by middle and upper classes, elected through manipulations by parties and media, are not really their governments: they do not and cannot represent their ideas or interests. All governments claim to govern "*for* the people," supposedly caring for their welfare. But the "social majorities," particularly the more marginalized among the marginals, are usually absent from the people cared for by national governments. "The people" have ceased to believe that great leaders, democratic or not, incarnate the people's will. "Democratic centralism" is fast becoming an oxymoron like "nuclear protection" or "military intelligence." Daily "the people" learn from experience that real democracy depends on localism: local areas where people live and exercise their power. "Democracy doesn't mean putting power some place other than where the people are" (Lummis, 1996, p. 18). "The people" have decreasing faith in the availability of opportunities to "have their say" or to be heard in today's large modern states, for they know that vicarious power is a very poor substitute for real power. They want real democracy: nothing more and nothing less than people's power. Instead, they continue to be offered placations by the state: more participation in the electoral processes; or reductions in its manipulations; or additional means of democratic control to the existing governmental structures. It is no secret for "the people" that these are not equivalent to real power. They are not bluffed by modern smokescreens conceived to conceal "the people's" powerlessness in all formal democracies, organized "of, by and for" the state.

Since "people's power," Douglas Lummis pertinently reminds us, is but "a translation into English of the Greek words *demos* and *kratia*" (Lummis, 1996, p. 11), it makes sense that the increasing focus of people's movements is directed towards organizing themselves to reformulate political bodies, enabling themselves to keep their government in their own hands. "Real" democracy means creating people's power – literally speaking. To really rule over their own lives, people's struggles are creating political bodies by which power can be held, in principle as well as practice, by themselves; not in the hands of elected or imposed leaders. In their new commons, they search for shared governance, where "democracy" is nothing but common sense. Lummis also recalls that "'common' comes from the Latin *communis* – a combination of *com* (together) and *munis* (bound, under obligation). The latter word is the opposite of *inmunis* (not under obligation, exempt)" (Lummis, 1996, p. 21). In their commons, "the people" are attached to each other by duties and obligations, not by abstract notions of rights. They are bound together by the common "sense" that is part of belonging; of participating in shaping or sharing common ways of living and dying.

People's rule, which Lummis calls "radical democracy," is not a kind of government, but an end to government as we have come to know it in modern times. Credos such as "government of the people, by the people, and for the people" (which define democracy for many) are not acceptable substitutes for the real exercise of people's power. Lincoln's formula in the Gettysburg Address does not define "democracy" (a word that does not appear in his speech). He was thinking not of a society where people have the power, but of a set of institutions designed to empower the people. He knew that the Union was not democratic – its slaves being only one of many undemocratic traits. The institutions of the governmment he imagined were not "the golden apple of liberty," but the "silver frame" by which the apple was (hopefully) to be protected (Lummis, 1996, pp. 23–4). Far from protecting it, those institutions of the government, "improved" and unrecognizably expanded since the time of Lincoln, have reduced people's power to a strict minimum. Increasingly, they prevent the rule of "the people," while sustaining that illusion within power structures which long ago co-opted control by "the people."

Radical democracy is not a historically existing institution, but a historical project which can only exist as a never-ending horizon. It is not about "a government" but about governance. It is not about any of the existing "democracies" or "democratic institutions," but about the thing itself, the root of democracy, the essential forms taken in the exercise of people's power. As Marx stated, "democracy is the solved riddle of all constitutions. Here, not merely *implicitly* and in essence but *existing* in reality, the constitution is constantly brought back to its actual basis, the *actual human being*, the *actual people*, and established as the people's *own* work. The constitution appears as what it is, a free product of man" (Marx, 1975, p. 29; emphasis added).

What is now adopted as "common sense" among politicians, experts and all those educated by them is the disqualification of this essential form of democracy. In the literature about democratic theory, "direct democracy" – with the implicit meaning of people's power – is mentioned to identify what is not possible. "'It may have worked in ancient Athens,' we are told, but 'the principle is neither descriptive nor feasible in any modern state'" (Lummis, 1996, p. 27). Paradoxically, the state thus described as democratic is precisely a system in which the very essence of democracy is impossible or unfeasible. The best that conventional theorists proffer is to cosmeticize that fact with the newly fashionable concept of "participatory democracy." It is in that vein that expressions like "direct democracy" are used, reducing it to the addition of initiative, referendum, recall, and other political tools; ensuring that they are conceived and applied in a manner compatible with representative government.[4]

From Aristotle to Marx, in contrast, the meaning of democracy as people's power was widely held. Elites shared Aristotle's view that such a system conspired against the health of the body politic, the common good, for it was the government of a faction – even if this faction was the majority. Marx assumed the opposite: that people's power was something good and desirable, while also recognizing that it was a mode of revolutionary action, as illustrated with the Paris Commune. Given the current rhetoric of "real socialism," it appears preposterous to present Marx on the side of the democrats; though some of his writings offer good reasons to do precisely that.[5] While in the tradition of Aristotle, modern critics question people's power, basing their critiques on the experience of contemporary democracies. They observe that when people do express themselves democratically, most of them vote for things that good socialists will call petit-bourgeois preferences: a little bit of pornography, more sports and TV than reading, etc. In other words, the contents of a typical contemporary popular journal offer good clues to the "stuff" of people's preferences.

Responding to such observations, it is noted that this outcome stems from the fact that the people have been continually exposed to manipulation, disabling them from making proper decisions. There is, therefore, the need to "educate" them about making correct or rational decisions. That is populism: an enlightened elite leading and conducting "the people." But populism has also failed. Since "popular decisions" seem ethically, philosophically and esthetically unacceptable to socialists as well as liberals, both have declared that an educated elite must guide "the people," making decisions on their behalf. They have accepted the thesis Hegel exposed in 1820, which has, since then, become conventional wisdom: *people lack the wisdom and capacity to govern themselves.* Yet "enlightened" elites have proved themselves to be no less corruptible than "the people." All elites have become corrupted. Tools of "direct democracy" – like the initiative, referendum and recall – are notoriously insufficient to prevent their corruption. And "the people" no longer put their trust in "democratic bodies" of the state, like parliaments or senates. The corruption of the latter are also well known by now. Thus, after the bankruptcy of state socialism along with all the variants of the populist, liberal or welfare state, the authoritarian option now seems open. To govern with the force of the market and the state is the new name of apocalypse. It remains well hidden behind the mask of democratic promises made by the propagators of the "Global Project."

Taming the Leviathan

Since state power naturally tends towards arbitrariness and injustice, there is the perpetual need to curtail and limit it. Currently, many are looking for alternative forms of control.[6] Communities are appearing as the only viable option taking us beyond a century of blindness: limiting political imagination to the dichotomy of socialist or capitalist ideologies. This option appeals to those for whom the future will be, one way or the other, a communitarian fact; that is, a world of communities. The wary warn that socialism also carried a message of communitarianism, and reality translated it into collectivism, statism and self-destruction.

Many among the "social minorities" refuse to recognize the communitarian political option as either viable or desirable. They view it as a step back in history; or, at best, as an illusion that hides the practical reality of massive modern societies in which we all live (or believe we live). Even those accepting the value and potentialities of communal power do not believe that it can counteract the forces of transnational corporations and the modern nation-state. How do we resist the blind and abstract logic of modern power, which exists beyond the human scale and, therefore, beyond any possibility of communal control? That question particularly paralyzes those who embrace modern certainties regarding political power. Modern societies have abandoned the tradition which derived power from heaven, while continuing to retain its structure and imagery. The modern transition from the Pope or the monarch to a president or a prime minister eliminated religious or regal intermediation as a source of legitimacy. But it did nothing for the relocation of power in the hands of "the people." That is why modern peoples still continue depositing their power in someone who is supposedly still "up there." Since political parties have sequestrated democracy and political life is increasingly a "media event," modern democratic regimes have become mechanisms for concentrating power in the hands of elites dedicated to reproducing themselves and protecting their own interests.

At the same time, the emptiness of modern power paraphernalia is increasingly evident. Power is, after all is said and done, nothing more nor less than the power to do something. Power means nothing without that capacity for action. Yet, every day, the powerful have decreasing capacities to do what they desire or intend. Every president or prime minister soon learns how difficult it is to implement even his or her favorite policies and programs. (Hillary Clinton's health program is perhaps one of the best known cases in point today.) In the economic arena, corporate executives recognize the acute limits of their real powers to do what they want. While the "rich and the powerful" still possess economic, military or political force, power eludes them. They can no longer conduct others without direct coercion. In spite of their continual use of the media to conserve or increase the power they still have, "the people" are increasingly challenging them through abandoning the dominant sets of religious beliefs in theocratic regimes; or political beliefs in democratic regimes. Those grasping for political or economic power find themselves increasingly prisoners of the logic or set of principles that constitutes the "Global Project." Within contemporary democracies, even "the powerful" find themselves unable to exert their real powers in directions they define themselves.[7]

Reflecting upon these increasingly empty political structures, supposedly controlled by leaders democratically voted in, the story of the Wizard of Oz offers a parable for deconstructing the myth of modern power. After crossing all the paraphernalia hiding the Wizard, Dorothy's little community discovers a small, timid, trembling man, who wisely explains to them that they already possess the power they have come to him for: their courage, intelligence and compassion lies within them, waiting to be revealed. Analogously, buried beneath today's vast state paraphernalia lies the source of real political power not exercised by modern men and women. The post-modern challenge is for "the people" to grasp what they already possess; and, shaking off the oppressive minorities, to begin exercising their power for their own common good.

Radical grassroots movements are revealing that the "social majorities" are not nourishing the modern "democratic illusion" of surrendering their own power to a political party, a leader or a vote of the masses. "Radical democracy envisions the people gathered in the public space, with neither the great paternal Leviathan nor the great maternal society standing over them, but only the empty sky – the people making the power of Leviathan their own again, free to speak, to choose, to act..." They are not pre-democratic. For they have "lived under a government, [have] watched critically as this government became increasingly corrupted, and [are] now in the middle of revolutionary action" (Lummis, 1996, pp. 27, 30). People at the grassroots are learning and teaching, as did Václav Havel, how to avoid the myths of constructing another utopia in the distant future. Slowly discovering the power they already have, "the people" are begining to focus on things that can be done and practiced now, today. These entail profound transformations in marginalizing the state and society that has marginalized "the people."

Bringing Back Human Scale to Political Bodies

Radical democracy is based on the autonomy of rural and urban commons. But the truth is that "the people" are not organized to perform the functions of contemporary states: including general functions like keeping national unity, avoiding local fundamentalisms, feudal structures or fragmentation, as well as specialized functions like those of a Central Bank or foreign relations. The principle of representation seems unavoidable. Therefore, are we not back to point zero: needing to identify democratic forms for constituting, exerting and controlling political power at the center, no matter how "decentralized," "localized" or "communitarian" the society can become?

Before the "Global Project," the structures of the modern nation-state seemed, in fact, an unavoidable political horizon for those struggling against their marginalization and the profound injustices of modern societies. So they continued joining the ranks of revolutionary movements attempting to capture the state, to reform it according to different ideologies, or to impose over the Great Society a "popular regime." That was clearly the model of the "dictatorship of the proletariat." Rather than the promised transitional structure for the communist society that dissolves the state, however, this focus of people's efforts has continued to have the opposite effect: it has continually strengthened the centralist state in both "socialist" and capitalist countries.

We are living in times during which enough has been elaborated on that experience. With their own eyes, "the people" have now seen how

conquerors are always captivated; how they are absorbed by the Leviathan they wanted to tame; how they are put at the service of interests or
ideologies conceived to serve them. Today, only the "social minorities"
still fail to discern why people's power cannot be exerted at the scale
and in the conditions of modern societies. The "social majorities," in
contrast, do not need to be convinced that it is possible to operationalize
and implement modalities of the "state" or the "nation" that harmonize
the coexistence of their communities by reserving some clearly limited
general functions to political bodies "at the center" of society. This need
not impinge upon or reduce their capabilities for retaining their own
democratic styles practiced at the grassroots.

Spheres for the independent action of civil society within modern
nations are in fact – although not in principle – defined as the residual
of what the state has not reserved for itself. The "social majorities'"
struggles seek to reverse that process: attributing only those functions
to central political bodies that cannot be absorbed by the commons or
communities where the people exert their power. Furthermore, their
initiatives seek to shape centralized bodies on the models of those that
are localized; whereas the opposite has been the case in the construction
of the modern nation-state. The latter has imposed its vertical design
wherever it has extended its tentacles.

The European design of the nation-state, definitively western and
capitalist, has acquired universal hegemony, dissolving diverse traditions
for organizing the state (Nandy, 1992). In their process of liberation from
colonial strings, peoples attempting to follow culturally diverse paths of
postcolonial independence were forced to adopt their colonizers' designs,
rather than those rooted in their own traditions and cultures. Instead
of the modern western state, Gandhi's struggles for independence were
inspired by the indigenous ideals of *Hind Swaraj* or Home Rule (Gandhi,
1946). He lost to the perverse coalition of the British, Nehru and Jinnah,
constructing independent India and Pakistan as modern states, substituting Gandhi's dreams for what has been – as he anticipated – a chronic
nightmare.

To resist the continuation of such nightmares, today many traditions
of state organization are beginning to be challenged at the grassroots.
Furthermore, today's grassroots endeavours are finding new historical
opportunities in the era of the "Global Project." This is weakening the
main function of the nation-state: administering the national economy.
In fact, this has already been weakened dramatically by the increasing
role of transnational corporations and international arrangements in
determining and conditioning economic activities. To prevent economic
chaos in the processes of transition, the critical functions of the state are

being transferred to macro-national structures or to the global market. At the same time, the contemporary renaissance of local/regional movements taking shape, spanning a very wide ideological spectrum, is launching new initiatives for resisting the dominion of the centralist modern nation.

This two-pronged attack on the nation-state is perceived as a major threat by its functionaries. On the pretext of protecting "the people" from fundamentalism, fragmentation and violence, they seek to strengthen the basic design of the modern state, restoring the most perverse forms of nationalism. (Former Yugoslavia is a clear case in point.) But the same events are also stimulating radical political alternatives to the modern state. Several scholars are studying the steps by which modern nation-states are being dismantled and the processes by which they will rapidly vanish (Guéhenno, 1995). Others, convinced that the demise of the nation-state is still not in sight, have begun suggesting ideas and actions for their progressive dismantling. They recognize that the strength of the contemporary state is basically nourished by ordinary people's fears or feelings of incapacity, continually fostered by its lackeys (Nicolau, 1993).

In the course of its demise, some suggest that the nation-state will be transformed into a set of rituals similar to the ones found in England or Holland, where the monarchic form is kept in spite of the fact that its content, the constitution and orientation of political power in monarchic terms, has already disappeared. Among those able to smell "the breakdown of nations," scholars like Leopold Kohr (1986, 1992) have a new relevance. What seemed a utopian dream only a few decades ago now appears as a sensible and feasible solution for contemporary predicaments and crises. More and more people are tracing these to the inhuman size and proportionality which currently undercut possibilities for the authentic exercise of people's power.

At the margins of all those debates, the different initiatives of "the people" are challenging the nation-state in order to return the government of their lives into their own hands. When they hear the liberal or neoliberal propaganda about "less government," grassroots groups express the urgency for more government than ever before; a self-government that protects them from the machinations of a blind market or a corrupt state. In liberal claims today, they recognize the old myth of the self-regulating market-hiding mechanisms like the closed doors of "directors' boardrooms" (that continue to misgovern people's lives). To repossess the autonomy needed for governing the behaviors and events that shape their daily lives, "the people" are searching for political bodies that respect their freedom and dignity. Their grassroots initiatives for radical democracy are distinctly demarcated from the leftist propaganda of resurrected socialists, advocating the resurgence of the state, or of the social democrats, seeking to soften and decelerate the "Global Project."

The new paradigms of political styles that are being used to put state governments at the margins of people's lives differ markedly in urban settings from rural ones. Social movements and initiatives in distant villages look nothing like those being experimented with in the *barrios* or ghettoes of modern mega-cities. To understand these differences, in search of the real meaning and consequences of what they are doing, it is essential to go beyond "the discourse" of what "the people" officially and formally say they are doing. All too often, modern research methods prove to be counterproductive in this quest for meaning. After ten years of close association with many people's organizations in the *barrios* of Mexico City, for example, it seemed appropriate to have a shared reflection on what they have done; to understand how they saw their own epic, in contrast with how the media, the government and other observers viewed them. We started our investigations with the standard technical design for "participatory research." After taping hundreds of hours of interviews, it became evident that the whole exercise was futile. We were not alien observers or outsiders; some of us have participated in their struggles for decades. Every time we posed formal research questions, "the people" began aping the mainstream discourse of the left or of the government. In doing so, they invariably said the opposite of what they claimed to have done before. Often, we were forced to stop our research interview and say: "Wait. Come to the street. Let us see what you really have done. Let us remember exactly how the struggle has been and what you said at the time" (Esteva, 1991). We learned how conventional research procures its conventional results, completely distorting the real nature of people's initiatives and struggles for radical democracy.

It is not easy to explain why "common people" do not want to or cannot translate into formal discourses their actual practices. When asked to report their experiences and struggles in abstract terms, "the people" abandon their own modes of discourse and description. Perhaps people of the living word can neither describe nor orient their actions according to the intellectual logic of modern peoples; of the text or logos. They use reason as a veto in exercising critical awareness. Following their impulses, coming from their gut, from their experiences in the flesh, from their cultures and long traditions, they seem to feel no need to produce abstract accounts of what they are doing for some unknown abstract audience. Even less do they seem to sense this need before they start to react to their difficulties with their oppressors. It is a mistake, we are learning, to conclude from this that "the people" are unable to use analytical tools for discussing their predicaments. In spite of all the inherent difficulties in articulating the "implicit meaning" of such contemporary initiatives for radical democracy, it is becoming increasingly explicit that these are not to be found at the centers of conventional power: universities, research centers, public agencies, international institutions, political parties or the scientific community. They are coming from those directly affected and "worst hit": the marginalized who have suffered the most severe damages to nature and culture caused by modernity, state democracy and development. They are coming from "the people," the "social majorities," the *barrios* and the villages, social activists and "incarnated intellectuals." Understandably, functionaries or employees of the party or the government do not know how to deal with these new initiatives and social movements, now affecting the very foundations of today's structures of national and global domination.

People's experiences at the grassroots cannot be reduced to any single new political theory or a global political counter-proposal. The diverse cultural styles that we are directly observing in India or Mexico, or are learning about indirectly from the stories and experiences of peers and friends documented in the burgeoning rich literature on local/regional movements, go far beyond the horizon of modern democratic institutions. They can no longer be taken to be marginal oddities and aberrations, as exceptions that are doomed to disappear under the norms of the "Global Project" taking firmer root among the "underdeveloped" peoples and cultures. The new actors that constitute these movements know all too well the forms of aggression they suffer from the forces they are resisting and struggling against. Nor do they suffer the illusion of possessing the blueprint or solution for their predicaments. In humility, they recognize the extraordinary limitations they confront in their current ventures. Yet they do not fail to express the kind of hope that asks: What if...? What if, in the middle of the current or the following turbulence, the opportunity emerges for their initiatives to flourish and endure? What if the continual weakening of their modern oppressors and the fragility of the older modes of oppression open up radically new options which they are ready to take? What if...? In this vein of humility, hope and tentativeness, grassroots movements and initiatives are putting into practice what radical thinkers have been suggesting for some time. Foucault insisted twenty years ago, for example, that we need to dispense with all ideals or models of a design for the "whole of society" as preconditions for social and political action. Radical democrats have similarly argued that people's power best expresses itself through actions that strengthen democratic behavior rather than by succumbing to the placations of conventional institutions and apparatuses.

None of today's modern institutions, including the nation-state, were the product of a specific blueprint or intellectual design historically implemented by the people or the elites. They emerged as the outcome of a complex interplay of many different initiatives and social forces. In observing how those institutions are being challenged and resisted by "the people" at the grassroots, and in reflecting about the social arrangements that will be required if and when these challenges do succeed, we are learning to avoid speculations about the post-modern state – or the non-state – that may succeed the dominant design. Questions which defy ready answers are emerging about ways to define the "transition period" or about the shapes of new societies waiting to be born. How, for example, do people's political bodies create links of harmonious coordination between them? How do "the people" ensure that the principle of "command by obedience" is nourished at "the centers" of their new social organizations? With hindsight, we conclude that "the people" need not answer such questions as preconditions for their movements and struggles, liberating their own creative forces. Since these inevitably confront the state's domination through regimes of juridical and constitutional procedures, they are expressing their creativity by critically challenging contemporary conventional relations between "the people" and "the law."

Beyond the Empire of the Law and its Illusion of Equality

The modern nation-state, centralist even in its more federalist forms, is based on the progressive elimination of the customs of "the people." It makes it very difficult for communities to develop new social patterns in customary ways: using their traditions to change their traditions. For the new social relations are increasingly codified and the legislative organs of the state (including their economic and political pressure groups) seek monopoly over the production of social norms and laws. Social order is increasingly shaped as legal dispositions. State law becomes increasingly the only source of claims and obligations. Through processes for the legalization of right and the statization of law, the state increasingly seeks to suppress the spontaneous bonds people create, reflecting their particular cultures, their small territorial communities, or even their larger collectivities. State machineries and apparatuses are specifically designed to prevent citizen-subjects from weakening their fidelity to the nation's economic design.

Indigenous peoples' struggles in every continent currently involve resisting the "Empire of the Law" in order to strengthen the autonomous

reign of their customs. At the same time, they are increasingly recognizing the value of "juridical procedures" which peoples of different
cultures (or villages) can use to establish social arrangements that resolve
intra-communal conflicts. "The structures of political and legal procedures are integral to one another. Both shape and express the structure
of freedom in history. If this is recognized, the framework of due pro-
cedure can be used as the most dramatic, symbolic and convivial tool in
the political area" (Illich, 1973, p. 109). At the same time, "any revolution which neglects the use of formal legal and political procedures will
fail" (Illich, 1973, p. 99). "The people" are learning to transcend the
adversarial nature of the common law, discovering convivial procedures
for recovering their own ways for dealing with conflicts; particularly for
keeping economic behaviors within commonly agreed limits, essential
for controlling the hands of the Leviathan.

These reflections offer a pertinent frame of reference for the rich
variety of initiatives being taken by many people in different parts of
the world to challenge the "Empire of the Law." Some of these initiatives call for new laws that limit state actions or attributions, creating
"legal umbrellas" for people's programs for autonomy. On August 30,
1995, for example, following a long struggle, the Indians of Oaxaca
(Mexico) succeeded in getting the enactment of a new disposition of
the law for respecting and recognizing the autonomy of "the people"
in designating their local authorities in their own ways. It is forcing the
electoral authorities to accept the legitimacy of their customs and traditions, especially where these are in open contradiction with the legal
procedures established for all Mexicans regarding the election of public
officials. Instead of continuing to be subject to the general procedures
of state law, or of codifying into it differentiated procedures for the
Indians, the new law limits state interventions. The Oaxacan Indians'
success has helped generate legitimacy for their autonomous political
spaces, governed by their own laws and modes of adjudication.

Like "the people" who constitute the "social majorities" elsewhere,
half of the inhabitants of Mexico City live practically without lawyers
or courts. Compared to the judiciary inflation of the "social minorities"
(directly paralleling monetary inflation), "the poor" reveal their success
in escaping the sorry plight of the privileged. Free of dependency on
western institutions designed for the equality of abstract individuals,
they find themselves less within state clutches: designed by and for
centralized and authoritarian bureaucracies of politicians, private businessmen, lawyers and judges. This freedom does not mean that "the
people" are flourishing. Far from it. Their limited successes in protecting their communities and *barrios* from the invasiveness of lawyers and

the law continually face wear and tear in the hostile environment of dominant policies and programs. To alter this hostile environment, they are reformulating it rather than seeking to conquer it by constituting themselves as yet another political party platform. Just as the ecological toilet makes the sewerage system unnecessary, and popular vigilance makes the police officer on the corner unnecessary, the daily actions of increasingly autonomous communities continue eliminating a variety of government functions. Modes of radical deregulation (not to be confused with the kinds proposed by Reagan) are beginning to take priority in their political agendas. Such deregulations are dismantling a number of state mechanisms of coercion or service. They are counteracting the modern inflation of litigation, legal services and courts of the judiciary. These deflations will contribute to the autonomy of their spaces only if they succeed in legally formulating "umbrellas" to protect themselves from the general law of the state, designed to benefit aggressive internal groups of "social minorities." Such challenges to juridical procedures do not seek to cancel the law, but to modify its scope, scale and meaning. Instead of accepting it as a mechanism which deprives people of their own power by depositing it in bureaucratic and professional structures, these challenges are limiting state juridical procedures, rendering them either unnecessary or molded to adopt the shape of people's power.

Grassroots initiatives to conceive and implement a regime based on juridical pluralism are unlikely to gain easy success in the modern state. It is inhospitable to those who challenge its principles declaring the unity and universality of the law. The modern state is constructed as the expression of one, and only one, body of law, supposedly applied under the principle of universality to everyone: all the individuals of the social pact. This pact is based on the assumption that there exist individuals, homogeneous and equal. Constitutional procedures supposedly enact the social pact which rules these individuals' lives and interactions.

Such homogeneity and equality are illusory. Real men and women are radically heterogeneous and different. The abstract category of citizen is a historical compromise, reducing real people to a marginal and unimportant dimension of their being: a bureaucratic and statistical condition (of citizenship or electoral majorities), adopted as the source of rights (the original right to enact the social pact or modify it, and all the rights that the law establishes for all the citizens). Such rights, made law, imply claims or entitlements to goods and services provided by the state. And this law, as we said before, is always the creation of a minimal minority who formally represent all citizens. They need to be represented, given the practical impossibility that all citizens – the whole constituted of homogeneous and equal individuals – come together to conceive, formulate and enact the law. Furthermore, the principle of representation, in turn, implies that the masses of homogeneous and equal individuals have no bonds or connections between them other than to get their unity through representatives identified by electoral majorities. These are but fictitious aggregates of individuals supposedly "educated" with the myth that they can express their rational interests, giving them political form through a vote.[8]

Based on such illusions and myths, state systems continue to be, not surprisingly, the source of the corruption and bad government found in all societies today. The assumption of equality continues to be the source of inequality and unjust privileges. Real men and women, who are radically different and deserve to be treated according to their differential beings and conditions, are instead treated as if they were equals, with the usual implications of great injustice. In time, the elimination of such differences, of the radical heterogeneity of Being, expressing the singularity and uniqueness of every man and woman, becomes an ideal, a social goal, to be accommodated to the homogeneity adopted as a premise and assumption. Such homogeneity does not derive from any need or aspiration of "the people" themselves, but from a very well-specified organization: the industrial mode of production, which needs to create and operate masses of homogeneous consumers. It does not allow "the people" to shape either their desires or satisfactions. Instead, these are manufactured to mutilate, mold and reshape "the people" to the needs of economic accumulation.

Breaking or escaping the prison of such illusions and myths, seeking to regenerate their social fabric, popular movements and their initiatives spring from the recognition of their fundamental differences from others, including those that differentiate and define every man and woman. People are different and want to continue being different as they strengthen their struggles against the profound inequalities suffered within contemporary "democratic" regimes. For harmonious coexistence with others, they claim recognition and respect for their communities and cultures; embracing diversity and equality in their interactions, while rejecting hypotheses about the superiority of any culture over others. Wanting to govern themselves, they seek to exert their own powers in coping with their personal and collective predicaments. Rather than transferring their power to corruptible state representatives, they want to reorganize themselves in political bodies functioning at a human scale; where people can put their trust in those whom they know personally; those capable of commanding and leading through obedience to people's will. Limited functions not absorbed by local political bodies can then be entrusted to larger umbrellas, webs, and other institutions which respect the principles applied at the grassroots. In some cases, their designs call for an assembly when they are together, and a web when they are apart. In such an assembly, entrusted by their groups and communities, men and women take decisions which require the full consultation of the peoples of their commons before any and all final enforcements. Among such decisions or agreements are the juridical procedures which, at a larger scale, express the will of "the people." There is nothing to stop these from evolving into constitutional procedures which follow naturally from this political style: non-pyramidal and well rooted in the communal and cultural soils of local groups. Some indigenous social and political movements now seem to be accumulating the strength to generate constitutional processes that do not ape the procedures used to establish the modern state. Non-modern concepts – indigenous to cultures of East and West, North and South – are being nourished by grassroots movements of "the people."

One Postmodern Story: The Zapatista Struggle for Autonomy and Dignity

> We have always lived here: we have the right to go on living where we are happy and where we want to die. Only here can we feel whole; nowhere else would we ever feel complete and our pain would be eternal. (*Popol Vuh*)

It is time once again to give these political reflections the flesh and blood which inspired them; to fully locate theory in the grassroots praxis from which it springs and receives its vitality. Full circle, at the end of our book, we return to the story of the Zapatistas, exemplifying the political styles and cultural alternatives that we seek to describe in this book. The Zapatista tale tells of only one among the innumerable initiatives of "the people" across the world; struggling today for the autonomy of their cultures and commons, their political and moral spaces.

No two stories of struggle can be mechanically reduced to the same formula, except by officers or representatives of the state; invariably classifying these as "national threats" or proofs that "the people" – poor, illiterate and underdeveloped – need to be educated and developed for their own good. For "the people" making their stories, each tale is unique, with its distinctive regional flavor; like the clime, clothes and comida of its own little niche, irreducible to any other on our vast earth. Far flung and remote though the location and context of their struggles, "the people" at the grassroots are learning important lessons from each other. Resisting the national melting pot or the designs of bureaucrats, professional experts, multinational corporations of the "Global Project," they are also learning much from the globalists. Selectively using the tools of the latter (particularly their use of media and communications networks), they are publicizing their shared oppression; their struggles to overcome the powerlessness they have suffered in their silence and their spatial separatedness or isolation. With these tools, they are creating post-modern bridges of solidarity between "the people" living at different ends of the vast, abundant and generous earth. By sharing their oft-repeated, common stories of oppression and suffering, they are revealing to each other that they are not cultural oddities; that they are not abnormal nor unnatural in their quest to escape the machinery of modern states, marching in military unison to the noisy, loud and abrasive "Global Project" grand band.

The International of Hope: Local Thinking Revisited

On July 27, 1996, from more than forty countries spanning five continents, several thousand people arrived in Oventic, a tiny village in the middle of Chiapas' rainforest called Selva Lacandona. Here, in their own cultural space, the Zapatistas hosted the inauguration ceremony of the Intercontinental Encounter for Humanity and Against Neoliberalism, convened by them. After leaving their hammocks and sleeping bags in their huts – large and very simply constructed – the people congregated in Aguascalientes II:[9] a big, open plaza, surrounded by rows of covered seats, fashioned like the amphitheaters where the ancient Mayan communities held their ceremonies. As in pre-Hispanic times, this Mayan amphitheater was surrounded by a vast jungle. In the middle of "nowhere," hunted and hounded for months by the state, the Zapatistas and the villagers of Oventic, with their bare human hands, created a vast auditorium – humble and magnificent – to host and celebrate the thousands coming from the earth's four corners to be gathered together. Strangers faced each other for the first time. At times hidden by the clouds that floated in and out of trees stretching beyond, mile after mile after mile, they sensed that they were part of a "historical event" with no clear precedents; with the density, depth and shape associated with turning points – with palpable far-reaching changes in movements that, starting small, can yet sweep over vast spaces of the world.

   Who knows how this day will unfold into the unforseeable future? Will it be analogous to the day when the Luddites first smashed the machines of the Industrial Revolution – gestures as futile as those that seek to roll back the ocean tides? Or, alternatively, will this day mark one of several first small steps taken towards the demise of global neoliberalism, bringing the monstrous "Global Project" down to earth, to be buried next to its dead Soviet twin? Unable to foresee the events that will follow this moment in the future yet to be born, one by one the guests were seated in the three thousand chairs installed in the open plaza, full of light and music. As the last person sat down, light and music vanished. The deep darkness and silence of the forest took over. Above stretched the vast open sky, barely illuminated by a pale moon. In the far distance could be heard the soft sound of approaching music, coming closer and closer with the long winding file of forest people, holding torches of fire. Slowly, they filled the center of Aguascalientes. They occupied it. At "the center," sat "the people" whose collective decision led to the war declared by the Zapatistas on the Government of Mexico three years previously. As the center, they are the *bases de apoyo*, who daily nourish and support the armed Zapatistas, women and men struggling for freedom and dignity in their commons.

After the people at the center sat down, the lights returned. Standing in the midst of floating clouds, Comandante David welcomed those who had travelled long distances from home to come to this strange and distant place. With the magic of the rainforest, suddenly the clouds lifted and disappeared. In the clear night, Mayor Ana María rose and broke the silence of the plaza. For thoughts and feelings that they usually only express in their Tzotzil, Chol, Tzeltal or Tojolabal – the languages of the Zapatistas – Mayor Ana María discovered words in Spanish. Unfamiliar and unusual even to those who speak it, Ana María's strange Spanish words made transparent the hopes with which her people convened the Encounter.

> Welcome to the mountains of the Mexican southeast…. We want to introduce ourselves. We are the *Ejército Zapatista de Liberación Nacional*. For ten years we have been living in the mountains, preparing ourselves for war. Inside those mountains we built an army…. Down there, in the cities and the haciendas, we did not exist. Our lives had less value than their machines or animals. We were like stones, like weeds growing by the side of the road. We had no word. We had no face. We had no name. We had no tomorrow. We did not exist. For the Power, that Power now clothing itself all across the world with the name of "neoliberalism," we did not count, we did not produce, we did not buy, we did not sell. We were a useless number in the accounts of big capital.
> Then we went to the mountains searching for the good and to see if we could find alleviation for our pain, of being forgotten stones and plants. Here, in the mountains of the Mexican southeast, our dead live. Our dead, who live in the mountains, know many things. Their dead spoke to us and we listened…. Little boxes that speak told us another story that comes from yesterday and points towards tomorrow. The mountains spoke to us; the *macehualob* – those who are ordinary and common people. Those who are the simple people, so the powerful say…. All the days and the harrowed nights, the powerful want

to dance the *X'tol* over us and to repeat its brutal conquest. The *Kaz'dzul*, the false man, governs our lands and has big machines of war that, like the *boob*, who is half-puma and half-horse, deliver pain and death among us. The false that is the government send us the *aluxob* – the liars who cheat and donate forgetfulness to our people. That is why we became soldiers. That is why we continue being soldiers. Because we do not want more death and cheating for our people; because we do not want forgetfulness.

The mountain spoke to us to take up arms in order to have a voice. It spoke to us to cover our face to have a face. It spoke to us to forget our name to be named. It spoke to us of keeping our past to have a tomorrow.... In the mountain the dead live, our dead. With them live the *Votán* and the *Ik'al*, lightness and darkness, wetness and dryness, the earth and the wind, the rain and the fire. The mountain is the house of the *Halac Uinic*, the true man, the high chief. There we learned and we remembered that we are what we are, true men and women.... Once with the voice as an arm in our hands, with the face born again, with the name renamed, our yesterday added the center to the four points of *Chan Santa Cruz in Balam Ná* and so was born the star that defines the man, and that remembers that five are the parts that make the world.

In the time in which the Chaacab rode delivering the rain, we came down again to speak with our people and to prepare the storm that will announce the time of the sowing.... We birthed the war with the white year and we started to walk this road that brought us to your heart and today brought you to our heart.... That is what we are.... The *Ejército Zapatista de Liberación Nacional*.... The voice that took up arms to make itself heard [*para hacerse oir*].... The face that hides itself to show itself ... The name that you do not utter aloud [*que se calla*] to be named.... The red star that calls the man and the world for them to listen, for them to see, for them to name.... The tomorrow that is harvested in the yesterday.

Behind our black face, behind our armed voice, behind our unnamable name [*innombrable*], behind the we that you see, behind we are you [*estamos ustedes*] ... Behind we are [*estamos*] the same simple and ordinary men and women that repeat themselves in all races, that paint themselves in all the colors, that speak themselves in all the languages and live themselves in all the places.... The same forgotten men and women.... The same excluded.... The same intolerated.... The same persecuted ... We and you are the same [*Somos los mismos ustedes*]. Behind us, we are you [*estamos ustedes*].... Behind our ski-masks there is the face of all the excluded women, of all the forgotten Indians, of all the persecuted homosexuals, of all the disregarded young, of all the beaten migrants, of all those imprisoned for their words and thoughts, of all the humiliated workers, of all those dead by forgetfulness, of all the simple and ordinary men and women who do not count, who are not seen, who are not named, who have no tomorrow.

Brothers and sisters: We have invited you to this Encounter to come to search and to encounter and be encountered [*encontrarse y encontrarnos*].... All of you have come to our heart and you must see that we are not special. You must see that we are simple and ordinary men and women.... You must see that we are the rebel mirror that wants to be a crystal and break itself.... You must see that we are what we are to cease to be what we are and to be the you that we are.... We are the Zapatistas. We have invited you for all of us to listen and to speak ourselves. For us to see the all that we are.

Brothers and sisters: In the mountain the little boxes that speak spoke to us told us ancient stories that made us remember our pains and our rebellions.... Our dreams will not end where we live ourselves; our flag will not surrender; our dead will always live.... So the mountains speak to us.... So the star that lights in *Chan Santa Cruz speaks*.... So it says that the *cruzob*, the rebels, will not be defeated and will continue on the path with all the others that are the human star.... So it says to us that the red men will always come; that the *Chachac-mac*, the red star, will help the world to be free.... So speaks the star that is mountain, that the people who are five peoples, that the people who are a star of all the peoples, that the peoples who are human and are all the peoples of the world, will come to help in their struggle for worlds to make themselves people. For true man and woman to live without pain and for the stones to soften.... All of you are the *Chachac-mac*, those who are people who come to help the human who is made of five parts in all the world, in all the peoples, in all the persons [*in todas las gentes*].... All of you are the red star mirrored in us.... We will continue on the good road if the you that we are walk ourselves together.

Brothers and sisters: In our peoples, the most ancient *sabedores* (those who know) have installed a cross that is the star in which the water-giving life births itself. So is marked the beginning of life in the mountain, with a star. So the streams that come down from the mountain and that bring the voice of the speaking star, of our *Chan Santa Cruz*, birth themselves. The voice of the mountain has already spoken, saying that the true men and women will live free when they make themselves the all promised by the five-pointed star, when the five peoples become one in the star, when the five parts of man that is the world encounter themselves and encounter the other, when the all that are five encounter their place and the place of the other.... Today, thousands of different ways that come from the five continents encounter themselves here, in the mountains of the Mexican southeast, to join their steps.... Today, thousands of words of the five continents keep silence here, in the mountains of the Mexican southeast, to listen one to the other and to hear themselves [*para oirse ellas mismas*].... Today, thousands of struggles of the five continents struggle themselves here, in the mountains of the Mexican southeast, for life and against death.... Today, thousands of colors of the five continents paint themselves here, in the mountains of the Mexican southeast, to announce a tomorrow of inclusion and tolerance.... Today, thousands of hearts of the five continents live themselves here, in the mountains of the Mexican southeast, for humanity and against neoliberalism.... Today, thousands of human beings of the five continents scream their *Ya Basta* here, in the mountains of the Mexican southeast. They scream *Ya Basta* to conformism, to doing nothing, to cynicism, to selfishness transformed into the modern god.... Today, thousands of little worlds of the five continents essay a beginning here, in the mountains of the Mexican southeast. The beginning of the construction of a new and good world, that is, a world where all the worlds fit [*quepan*].... Today, thousands of men and women of the five continents start here, in the mountains of the Mexican southeast, the First Intercontinental Encounter for Humanity and Against Neoliberalism.

Brothers and sisters of all the world: Welcome to the mountains of the Mexican southeast … to this corner of the world where we are equal because we are different…. Welcome to the search of life and the struggle against death.

Once she stopped, "the people" responded to Ana María's words with the long thunderous clapping that did not overcome their "emotional shock." While only the ski-masked people and their *bases de apoyo*, sitting in the center of the amphitheater, had actually undergone the anguish of namelessness, voicelessness and facelessness in Ana María's song, all those present recognized it in their hearts; from the experiences of their own places, however dispersed these were across the globe. Those local experiences and understanding create the solidarity that brought people to this International Encounter Against Neoliberalism.

The Zapatistas cannot be more local: firmly rooted in their own communities and traditions, they do not pretend to represent others, beyond the four municipalities in Chiapas where they live; not even the Indian peoples of Mexico, whose claims and interests they have assumed and continue to give voice to as their own; or all the groups and organizations that have explicitly claimed solidarity and association with them. Ana María's words revealed how alive and present for them are the voices coming from their past, how localized they are in their endeavor. Yet the media's treatment of the event seemed to offer an alternative interpretation, as if their international success was turning them global. Some journalists and participants are asking themselves if *Zapatism* or *Neozapatism* has not become a new global chic, ideology or organization. Was the intercontinental or "galactic" Encounter an example of the alternative global thinking and action criticized in Chapter 2?

The Intercontinental Encounter offers, in fact, a good illustration of the new political styles being created at the grassroots. These prevent isolation, fundamentalism or parochialism in local thinking and action. Several social movements struggling around the world against the "Global Project" had representation at the Encounter: feminists, gays and lesbians, blacks, workers, peasants, the unemployed, national liberation movements, leftist political parties or organizations, and former *guerrilleros*. People coming from different social and political struggles of the last fifty years from all over the world, while speaking on their own behalf, also presented the predicaments of those who could not be present.[10] But they did not attempt to think the globe, or even less to manage it. They did not abandon their own cultural roots and backgrounds. They prevented each other from falling into the trap of nice-sounding abstractions or plastic words – aping their counterparts in the "Global Project."

The international web of solidarity, taking new shapes and forms in La Realidad, is clearly heir to myriads of movements and traditions. "Some of the best rebels of the five continents arrived in the mountains of the Mexican southeast," subcomandante Marcos observed in the closing ceremony. "They brought many things. They brought words and ears. They brought their ideas, their hearts, their worlds. They came to La Realidad to encounter themselves with other ideas, with other reasons, with other worlds." One of the lessons they reminded each other of was the importance of avoiding any centralized structure or common ideology. None of the "key" words they used – humanity, neoliberalism, democracy, freedom, justice – were defined with precision. They recognized that the common "No's" against global forces and their logic and ideology incarnate differently in diverse places and circumstances; express differentiated "Yes'es"; defining incommensurable conceptions and hopes. This implies that their webs of solidarity should reflect the pluralism of their reality, renouncing the standardization of one religious, scientific or ideological credo. The Encounter became one context for sharing beliefs, ideas, experiences and understandings of what the neoliberal "Global Project" is: how it was born, what its logic is, etc. But it resisted being an academic workshop to bring about definitions or unified conclusions about specified issues; or a political convention to produce the platform, the political line.

The "structure" of the web of initiatives emerging out of La Realidad implies a conception of political organization which can be illustrated with reflections on the current challenge of the Indian peoples of Mexico. For the first time in history, they are currently trying to coordinate their initiatives, their resistance and their struggle. To do so, the Indian peoples of Mexico confront even more serious challenges and obstacles for their interaction than the participants of the Encounter. They speak more than fifty languages, they live in dispersed communities all around a big country and most of them have no access to phone, fax, e-mail or other modern means of communication. There is the continual pressure of some "visionaries" to create a national coordinating body for facilitating contacts and interactions between all of them. The Indians have resisted such proposals, given their long experience with political organizations that bureaucratize and corrupt themselves by achieving a vertical structure. To avoid this corruption, they have taken the decision to be an assembly when they are together and a web when they are separate. When there is an encounter of representatives trusted by the communities, they make decisions which must always be consulted upon with the communities before enforcement. When they are separate, they use the knots of their webs: small groups with access to modern means of communication, distributing any information coming to them among a specified number of other groups or communities through all possible and impossible means: word of mouth, a mule, a pamphlet, community assemblies ... This approach, well known by many people at the grass-roots, has been pretty effective among the Indian peoples of Mexico – in spite of increasing military pressures and controls.

The "International of Hope" is now using this approach. The Encounter resisted the dissolution of differences into any universal ideology or global organization. However, recognizing the global nature of the forces each is confronting in their own local settings, articulating their shared need to break the isolation and division promoted by the dominant power structures, they wove webs of solidarity which respect the full autonomy of each local group represented. They do not need to cease being themselves. Nor do they become atoms, conducted and manipulated by an enlightened leader, a bureaucratic structure, an ideology, a slogan. Instead, they respect and cherish differentiation in their webs. The "One World" of the "Global Project" lacks respect for this differentiation.

The Historical Subject: People Who Have Suffered Enough

> "Do you consider yourself a hero of modern times?" asked a journalist of the now famous subcomandante Marcos, the speaker of the Zapatistas; a faceless person behind a ski-mask; one among billions joined together by the solidarity of today's suffering "social majorities."
>
> "I am a man of the people," he answered, "who struggles so that these terrible inequalities will no longer be suffered in our country. I am a combatant." (Autonomedia, 1994, p. 72)

Who is this man? Learned in more than book knowledge, this person understands in the flesh what it means for "the people" to suffer in today's modern democratic states. He gives different answers to those curious about the identities of the persons who dare to speak truthful words behind the anonymity of their ski-masks. Who is Marcos? What kinds of leaders lead behind ski-masks?

> Marcos is gay in San Francisco, a black person in South Africa, Asian in Europe, a chicano in San Isidro, an anarchist in Spain, a Palestinian in Israel, an indigenous person in the streets of San Cristóbal, a gang member in Neza, a rocker on a (university) campus, a Jew in Germany, an ombudsman in the Department of Defense, a feminist in a political party, a communist in the post-Cold war period, a pacifist in Bosnia, a Mapuche in the Andes, a teacher in the union, an artist without a gallery or a portfolio, a housewife in any neighbourhood in any city in any part of Mexico on a Saturday night, a guerrilla in Mexico at the end of the twentieth century, a sexist in a feminist movement, a woman alone in a Metro station at 10 p. m., a *campesino* without land, a non-conformist student, a writer without books or readers, and a Zapatista in the Mexican

Southeast. In other words, Marcos is a human being in this world. Marcos is every untolerated, oppressed, exploited minority that is beginning to speak and every majority that must shut up and listen. He is every untolerated group searching for a way to speak, their way to speak. Everything that makes power and the good consciences of those in power uncomfortable – this is Marcos. (Autonomedia, 1994, pp. 312–13)

What kind of "we" constitutes his "I"? "This pain united us and made us talk," he wrote in 1994.

We recognized that in our words there was truth. We knew that it was not just pain and suffering inhabiting our tongues. We knew that there was still hope in our breasts. We talked with each other. We looked within ourselves and we looked at our history. We saw our elder parents suffer and struggle. We saw our grandparents struggle. We saw our grandparents with fury in their hands. We saw that every thing had not been taken away from us; that we had something more valiant which made us live; ... which made the rock be under our feet. We, brothers and sisters, saw our DIGNITY. That was all we had. And, we saw that it was a great shame to have forgotten this. We saw that DIGNITY was good for men to be once again men. And dignity returned to inhabit our hearts. The dead, our dead, saw that we were still new. They called us again – to dignity and to struggle. (Autonomedia, 1994, p. 122)

Their post-modern "we" is not constituted by abstract categories: passengers, consumers, owners, members of a club, a church, a party. These "we's" are but the stuff with which elites build and operate "organizations." A collection of billiard balls cannot stand up by itself; it needs an external force to keep it within a specific structure. The thousand faces of Marcos, in contrast, constitute a "we" of peoples whose survival depends upon their solidarity. Learning and fighting to stay with their "we's," the post-modern "social majorities" are still surviving the doom the social engineers of modernity have designed for them. There is no hint of necrophilia in their "we's." They hold joyful celebrations even in the middle of jungles and urban ghettoes. Their "we" knows how to regenerate their traditional arts of living, enabling them to escape from the despair of suburbia.

Uniting all those who suffer the fundamentalisms of the "Global Project" and the state, the EZLN explicitly rejects any and every variety of fundamentalism. They resist the machinations of the state to separate them as an isolated ethnic movement. Their members come from the different Indian peoples of Mexico, professing different religions while explicitly manifesting ecumenism. They are not tempted by the standard political ambition for power: of becoming a small state, a kind of Indian republic, or even an "autonomous" administrative district, following the models sought by some minorities in the states of Europe, Africa or Asia. Although their members are mainly Indians, they do not identify themselves as an Indian movement. with the limited goals of a specific people. They know that the causes of their predicaments are not limited to their place in Chiapas' jungles; that getting "everything" for themselves means nothing as long as the sources of the suffering of "the people" – now in the form of the "Global Project" – remain in full operation. What about their ski-masks? Why do they still wear them? First, for reasons of security: their masks offer them some personal protection against selective repression by the police, the military or paramilitary groups. They also protect the communities which originally designated them to be combatants in the Army, and to which they regularly return for their daily life after each military mission. However, apart from concerns for personal and communal security, they have other reasons as well. The anonymity of the mask, they hope, will prevent the emergence of a personality cult: the glorification of specific leaders – their names, faces, biographies of heroic behaviors. Yet, this seems a false pretext for many, given that the media have made well "known" comandantes David, Tacho, Trini, Zebedeo, Hortensia and many others, and particularly subcomandante Marcos, recognizable "leaders" despite their masks. The more fundamental and symbolic reasons for their masks were identified by Mayor Ana María in her inaugural message for the Encounter. For their own people, the Zapatistas have no ski-mask: they are not heroes or leaders, but men and women who command by obeying; receiving instructions from their communities, after submitting for their discussion all proposals discussed with the state. After explicitly renouncing any ambition for power, these women and men are chosen by their communities to perform specific duties. Nothing more. For the others – the public and the media – keeping the ski-mask allows them to underline the invisibility of marginalized, discriminated groups all over the world. Their masks serve to remind their audiences of the real conditions of the unknown sufferers of the world: the faceless ones – everybody, everyone and nobody. Time and again, talking to them face-to-"face," we have been challenged to read their reactions; to see ourselves in their "face," to face it as one does a mirror. Paradoxically, their ski-masks render them more transparent than the famous personalities whose faces appear regularly in magazines, newspapers and on television.

When the Word Became Verb

The dominant view at the end of 1993 was that no power could stop Mexico in its accelerated incorporation into the global economy. It was a mortal swell, overtaking entire cultures, leaving their natural spaces or "environments" devasted with dramatic violence.

Words stopped that global march into Mexico; words piercing, without violence, the mantle designed to cover up the deceit of modern democratic elections and rule. Time will tell whether the halt called by the words of the Zapatistas has any long-term impact. In the short term, the international economic community lost confidence in a country that still harbors guerrilla peasants. Overnight, the peso fell to half the value it had in the hour that Mexico triumphantly joined NAFTA; overnight, half of the "foreign investment" former President Salinas had attracted into the country flew away. The Zapatista uprising never posed a military threat to Mexico's national security. The guerrilla warfare into which the government has been seeking to doom them will continue to cause severe sufferings for the peasants. While guerrilla warfare is unlikely to modify the course of Mexican society, the words of the Zapatistas are bringing down the pyramid of democratic oppression, brick by brick. The Zapatistas and their speaker, subcomandante Marcos, make a masterly use of words. With words so powerful and effective, they could have built a political party platform. Yet, resisting that co-optation by the state, they give voice to the unheard; to the millions rendered impotent; to articulate the feelings of those oppressed into silence.

A few days after the uprising started, attempting to take control of the situation, President Salinas sought the surrender of the Zapatistas. The government used all kinds of political pressures, including an amnesty law. Worded to promote the image of the government's generosity and humanity, it craftily sought to cast a veil over its brutalities against peasant civilians, its ruthless violations of "human rights" during the first ten days of the uprising. The words of the Zapatistas, however, pierced through the state's deceit, unveiling the motives of the pardon. Revealing the innocence of the subjects supposedly being pardoned, Marcos sent a communiqué that has travelled around the world:

> Up to today, January 18, 1994, the only thing we have learned is that the "pardon" which the government offers to our forces has been made official. What do we have to ask forgiveness for? What are they to "pardon" us for? For not dying of hunger? For not accepting our misery in silence? For not humbly accepting the huge historical burden of disdain and abandonment? For having risen up in arms when we found all other paths closed? For not heeding Chiapas's penal code, the most absurd and repressive in history? For having shown the country and the whole world that human dignity still exists and lives in the hearts of the most impoverished inhabitants? For having made careful preparations before beginning our fight? For having brought guns to battle instead of bows and arrows? For having learned to fight before having done it? For being Mexicans, every one of us? For being mostly indigenous? For calling the Mexican people to struggle, through whatever means, for what rightfully belongs to them? For fighting for freedom, democracy and justice?

For not following the leaders of previous wars? For refusing to surrender? For refusing to sell ourselves? For not betraying one another?

Who should ask for forgiveness and who can grant it? Those who, for years and years, sat before a full table and satiated themselves while we sat with death, as such a daily factor in our lives that we stopped even fearing it? Those who filled our pockets and souls with declarations and promises? The Dead, our Dead, who mortally died a "natural" death, that is, of measles, whooping cough, dengue, cholera, typhoid, mononucleosis, tetanus, bronchitis, malaria, and other gastrointestinal and pulmonary diseases? Our dead, who died so undemocratically of grief because nobody did anything to help them, because all those dead, our Dead, would simply disappear without anyone paying the bill, without anyone finally saying "Enough!" Those who give feeling back to these dead, our Dead, refusing to ask them to die over again, but now, instead, asking them to live? Those who deny us the right to govern ourselves? Those who treat us as foreigners in our own land and ask us for papers and to obey a law whose existence we ignore? Those who torture, seize, and assassinate us for the great crime of wanting a piece of land; not a big piece; not a small one; just one enough to grow something with which to fill our stomach?

Who should ask forgiveness and who should grant it? The President of the Republic? the Secretaries of state? the senators? the deputies? the governors? the municipal presidents? the police? the Federal Army? powerful businessmen, bankers, industrialists and landowners? political parties? intellectuals? the media? students? teachers? our neighbors? workers? *campesinos*? indigenous people? Those who died a useless death? Who should ask forgiveness and who should grant it? (Autonomedia, 1994, p. 108)

The impact of this communiqué was immediate and general. It doomed the Amnesty Law to all the agonies of a slow and tortured death; to complete political failure. Those words suddenly eliminated the anesthetizing effects that the media, controlled by the dominant interests, like the government, have upon all levels of society. It immediately added the claims of Indian peoples to the national agenda, pressing, "legitimate" and long overdue. It brought sympathy from all those finding in these words a complete and poetic expression of their own suffering and anguish. It inspired the anesthetized to abandon their indifference, apathy and numbness, their own dehumanization.

In a communiqué, the Zapatistas revealed their full awareness of the power of their words, which, while not able to kill, are more lethal than bombs. It is words, not bullets, that have been "shot" in their thousands and that stopped the war waged by the government on the Zapatistas in January, 1994. It is these words, proclaiming the Zapatistas' truth (not, they acknowledge, a universal truth), of which the government is afraid.

The words of the Zapatistas deeply affected the regime that dominated Mexico until 1993. Their statements rang the death knell for a vast number of the "statements" governing Mexicans under the existing regime for six decades. The statements of the Zapatistas articulated with genius the unarticulated intuitions of millions of Mexicans. They revealed their well-rootedness in the traditions of the land. True, the Zapatistas continue to be very effective in dissolving existing statements, rather than in constructing new ones. The new statements by which Mexicans can govern themselves are yet to be formed and uttered. As a consequence, the people sense a vacuum of power. Existing structures are increasingly empty and will continue falling, as did the Berlin Wall, until new statements begin creating new institutions. The Zapatistas know their own limitations on this matter. And celebrate them. They do not pose as an enlightened vanguard, an elite, making decisions for everyone. Unlike all other guerrillas, they have made no bid to seize power. They have refused to accept the prevalent view that power is something that exists "up there." They have not been tempted to establish a new political party or to proliferate the preferred and privileged ideology of a new regime.

People and Power

"I am my people's leader. There go my people. I must follow." This statement of Gandhi's, like others, defines his experiments in a radical notion of leadership: of non-elitist leaders who live with "the people," permanently forsaking grandeur, in form as well as content.

The challenge of that leadership has been embraced by the Zapatistas. They live as humbly and simply as their people, suffering in solidarity their physical and economic hardships, as well as other difficulties. Struggling to transform the "civil society," they model what it means for the oppressed to exert their freedom and power; taking responsibility for altering the political structures which affect their lives every day. Daily, they find the courage to reveal that the Emperor is naked. Daily, their words open doors for "the people" to reaffirm their power, taking steps towards precipitating the fall of the dominant political ideologies. Like Gandhi, the Zapatistas do not place their principal focus on negotiating deals with the government or the prominent political parties. Instead, their primary attention is upon dialogues among "the people." While these dialogues shame the government into reducing its use of police force, more importantly still, they reveal to "the people" their own strength; forcing them out of their long silence; challenging the oppressed "social majorities" to seek democratic participation in the creation of new political spaces; of a "civil society" in which they exert themselves more fully. They continually reiterate the need to reinvent a new regime: juxtaposing conventional democratic power (constructed from the top down) with styles of power that rise from below, from the very bottom of society. This power involves commanding through obedience.

Is it really possible for "the people" to directly exercise power that is just, democratic and liberating? Can people's power take hold in a society that has not even succeeded in obtaining western-style "formal democracy"? In their search for answers, the dialogues initiated by the Zapatistas are steps daily taken for the construction of alternatives to the existing structures of the modern democratic state.

In the Freedom of Being Together

"Freedom" is another word for nothing left to lose, suggests a once-popular American song. Its assertions are painfully reiterated by Indian peoples in the mountains of the southeast in Chiapas. Three years ago, they wore the Zapatista ski-mask and picked up guns when they had nothing left to lose: face-to-face with their final extermination; to disappear in silence, without a murmur; rendered mute, hopeless or cowardly by the state's machinery.

The government, media and the "social minorities" of the state prefer their silence; their mute disappearance; so that they may easily forget the fate they impose on the "social majorities." For decades, the Mexican state ignored and dismissed the legal petitions made by the Indians of Chiapas for reclaiming their commons. After ten failed years of using every available legal channel, of knocking on all the official doors shut with indifference in their faces, of trekking the thousand miles to Mexico City that was the walk to nowhere – the Indian peoples of Chiapas found themselves at a dead end; literally at death's door, their own end. Their voices remained unheard by the government and the social "minorities"; their commons continued to be daily raided; their children and elders continued to drop dead like flies of curable diseases. Finally, faced with their own mute extinction, they chose freedom; the freedom to die a dignified death – not the silence of lambs headed for their slaughter.

As their last resort, they took up arms against the state. They became faceless, losing their faces behind the anonymity of ski-masks: "We were forced to lose our faces, in order to have a face," remembered Mayor Ana María on the first day of the International of Hope – the Intercontinental Encounter for Humanity and Against Neoliberalism. "We were forced to lose our names, in order to have a name; we were forced to lose our voices in order to have a voice."

That voice, finally heard, reached the far ends of the earth. It brought thousands – of different colors and creeds, religions and histories, problems and predicaments – to gather together at the Encounter held in the middle of the rainforest; to see what they could learn about their shared pain and how to overcome it from listening to each other's stories

of struggles for survival and dignity; to exercise the freedom that comes
through the solidarity of those who suffer.

After the inauguration of the Encounter in Oventic, the people
dispersed to the five Aguascalientes (see n. 9) for reflections on five
main themes. In Roberto Barrios, the focus was on economic issues; in
Oventic, on the civil society; in Morelia, on the cultures of the people;
in La Garrucha, on the diversity of having many worlds, Indian and
non-Indian; and in La Realidad, the political aspects of transforming
the state. At each of the five gatherings, there were presentations of
"papers"[11] offering different, even opposed, conclusions, while elaborate
procedures were discovered for reaching consensus. Six days later, at
the conclusion of the Encounter, everyone gathered in the village of La
Realidad. Here, their web of new social movements was announced;
of movements that are firmly local while being, at the same time and
without contradiction, international in expressing the shared hopes of
liberation across the world; of the people struggling to free themselves
from the menace of global neoliberalism.

> A world made of many worlds encountered itself in the mountains of the
> Mexican southeast.... A world made of many worlds opened itself a space and
> conquered the right to be possible, waved the flag of being necessary, rooted
> itself in the reality of the Earth to announce a better future. A world of all
> the worlds that rebel themselves and resist the Power, a world of all the worlds
> that inhabit this world opposing themselves to cynicism...
>
> But, what is next? ... A new number in the useless numbering of the
> numerous internationals? ... A new scheme which tranquillizes ... anguish
> ...? A world program for the world revolution? ... A theorization of the
> utopia for maintaining a prudent distance from the reality anguishing us? ...
> An organization chart giving us all a position, a cargo, a name and no work?

Such questions challenged the people to reflect upon those "spontaneous" organizations of "the people" – informal, dispersed, solidary –
needed to resist the "Global Project." In the absence of clear alternatives,
what must follow this Encounter? If not committees and organizational
charts, what comes next?

> The echo follows, the reflected image of the possible and forgotten; the possibility
> and need to speak and listen.... It is not the echo which slowly extinguishes
> itself or the force that diminishes after it reaches its highest point.... Yes, the
> echo that breaks and continues.... The echo of the propio pequeño [the small
> that belongs to you] of the local and particular, reverberating in the echo of the
> propio big [the big that belongs to you], the intercontinental and galactic....
> The echo which recognizes the existence of the other and does not put itself
> over the other or attempts to make the other mute.... The echo that takes
> its own place and speaks its own voice and speaks the voice of the other....
> The echo that reproduces its own sound and opens itself to the sound of the

other.... The echo of this rebel voice transforming itself and renovating itself in other voices.... One echo that becomes many voices, in a web of voices that, before the deafness of Power, opts for speaking to itself, knowing that it is one and many, knowing that it is equal in its aspiration to listen and make others listen to it, knowing that it is different in the tones and levels of the voices constituting it.

A web of voices that resist the war that the Power makes.... A web of voices that not only speak, but also struggle and resist for humanity and against neo-liberalism.... A web of voices that are born resisting, reproducing its resistance in other voices still mute or solitary.... A web that covers the five continents and helps to resist the dead that the Power promises.

It follows the reproduction of resistances, the "I am not a conformist," "I am a rebel." ... It follows the world with many worlds that the world needs.... It follows the humanity recognizing itself as plural, different, inclusive, tolerant with itself, with hope.... It follows the human and rebel voice consulted in the five continents to make itself a web of voices and resistances.

"The Indian communities," said Marcos after reading the Declaration, "have taught us that to solve a problem, no matter how big it is, it is always good to consult with the all that we are." The Encounter created a "collective web" of all the particular struggles and resistances that support each other. "This intercontinental web is not an organizational structure, it has no center to direct or take decisions, it has no central command or hierarchies. All of us that resist are the web." There will also be a web "for each word to walk all the ways that resist." The place for the consultations and conversations that make us into a "we" start at home, within the local spaces where people are able to speak face-to-face. Without these strong, local alliances, solidarities between groups are difficult to differentiate from the alliances that constitute global neoliberalism.

Beware of whom you consider your enemy, an arab elder once warned; for you are in danger of becoming like him. That threat was not ignored at the gathering:

> We are not the escape valve whose existence legitimizes the Power.... The Power is afraid of us. That is why it prosecutes and encircles us. That is why it puts us in jail and kills us.... In reality we are a possibility that can defeat it and make it disappear.... Perhaps we are not too many, but we are men and women who struggle for humanity, who struggle against neoliberalism.

LIKE THE SHADE OF A TREE

Post-modernists are reflecting on profound transformations in the structures of the modern state; archaic, these are left-overs of bygone days and events, like the Treaty of Westphalia. The new liberals advocate as much society as possible, and as little government as necessary. They include in "society" both competition and corporations, assuming that the global market, transnational corporations and strong local governments will be more efficient in performing many of the functions previously attributed to the centralist state. The new leftists, on their side, reason that there is still much to be said about the way in which they dismantled bureaucratic apparatuses which shaped the modern welfare state. They think that rigorous re-examinations of the privatization process will pave the way towards an innovative political agenda, in order to socialize, rather than privatize, activities and functions previously concentrated in the state.

Radical democracy, sought at the grassroots by "the people," affirming the power of their commons, is clearly at odds with the contemporary political agenda of the "social minorities." Their own traditions are opening the doors of radical democracy for indigenous communities. We end with one of their stories. It comes from the Indian peoples of the state of Oaxaca in Mexico. They constitute almost 70 percent of the state's population. In 1988, an Indian was nominated to be the governor of the province – the first time in a century. On the day on which he launched his political campaign, representatives of the sixteen Indian nations living in Oaxaca were present. For many hours, they spoke in their own languages, without interpreters. At the end of these extended conversations held in sixteen different tongues, an old man crossed the immense hall to tell the Indian candidate what "the people" wanted from the government.

We were prepared for the presentation of the usual list of claims for schools, roads, sewerage, hospitals, housing, jobs and the like. Instead, with dignity and simplicity, the elder announced:

We want you to be for us like the shade of a tree.

Not understanding it, we inquired about the meaning of their metaphor for the governance of "the people." They replied:

How can the new governor pretend to govern us, if he cannot even understand our languages, the supreme expression of our cultures? How can he talk for us if he can only speak Spanish, the language of the colonizers? We are not rejecting the idea of having a governor. We want a governor; and it is better for us to have an Indian. But we want the governor and his government to remain in a specific place. Like a tree. We don't want a government trying to govern us all the time, everywhere, even against our will.

We want a government which can offer us protection and support in case of calamity or conflict. When we want its support, we go to it ... for shade. It stays in its place; it does not meddle with our internal affairs.

Most of the time, we are able to take care of ourselves. Sometimes we need the help of others – like the government. And we want a government that is for us like the shade of a tree.

NOTES

1. The forms studied in democratic theory can be classified as follows:

(a) *The constitution of political power:* universality and effectivity of suffrage, widening the electoral base, preventing electoral frauds or manipulations, etc.

(b) *The structure and operation of political power:* the division of power, the independence of each power base in relation to the others, the existence and operation of countervailing powers, etc., as well as different options for the structure of political power: centralist or federalist, bi-partisan or multi-partisan, etc. The interaction between political power and economic or ideological power is also examined.

(c) *The control of political power:* the conditions to establish its limits, widen citizen participation or institute effective mechanisms of accountability.

2. Bishop cites the editorial "Freedom of No Choice," in *The Nation*, April 17, 1989, p. 505, which adds that "more than 98 percent of House members and 85 percent of Senators who ran for re-election in 1988 won − giving Americans a collection of politicians not widely known to be unconventional contenders."

3. *Comulgar:* to take communion. (Rel.) *Ruedas de molino:* millstone. The expression inplies the attempt to cheat someone with something too difficult to believe. To make someone *"comulgar con ruedas de molino"* implies to submit him/her to the humiliation of believing in something unbelievable. Following The Oxford Spanish Dictionary, "*A mí no me vas a hacer comulgar con ruedas de molino:* I'm not going to fall for that (colloq.)."

4. See M.J. Rossant, Director, The Twentieth Century Fund, "Foreword," in Cronin (1989).

5. See Norberto Bobbio, "Democracia," in Bobbio and Nicola Matteucci (1981), pp. 493 ff. See Shanin, 1982. Searching the past and present for manifestos celebrating "radical democracy," Douglas Lummis could only quote from Marx's chapter "On Democracy" in his *Critique of Hegel's Philosophy of Right.* For Lummis, "after he became a communist, Marx never returned to address the question of democracy at any length, at least in the same way." Maximilian Rubel argues that he only "sublimated it"; for in his communism "democracy was not only maintained, but acquired even greater significance." But the chapter in the "Critique," Lummis insists, "stands alone in his writings as a sustained discussion of democracy itself" (Lummis, 1996, p. 167). (Such a conclusion applies only to the *formal* discussion of democracy, as we examine below.)

It must be taken into consideration for this debate that in his writings about the Paris Commune Marx celebrated its political bodies, which were but the expression of people's power. He observed that the people used universal suffrage to constitute their communes, not a separate power, for "nothing could be more foreign to the spirit of the Commune than to supersede universal suffrage by hierarchic investiture.... The Communal Constitution would have restored to the social body all the forces hitherto absorbed by the state parasite feeding upon, and clogging the free movement of, society." (Marx and Lenin, 1968, pp. 58–9). Furthermore, in an introduction to an edition of writings commemorating twenty years of the Paris Commune, Engels wrote: "Do you want to know what the 'dictatorship of the proletariat' looks like? Look at the Paris Commune. That was the dictatorship of the proletariat!" (Marx and Lenin, 1968, p. 22). Lenin found inspiration in those reflections to establish a democracy based on workers' councils. Socialist theoreticians extensively discussed the issue in the 1920s. This conception of democracy as people's power, needed for both socialism and communism, seems coherent with the position of the Young Marx, which is far from alien to the Late Marx (Shanin, 1982): both assert that man is only man in community (which is not the simple addition of individuals); man is only man in the measure that he is intrinsically in community with others; and only that man, as such, should be in power.

However, the face of the dictatorship of the proletariat that the world knew was that of Stalinism, not of the Paris Commune. Furthermore, neither Marx nor Lenin presented a critique of the industrial mode of production and its organization of work, a critique that is a necessary condition for giving feasibility to radical democracy, to people's power.

6. In Russia, many people still place their hopes on capitalism and the market as the only way to limit the power of the state. They remain innocent of the workings of the reigning market regimes; while those learning fast about their consequences have started to exhibit nostalgia for the "good old times" of Stalinism.

7. Promoters of the "Global Project" are of course real men and women, in private or public corporations, who derive dignity and income from what they are doing. But they are trapped in their own game: they are masters of a mechanism that enslaves them; a logic that they can no longer control. Yet, these reflections do not eliminate their responsibility in the implementation of the "Global Project"; just as Nazi commanders were not liberated from their responsibility when they attempted to wash their hands of the horror in which they were active agents by arguing that they were just following orders. Political leaders, corporate managers, and the expertocracy "ruling" international institutions are increasingly following the Nazi example: legitimizing their participation by declaring that they cannot but follow the rules of a game they did not formulate. They obviously prefer to ignore the dignity of saying "No" to their global horrors; accomplices who prefer to mask the technological and economic "bluff."

8. Hobbes clearly revealed why political power based on the unity of men is transferred to the head of the state (the King or the President, the Prime Minister or the Parliament): "A multitude of men are made One Person, when they are by one man, or one Person, Represented; so that it can be done with the consent of every one of that Multitude in particular. For it is a Unity of the Represented, that maketh the Person One. And it is the Representer that beareth the Person, and but one Person" (Hobbes, 1914, p. 85).

9. In August 1994, the Zapatistas convened a National Democratic Convention to open a national dialogue within "civil society." To host the six thousand people, coming from almost the whole ideological spectrum and the most diverse groups and organizations, the Zapatistas built, in the middle of the jungle, an "auditorium," surrounded by a group of large huts, which they planned to use as a library, health center, etc. They called the place Aguascalientes, thus evoking the Convention held in that city of Central Mexico, during the Revolution of 1910, to open a dialogue among all revolutionary forces and to pave the way for a new Constitutional Congress. In February 1995, the Mexican Army launched an attack against the Zapatistas. Both the *milicianos*, the members of the Zapatista army, and their *bases de apoyo*, the people of the communities supporting them, were forced to escape to the jungle, where they stayed for several months, until the dialogue with the government was again restarted. During the operation, the Mexican Army

destroyed the Aguascalientes and occupied Guadalupe Tepeyac, the village in which it was located. On January 1, 1996, the Zapatistas inaugurated five Aguascalientes in Oventic, Roberto Barrios, La Garrucha, Morelia and La Realidad, as cultural centers for the communities surrounding those villages. The Intercontinental Encounter took place in all five places.

10. In fact, the people who could not come for different reasons organized parallel Encounters in their own countries.

11. All groups held intense discussions about the format of the Encounter. Different cultural styles were in open contradiction. While the people coming from the northern part of the globe struggled for efficiency in the use of time for concentrating on the "important" presentations, people from the southern part of the globe wanted everyone to have a chance to talk and to listen. A compromise was reached, allowing for short presentations of anyone wanting to make his/her point. This arrangement did not satisfy everyone. Other problems arose, including repetitiveness. "We did not travel five thousand miles to hear this," said some impatient participants, overconscious of the historic importance of the event ... and of the importance of their own ideas. But once everyone had had his/her say, and ideas started to be woven around the main themes, most people appreciated the meaning of the extended listening to all those who chose to speak. Something similar happened with the "cultural activities": all kinds of music, poems, dancing in the mud under heavy rain . . . For some, too many hours were "lost" in such activities, which meant reducing time spent upon "serious" discussion. But after seeing the impact of those "extra-curricular" activities upon the participants, and how they helped to open minds and hearts in the common adventure of hosting the Other, earlier critics came to express appreciation for these key components of the Encounter.

SIX

EPILOGUE: THE GRASSROOTS
POST-MODERN EPIC

Still rooted in their traditions and local cultures, the "social majorities" are creating post-modern paths, taking us beyond modern thinking and behavior. Neither trapped by modern certainties nor institutions, urban as well as rural marginals, peasants and small farming communities, along with others who constitute the "social majorities" are the pioneers of grassroots post-modernism.

They are not attempting to go back to any lost paradise. Nor are they falling into nostalgia or revivalism. In fact, they are dissolving the historical break imposed by modernity. Their search for continuity gives them the spirit of old wine. But they are not merely new bottles. They are coming from different grapes; the wine is different. Their initiatives are so new, in fact, that we have to go beyond modern words to express them in their own terms. Formal modern categories are irrelevant or useless. We clearly need new discourses to articulate the wide variety of contemporary grassroots initiatives. The new discourses are not re-inventing the wheel, as does the "education" of the "social minorities." They are simply plumbing the depths of "the people's" traditions, escaping the folly of modern arrogance and disrespect towards the experiences of their elders, their dead.

The people's experiences are concretely located – or, better yet, rooted in particular soils.[1] They belong to local spaces and cultures. That is why the modern attempt to reduce them to a single global discourse is both impossible and preposterous.

They do, of course, have in common their radical post-modernity. This is not only something that comes after modernity, but also something that happens against modernity. In their own spaces, they are reacting against and resisting modernization, with its economic cancer metastasizing across the globe.

These grassroots initiatives sustain the hope that after modernity we will not be oppressed by universal, unique truths nor by the global certainties of globalists: whether the conventional or alternative managers of the development discourse, including those offering the salvation of the Universal Declaration of Human Rights to all peoples, regardless of culture, caste, color or creed. After modernity, once again, we may have the flourishing of diversity: with "a good life" defined in local, rooted terms; incommensurable truths or perceptions regarding the nature of Nature, of Reality. "The people" are revealing a multiplicity of different cosmic visions conceived at the local level, emerging from the ruins left by modernity. After "the end of History," we can have the continuation and regeneration of thousands of histories.

The differentiated responses we are now observing and articulating in this book are reactions to a common enemy – shaping the struggle itself and its basic thrust. Grasping the commonality of those diverse experiences demands the verbal inventiveness that matches the inventiveness of the "social majorities" in their daily actions. Inventing that discourse is required of intellectuals who are joining the thousands of local struggles challenging the gigantic forces and institutions created by modernity. The strength of the "social majorities" can be increased through the articulation of unifying discourses, capable of shaping coalitions of the dispersed and diverse struggles located in different heads of the modern hydra. The contemporary challenge of articulation is to carefully avoid the tyranny of globalizing discourses.

Part of the challenge of writing this book has been one of groping for the terms and words of the new era being experienced at the grassroots by "the people." It is in the experiences and stories of the "social majorities" that we continue searching for images and metaphors, for concepts and words capable of revealing what is emerging as millions seek to bury the pestilent corpse of modern times. Radical thinkers are helping us by breaking our modern intellectual chains, offering images, experiences, concepts and words that help us to bridge the chasm that separates the grassroots world from the landscape of the modern mind.

How do we see and touch and smell the post-modern reality of the "social majorities"? How can we join with others in constructing dialogues inspired by the spirit of radical pluralism? The "social majorities" are showing us that we can learn from our ancestors how to walk the paths of escape from the horrors of modernity. There remains the need to go farther still; to give appropriate articulation and expression to the epic our book has barely started to sketch.

The post-modern ethos of liberation eludes the economic men and women who work for modern institutions wedded to spreading the global economy. It proceeds unseen by individual selves whose lives are defined by demands for the global dissemination of an economic system with its glamorous guarantees of social or human rights for every man, woman and child on earth. The post-modern liberation of the "social majorities" cannot be reduced to merely suppressing money or stopping trade. The political design establishing modern economic societies has implied installing the economic sphere at the center of politics and ethics. That brutal and violent transformation, first completed in Europe, was always associated with colonial domination of the rest of the world. In the postcolonial era, supposedly ushered in at the end of World War II, it re-entered every culture under a moral mantle, now piously worn by the descendants of those who "discovered," looted, pillaged and raped with justification the inferior or subhuman species. To make amends to the "social majorities" no longer willing to suffer the myth of their inferiority, the latest agenda of recolonization means transforming all the different peoples of the world into economic men and women, independent individual selves, now promised security and protection under the grand umbrella of the global economy, with democracy and human rights for all.

Post-modernity already exists where people refuse to be seduced and controlled by economic laws. It exists for peoples rediscovering and reinventing their traditional commons by re-embedding the economy (to use Polanyi's expression) into society and culture; subordinating it again to politics and ethics; marginalizing it – putting it at their margins: which is precisely what it means to be a "marginal" in modern times.

But what is it that the "social majorities" are marginalizing? It is not material things or money.[2] It is scarcity, a principle, a logic. This scarcity should not be confused with age-old rarity, shortage, restriction, want, insufficiency or even frugality. The "law of scarcity" was constructed by economists to denote the technical assumption that human wants are great, not to say infinite, whereas human means are limited, though improvable. The assumption implies choices about the allocation of means (resources). This "fact" defines the "economic problem" par excellence, whose "solution" is proposed by economists through the plan, the state, the market and now the "Global Project."

The "social majorities" are leading the way in keeping alive their traditional rejection of that assumption. Just that. An assumption. A belief; a statement through which modern people continue oppressing themselves and others. Marshall Sahlins (1972) and Pierre Clastres (1987), among others, have given detailed and well-documented accounts of cultures in which non-economic assumptions govern the lives of peoples, rejecting the assumption of scarcity whenever it appears among them. In our experience, this is not something that only happened in the past, something to be remembered with nostalgia. Rather, it is a contemporary, daily practice among the "social majorities" of the world. They see it as the very condition for their survival in the midst of the depredations of modern individual selves into their cultural spaces, promising "the American dream" or its moral better half: human rights.

Of course, the "social majorities" are suffering the massive damage of the "Global Project," with its myths of "global commons" and of the individual self, claiming human rights. They are, after all, living on this planet, not in some extra-terrestrial world or hyper-reality. Day after day, they must resist the modern mind's economic and technological invasions into their lives; frequently with bulldozers and the police; always at the service of development, education or human rights agencies.

The better the "social majorities" get to know their modern enemy, the more fully they appreciate the support they find in their commons and communities; in their traditions; in their well-rooted or indigenous ways of living, suffering and dying. Their own traditions teach the "social majorities" the wisdom to challenge the assumptions by which the minorities maintain the myths of modern reality. Minus these assumptions, there remains no foundation for the "Global Project" or the universal human rights for which the modern individual self kills today, and then dies a prolonged, lonely, slow death.

The new grassroots commons look fragile when confronted with the disturbing uncontrolled flood of transnational economic forces still in operation. But new and extended coalitions continue to emerge, becoming stronger step by step. In these spaces, in ordinary people's humble local initiatives, we find hope for starting political inversions of economic domination. Recent as well as ancient history teaches us how grandiose pyramids cave in; how the great walls constructed by the big and the famous come crumbling down.

It would be criminal to idealize misery. The new commons are more often than not suffering extreme restrictions. But modern blindness fails to recognize that their suffering is the source of the amazing capacities "the people" have for reinvention and innovation. Their post-modern commons are not forms of mere survival or subsistence. They are contemporary forms of life, spaces for solidary and convivial life, sociological novelties which regenerate the traditions of the "social majorities," while re-evaluating modernity. They are conceived in an era in which all that men and women need for their delight in living can be obtained, given that the technical means are already available; and *for* an era in which non-economic relationships will liberate men, women and children to freely look for what they want with dignity and wisdom. These new horizons and commons are supporting the "social majorities" in the small, human steps they are taking to leave behind them the era of *Homo oeconomicus* in which the explicit goal of unlimited improvement has further concentrated the economic privileges of the "social minorities" and imposed untold sufferings on the "social majorities" – behind the "mask of love," the farce of promoting the welfare of the latter (Illich, 1977).

We have no desire or intention to do the "noble savage" on the "social majorities" – to dehumanize them by stripping them of what is part of the human condition: the bad and the ugly in conjunction with the good. We see no need to idealize them into a "perfection" that is neither real nor humanly feasible; that is, literally and metaphorically, out of this world.

The good, the bad and the ugly, like the virtues and vices of the "social minorities," have their own variants of degree or shape, scale or form among the "social majorities." Our *Popol Vuh*, *Ramayana* or *Mahabharata*, like other epics, teach us how our gods are flawed. How, then, can "common people" be perfect? Despite the absence of "objectivity" in our study and reflections on the "social majorities," we are not blind to their many flaws. These hardly need further recording or elaboration. For five hundred years, that is all their enslavers, colonizers or hunters have done; and still continue to do today.[3] It is urgent that we explore the missing half: their impressive strengths and capacities, their knowledge and understanding of survival and flourishing acquired through overcoming all the odds stacked up against them.

According to an ancient African proverb, until the lions find their own historians, the histories of hunters will continue to celebrate hunting. Some lions have had to become extinct or to border on the edge of extinction in order to finally find their historians among environmentalists. Eco-developers are throwing out indigenous peoples from their homes in jungles and forests, being cordoned off as national reserves for the preservation of threatened animal species. Peoples of forests and jungles, like other members of the "overpopulated" "social majorities," lack the privileges being accorded to the animals which make it to the list of "endangered" species of the "social minorities." Faced with these peculiarities of our times, we find ourselves trying to be one of the historians of the currently hunted, including those classified as "overpopulated." Undoubtedly, it is modern hubris to aspire to write the global history of the world's "social majorities." They are so numerous, so rich, so magnificently diverse that no single history could do them justice. How many millions would need to be employed to even begin the monumental task of recording their ongoing epic? Of capturing on the printed page or in hard disk "memory" their practices, traditions and cultures, still alive and exuberant after thousands of years?

For most writers of the printed page or electronic text, these traditions are either dead or doomed to extinction; only worth remembering as museum curiosities that have been retrieved from anthropological trips or archeological digs. We hope that more members of the "social minorities" will abandon such certainties, going beyond the grave limits of their hard print or electronic text in order to enjoy the lived practices that constitute grassroots post-modernism. These reveal to us the simplicity and transparency of the commons which teach the "social majorities" how to adapt and survive. They also reveal to us our maladaptations to the opaque systems of the "social minorities" which we were educated to fit into, however uncomfortable or unnatural.

The current endeavors at the grassroots, of course, raise more questions than they answer. In our quest for answers, we are learning of the multiplicity of ways in which "the people" are once again beginning to root and re-root themselves in their own spaces. They do not feel limited by frontiers, with the signs of the minorities that declare "No Trespassing"; but by the thresholds and horizons that define their own cultures. At first glance, their new commons might appear as inverted ghettoes. When we learn to look further, however, we discover the marvellous ways in which these creations are free of the controls of experts and administrators; brought into being by "common" women and men despite the ordinances of municipalities; created to be places where they can be themselves and not the shadows of the upper classes who seek to control them, preventing them from being free like the wind.

"Most people want economic development or progress," insists the standard modern axiom. It is analogous to the fake question: "What do you prefer? To be rich, young and handsome, or poor, old and ugly?" If development is publicized as the first, and underdevelopment as the latter — as politicians, professionals and the media are doing everyday — most people do "vote" for development. But "common" men and women are not stupid. They may still be illiterate. Yet, without needing to enter the World Wide Web, they know from their daily experience that most of the marvels of development are not for them; furthermore, that these are not the marvels their advertisers claim them to be. They know that most of them will not possess a family car, but will suffer as pedestrians in urban developments built for the cars of the minorities, not for the feet and bicycles of the "social majorities." Once upon a time, they admired the "miracles" of fertilizers and pesticides and wanted their magic. But they are now painfully recovering from the damage done to their land, lives and social groups by the Green Revolution. In going beyond development, they are not enjoying a paradise, exposed as they are to all kinds of restrictions; but they are giving up counterproductive illusions and adopting sensible attitudes to deal with their predicaments as well as to realize their hopes. Rather than "rights," "economic development" or the "miracles" of genetic engineering, they are now claiming respect and political autonomy; recognition for their dignity, initiative and imagination, enabling them to create their own worlds.

How do we articulate their claims in a world defined by frontiers – including the frontiers of the modern individual self that separate men, women and children from their possible "we's"? How do we learn to put into words what the rich multiplicity of peoples are claiming and living at the grassroots? When Indian peoples claim their autonomy, they dream of self-determination. But the determination of each community differs. Each group has a different gaze. How do these come to be interwoven in the absence of common words?

Clearly, questions like these do not pose an easy challenge. It is cowardice to run away from the challenge of reflecting upon them by hiding behind the deceptive protection of modern certainties. "The people" are learning to dismantle the "truths" imposed upon them from outside; the global truths of top-down regimes that mass-produce them. From "down below," communities are now weaving their own truths with growing confidence, using some of the threads that have come to them from their dead, from the past, along with some that belong to the present. In the meantime, all the "truths" inherited from the nineteenth century are crashing around them, creating dangerous vacuums. How can these vacuums be filled?

The challenge of the "social majorities" is to continue improvising creative transitions from an imposed universe to the regeneration of their more familiar pluriverse. Today, their struggles of resistance seek to go beyond the new universe, more simplified and aggressive, trying to control the modern state by redefining its function. Both transnational corporations and authoritarian, fundamentalist factions are currently eroding the homogenizing projects of nation-states. How do the "social majorities" create spaces for harmonious coexistence, preventing the decadent structures of the state from falling into the authoritarian hands of those reinventing racism and nationalism to control what remains of it? How do the "social majorities" create protective umbrellas for their rich and vigorous pluriverse in the process of being reborn?

This epilogue ends with many unanswered questions. Our images, stories and reflections offer invitations to our readers to discover their own answers, in their own places, with roots that tap deep into the genius of their traditions.

NO NEW TRUTHS, REOPENING OUR HORIZONS

> The open horizon ... is meant to preserve the validity of this trend towards unity and universality, but without closing it up in any single perspective, vision or system. We need a horizon in order to see and to understand, but we are aware that other peoples have other horizons; we aspire to embrace them, but we are aware of the ever-elusive character of any horizon and its constitutive openness. (Vachon, 1995b, pp. 54–5)

The people are learning to deal with the nation-state, with what remains of it, as a form of taming its impulses and softening its agony. They are dispensing, as Foucault recommended, with any image of the new society's political construct. The disparate initiatives and movements of "the people" appear in the form of rainbows, vague horizons full of different colors that no one may ever reach. They are creating different social and political spaces, making new paths by walking through them; learning to circumvent the pathological reactions of the privileged minorities threatened by these new impulses at the grassroots.

"The people" are leading the way, teaching us how to once again transform needs into localized verbs. Instead of waiting for the state to provide classrooms to fulfill the modern "need" for "education," they are learning from each other. Instead of waiting for the state to provide "health services," they are using their traditional knowledge for healing themselves. Instead of depending upon the housing and urban services of the state, they are settling in the dwellings that distinguish and differentiate their unique spaces and commons. Instead of food intakes and nutrition defined by the professionals of industrial eating, they are enjoying their comida. In their struggles, "the people" are localizing and re-rooting themselves in their immediate spaces, while at the same time opening these to extensive coalitions with others.

Step by step, they are learning to escape from the extravagant idea that political struggle requires, as a premise, a clear conception of the desirable social regime that is the "ultimate" goal. In rebelling against the tyranny of globalizing discourses which impose an authoritarian vision of "the society as a whole," they are discovering that the latter is nothing but a diffused horizon, produced by a myriad of personal and communitarian initiatives; shifting and moving away, as do rainbows, with their growing interactions among and between them. They are rediscovering how to resist universalizable "normality," abandoning the egalitarian struggle for rights. The latter, they are finding out, only create bureaucratic apparatuses by redefining "needs" in terms of professionals' expert services. Rescuing their spaces for the autonomous satisfaction of their culturally defined desires, they are liberating themselves from norms which increase dependencies upon the globalizing service industry. Each step in this direction enables them to enjoy the freedoms that define their post-modern commons.

These transformations are occurring right under the global monoliths that hide the small, local endeavors where people can face each other as I–Thou. All the words and concepts needed to fully capture what we are gazing at with our new eyes remain elusive and unarticulated. We are struggling for ways to take our experiences of people at the grassroots out of the jail of modern abstractions, searching for the institutional inversions so desperately needed. Ours are mere preliminary steps taken to escape from the opaque vision of conventional thinking and the frozen language of modern ideologies and formal categories.

REGENERATING PUBLIC VIRTUES

Over centuries of colonization and development, continually exposed to foreign repression and threats, the "social majorities" were forced, all over the world, to concentrate their resistance inside their own spaces. From inside, they tried to hide their truths: their forms of governing themselves, their living and changing traditions. Hidden and protected from the Outsiders' stare or meddling interference, the traditions of the "social majorities" mutated and survived. Some anthropologists, perceiving this, refused to reveal their findings to the colonizers; it was their way of expressing their love and respect for the peoples' and cultures that hospitably opened their hearts and minds to them. Unfortunately, other anthropologists, more interested in their own professional advancements or convinced of the intrinsic merits of universalizing their own cultural norms (including their systems of domination), had no compunctions about revealing those cultural "secrets." These were extensively used by colonizers and developers to practice their genocides or culturcides. Today they continue to be used by the neo-colonizers for similar aims and purposes.

The epic now unfolding at the grassroots reveals further mutations of people's traditional struggles of resistance. These are being forced into the open, and thus being transformed into struggles for liberation. For "common" men and women know better today that to remain silent and hidden in their commons is all too often equivalent to being annihilated without a murmur or a ripple; without any press or media coverage. They are learning from the "social minorities" the tricks needed to put the *mass* media to the real and actual use of the masses. Some of the global noise made by the press is useful for broadcasting their provincial struggles of liberation.[4]

Seeking allies wherever they can get them, organizing coalitions of solidarity to resist the contemporary threats of the "Global Project" which is dooming them to extinction, "the people" are now emerging in the public arena. Publicly affirming, reclaiming and regenerating their commons, they are bringing out into the open what was previously confined to their inner spaces. Their discarded camouflage teaches us that the dawning millennium requires a whole new "survival kit."

Their emergent "public phase" has its dark side; its pathos of wars lost, of men, women and children killed. On the light side, their post-modern initiatives of liberation are enriching our lives with non-modern public virtues. Given their profound roots in the traditions of "the people," the public virtues exemplifed by them are, as Gandhi put it, "as old as the hills." Yet, these old hills have been so severely denuded by modernity that they almost disappeared from the public arena dominated by the "social minorities." The latter transformed them into vices, weakness or fatal flaws. The "social majorities" are leading the way in reclaiming and revaluing them as the moral principles to rule social life. From down below, at the grassroots, the traditional public virtues are springing to new life.

Disseminating Humility

Humility, traditionally designated a virtue or quality, is the opposite of vanity, pride and haughtiness. To be humble means to return to our senses, to balanced or virtuous ways of being and living.

In the contemporary discourse of progress or development, of becoming a military or economic superpower, humility has become associated with humiliation, an undignified condition. The "social minorities" do not aspire to be humble. In fact, their word "humble" is synonymous with another ugly modern word: "underdeveloped."

"The people" have never ceased to be humble. They have no reason to be other than humble. They reveal their humility by refusing to substitute their traditional hopes with modern expectations (Illich, 1970b). The latter challenge the gods with the hubris of science. A "common" woman who is pregnant does not speak of *expecting*; she expresses attitudes of *hoping* that the gods will bless her with the birth of a child. Some of the common myths of the "social majorities" reveal the "bad luck" of substituting the humility of human hopes with the arrogance of planned and managed modern expectations; for the latter evoke the wrath of the mysterious gods, tempting the Fates or the forces of evil and destruction. In celebrating the blessings of their gods, their customs resist the vanity of the "social minorities'" science: its certainties, predictions and expectations.

The humility of common women and men is usually disqualified as "primitive," "innocent" and "childish" by "the educated."[5] Currently revealed in their struggles from the margins, long absent at state centers, these virtues are desperately needed to put an end to the era marked by the hubris of modern man and woman. In their arrogance, they find their nemesis; while "the people" offer hope at the margins, emulating and applying both epistemological and political humility in their endeavors. Their humble political agendas reveal the premises or preconditions needed for intercultural dialogues which encourage the harmonious coexistence of diverse peoples and traditions.

Humility is not to be confused with or reduced to cultural relativism. Being true to their own cultures, "the people" affirm themselves in their own truths. They assume (with or without consciousness of it) that their "we" constitutes the center of their universe: a microcosmos which reflects entire Reality. But precisely because they assume themselves as the center, they can be open to the whole that they see reflected in their microcosmos. Humbly recognizing and affirming its own center, each culture can open itself to dialogues with other cultures (Panikkar, 1993).

Epistemological humility does not imply relativizing all knowledge. Going beyond the philosophical method of Cartesian doubt, it also escapes Marx's motto – *omnia omnibus dubitandum* – for de-absolutizing knowledge (including his own). It is epitomized in Gandhi's truth – at once a personal and cultural experiment. Repeatedly and in full faith, Gandhi affirmed his truth. While sharing with others his indubitable beliefs, he nonetheless described his incredibly rich, fruitful life as nothing more than a series of humble and humbling "experiments with truth." Epistemological humility means recognizing and accepting the limits not only of "science," but of any established knowledge; noting the personal limitations of the knowing subject as well as continually delineating the limits of the logos. The wise retain their humility, knowing all that they do not know.

Political humility also does not imply relativizing all claims. Recognizing the unity and integrity of each people's traditions, it calls for respect for the otherness of the Other; with their unique ways of being on Earth; with their own "science" and arts of living and dying. Political humility struggles for the dignity of all peoples, embracing the premise which rejects the supposed superiority of any culture, any ideology, any political position, over the others. It dreams of a world in which everyone can pose and propose their views and intentions to others, but no one can impose their own on others.

Recovering Austerity

Austerity is an ancient word, whose original meaning has virtually disappeared in the modern world, along with the conditions that made it possible. As a personal virtue, it is now taken to mean some kind of self-imposed deprivation by people who decide for reasons, religious or other, to live *out of the world* – as some type of pilgrim or monk. In the modern world, it can be requested from others – the government, public officials, etc. – when they become too ostentatious or wasteful with taxpayers' money. It lacks prestige today as a personal ideal for people interested in enjoying their lives *in the world*. Regardless of the remains of the Protestant ethic found in some of the behaviors of modern men and women, frugality is seen among the "social minorities" solely as a means, and not as an end: that is, the astute administration of time and money helps to make a good living, but the good living itself is not defined as frugal; in fact, it is precisely the opposite. The promise of modernity is fulfilled in overcoming the forced frugality of the past, when natural and social restrictions prevented people from enjoying the full satisfaction of their wants (assumed to be limitless).

The tradition of austerity, as a personal and collective way of being, remains alive and flourishing among the "social majorities." For "the people," it means nothing less than common sense – particularly, the sense of community. (The two senses clearly nourish each other.) "The people" view frugality as a basic desirable fact of life; the condition without which simple survival as well as endured flourishing are threatened. Losing austerity means losing sense: being "foolish" or "out of your mind."

How do humans conceive unlimited ends when their means are necessarily limited? "The people" continue experiencing the pain of destruction to their commons when these are attacked by behaviors stemming from the basic assumption of modern society: human wants are great, not to say infinite, although human means are limited, but improvable (Sahlins, 1972). Their traditions have antidotes for attitudes that stem from such an assumption. Only by preventing the scarcity and envy – chronic and insatiable – imposed by modernity can they circumvent the cultural extinction to which it dooms them.

Common sense maintains a sense of harmony and proportionality – the appropriate scale – in human activities (Illich and Rieger, 1996; Mokos, 1996). Among "the people" (those who have successfully avoided the process of individualization), common sense reveals sensible ways for perceiving self and world. These necessarily include the sense of community which, in its turn, means a sense of harmony and proportionality within the commons. The self, the very fact of Being, is necessarily conceived as a form of relationship: a knot in a net of relations.

Austerity or common sense is the condition of friendship – ways of being in the world that enhance "graceful playfulness" (eutrapelia) in personal relations. Austerity does not mean giving up wine, women or song. It is not equivalent to frugality (renunciation for mundane or superior purposes – either to save money or the soul) (Hoinacki, 1995). It "does not exclude all enjoyments, but only those which are distracting from or destructive of personal relatedness" (Illich, 1973, p. xxv).

Austerity is being promoted in the grassroots mobilizations of "the people" as a public virtue. They are not giving public discourses on this virtue. Nor are they reducing it to a matter of prudence in public budgets or to "mass education" preaching the reduction of modern waste – although this waste and contemporary public budgets do clearly reveal the foolishness of the dominant patterns in governmental expenses as well as public or personal consumption. In its essence, austerity means bringing common sense back into political life. Displacing the economy from the center of the society, while re-embedding it within culture and commons, "the people" are teaching us how to recover a sense of proportion and harmony in social life. Their virtue of austerity takes us to the very core of justice. Breaking the isolation of "the masses" (constituted by the individual self), their virtue of austerity calls for recovering the sense of community in personal relations,

Announcing Hope and Prosperity

The "revolution of increasing expectations" has never taken hold among the "social majorities." Defining the modern era, this revolution represents a radical break with the past; promising an escape into some fantasy future, an Eden of unlimited economic growth, bringing limitless freedom for the pursuit of unending happiness. Dangling such promises for the genuinely naive among the "social minorities," the "Global Project" is rapidly transforming that "revolution" into the Apocalypse of frustrated expectations. People still continue claiming their rights but no state can satisfy their claims. Increasing numbers among the "social minorities" are finally waking up to the fraud, perpetrated in part by the "education" that builds unreachable expectations.

Radical hope is the essence of popular movements, Douglas Lummis (1996) observes. Hope is what "the people," in all their simple and transparent dignity, are now bringing to the world. To those spoiled by splendor and high expectation, "the people" exemplify dignified ways of coping with their predicaments while challenging the "Global Project."

Their ways of hoping light the horizon, darkened today by the specter of the "Global Project." "The people" are no longer trapped in the fatalism of traditional societies, doomed by destiny. Instead of the modern illusion of escaping into some planned future, they are recovering the present, their present. This means counting the blessings of what they still have, in spite of colonization and development. In their reclaimed or regenerated commons, they are constantly rediscovering motives for their renewed hopes of liberation.

They nourish their own ideals of prosperity. Modernity doomed to oblivion the original meaning of this word, coming from the Latin *pro spere*, which means: "according to hope." Side-stepping the dangerous illusions and false expectations of the "social minorities," dismantling economic interactions inside their modes of living, they are opening roads to prosperity. Giving up such illusions brings "the people" a new sense of well-being as well as real and reliable improvements. Their modest successes, stemming from their courageous efforts, daily nourish their humble hopes.

Private hope and public desperation explain the collective manipulation of "the masses" in modern societies. Their "democratic" leaders make political careers misdiagnosing the daily disasters of modern life, raising false expectations, while stimulating the spirit of individualist competition among the remaining survivors of "downsizing" and collapsing economies.

Down below, at the grassroots, "the people" are busy at work removing the false promises of national development and the welfare state. They are regenerating social fabrics within which personal and collective hopes can be interwoven into a whole. Less and less gullible about the carpetbagging activities of national political parties, "the people" are experimenting with alternative democratic styles. These experiments reveal that the art of the possible always extends it: creating the possible out of the impossible.

To live in this world demands more than simply understanding it. At the end of this journey, we cannot but fathom the need to think everything through again; to question the modern certainties that have made us prisoners of the separate, small, possessive, individual self from whom we daily endeavor to escape.

We have learned from peoples at the grassroots that the restricted "we" of all those with whom we share our quest are poised at the beginning of an immense, unfolding epic, taking us on radically diverging paths beyond the monoculture of the modern era. However fresh and new the segments of the unfolding epic, they are continuing chapters in the ancient epics about the *conditio humana*.

The lives of "the people" in our cultures have always been filled with amazing grace and profound beauty, stemming in part from the solidity of Being which is nothing more and nothing less than communal power. From the ancient frescoes of Ajanta and Ellora to the contemporary paintings of a Diego Rivera, that grace and beauty are rendered transparent.

Our book invites others to our celebration of the re-emerging "commons" of "common" women, men and children; to walk with us, together finding our footsteps; taking us deeper into the ancient roots of our traditions; closer to the truths of our elders, our dead, with their hopefulness and humility, austerity and abundance, not to be forgotten.

NOTES

1. We know that "concrete" is generally used today as the opposite of "abstract." We continue to seek a better substitute to express that opposition. For the more we traverse concrete roads and superhighways, the less we like to use the word "concrete" to identify the rooted experiences of those who live in gobar (cow dung) or adobe (mud), practicing the "earthy virtue of place" (Groeneveld et al., 1991).

2. As we said before, we applaud alternative currencies, like the Ithaca Dollar, being coined by peoples seeking to escape the modern mold of economic selves. Hopefully, these new currencies will transform relationships of barter into the bonds of community and *communis*.

3. In 1875, the fifteenth edition of the *Abstract of Universal Geography* was published in Paris. It taught its readers that the inhabitants of Guinea were "black, robust and candid; but lazy, revengeful and thieves"; that the Persians were "sober, effeminate, skilled, given to poetry, ardent and revengeful"; that the Bedouins were "thieves, though occasionally they can be hospitable and compassionate with travellers"; while the British were "courageous, cultured, honest, industrious, loving freedom and their fatherland, entrepreneurial and dedicated, given very much to commerce and to useful crafts." There are many thousands of examples of these kind of books, through which western people have been educated.

If those perceptions seem crude and "politically incorrect" in the era of multiculturalism and Pocahontas, let's take a look at the Microsoft Word 6 Spanish Dictionary, now in the hands of 200,000 users in Mexico alone. The synonyms for "Mexicano (Mexican)" are "Azteca, charro (cow-boy), basto (coarse), vulgar, chillón (shrieking), ridículo (ridiculous)"; for "Indio (Indian)" are "salvaje (salvage), antropófago (cannibal), primitivo (primitive)"; for "Mestizo (a man of mixed blood)" are "Híbrido (hybrid), cruzado (crossed), mezclado (mixed), bastardo (bastard)"; for "Negros (Blacks)" are "indígena (Indian), salvaje (savage), bárbaro (barbarian), antropófago (cannibal)." Following the media scandal, Microsoft's makers apologized for the mistake and offered its users a new Spanish Dictionary for free. Their commercial cover-up will do little to hide the fact that today's ultramodern language, now being communicated all over the world by politically correct experts, shows the same lack of hospitality as did the ancient Greeks. It also reveals the same ignorance about who the Other really is, the same devaluation, the same exclusion.

4. For the most part, however, the media take only the perspectives of the "social minorities."

5. These are only some of the disqualifications that "the uneducated" receive from "the educated." Like other disqualifiers, these are justified and legitimized in all the histories of education written from the perspective of the educated. For an alternative, grassroots perspective of "education" and "the uneducated," see Prakash and Esteva 1997. In this book we deliberate upon what we have learned to learn from those who have no access to education; who cannot get the developed person's prescribed quota or recipe for education; or those who, having trustfully and diligently undergone the education planned for them, have by now come to know too well the bitter taste of false expectations, dubious benefits, or failed promises. While doing so, we celebrate the wellbeing still enjoyed in the commons and cultures of peoples living and learning at the grassroots; the "social majorities" who have not forgotten their diverse arts of survival and flourishing "in lieu of education." Escaping education is critical for their success in going beyond the myth-making processes that the modern mind has engineered to support and cement the other modern "certainties" – including the desirability of development, the individual self and universal human rights.

BIBLIOGRAPHY

Achebe, C. (1961). *No longer at ease*. New York: I. Obolensky.

———— (1969). *Things fall apart*. New York: Fawcett Crest.

The Aisling Quarterly, Inismor, Árainn, Co na Gaillimhe, Eire.

Agnoli, J., and Bruckner, P. (1971). *La transformación de la democracia*. México: Siglo XXI.

Alvares, C. (1992). Science. In W. Sachs (ed.), *The development dictionary: A guide to knowledge as power*. London: Zed Books.

———— (1995). *Turtles all the way down: The growing resistance to the West's intellectual discourse*. Presented at the International Conference on Knowledge and Power, Decolonizing Our Minds, Redefining Knowledge, Temple University, Philadelphia, PA, March.

Ames, R. (1993). Introduction. In Sun-Tzu, *The art of warfare*. New York: Ballantine Books.

An-Na'im, A.A. (1992). *Human rights in cross-cultural perspectives*. Philadelphia, PA: University of Pennsylvania Press.

Apffel-Marglin, F. (1990). Smallpox in two systems of knowledge. In F. Apffel-Marglin and S. Marglin (eds), *Dominating knowledge*. Oxford: Clarendon Press.

———— (1995). Development or decolonization in the Andes? *Interculture*, XXVI (1), Issue 126, Winter, 3–17.

———— (ed.). (1998). *Production or regeneration? An Andean perspective on modern western knowledge*. London: Zed Books.

Arendt, H. (1958). *The human condition*. New York: Anchor.

Ariès, P. (1962). *Centuries of childhood: A social history of family life*. New York: Vintage.

———— (1985). *History of private life* (5 vols). Cambridge, MA: Harvard University Press.

Aubry, A. (1994). *¿Qué es la sociedad civil?* San Cristóbal de Las Casas: Inaremac.

Autonomedia (1994). Zapatistas! In *Documents of the New Mexican Revolution*. New York: Autonomedia.

Banuri, T., and Apffel-Marglin, F. (1993). *Who will save the forests? Knowledge, power and environmental destruction*. London: Zed Books.

Bell, D. (1962). *The end of ideology: On the exhaustion of political ideas in the fifties* (rev. ed.). New York: Free Press.

———— (1989). American exceptionalism revisited: the role of civil society. *Public Interest*, 95 (56), 48, Spring.

Bellah, R.N., Madsen, R., Sullivan, W.M., Swidler, A., and Tipton, S.M. (1985). *Habits of the heart: Individualism and commitment in American life*. Berkeley: University of California Press.

Berger, J. (1984). *And our faces, my heart, brief as photos*. London: Writers and Readers.

———— (1996). El alma y el estafador. *La Jornada Semanal*, 74, 6–7, August 4.

Berger, P. , Berger, B., and Kellner, H. (1973). *The homeless mind*. New York: Random House.

Berry, W. (1972). *A continuous harmony: Essays cultural and agricultural*. New York: Harcourt Brace Jovanovich.

———— (1977). *The unsettling of America: Culture and agriculture*. San Francisco: Sierra Club Books.

———— (1983). *Standing by words*. San Francisco: North Point Press.

———— (1987). *Home economics*. San Francisco: North Point Press.

———— (1990). *What are people for?* San Francisco: North Point Press.

———— (1991a). *Out of your car, off your horse*. Atlantic Monthly, 61–3, February.

———— (1991b). *Nobody loves this planet*. In Context, 27, 4, Winter.

———— (1992). *Sex, economy, freedom and community*. San Francisco: Pantheon Books.

Bishop, J. (1989). *Democracy, Aristotle, Marx and contemporary myth*. Pennsylvania State University, Science, Technology, and Society Program Typescript (Spanish: El mito contemporáneo de la democracia. Opciones, 35, May 1993).

Blair, D. (1996). Eating in the bioregion. In J. Chesworth (ed.), *The ecology of health*. Thousand Oaks, CA: Sage Publications.

Bobbio, N. (1976). *La teoria delle forme di governo nella storia del pensiero politico*. Turin: G. Giapichelli Editore.

Bobbio, N. and Matteucci, N. (eds) (1982). *Diccionario de política*. México: Siglo XXI.

Bollier, D., and Helfrich, S. (2012) *The wealth of the commons: A world beyond market and state*. Amherst, MA: The Commons Strategies Group, Levellers Press. .

Bradford, G. (1991). We all live in Bhopal. In J. Zerzan and A. Carnes (eds), *Questioning technology: Tool, toy or tyrant?* Philadelphia, PA: New Society Publishers.

Brundtland, G.H. (1987). *Our common future: A report of the World Commission on Environment and Development*. New York: Oxford University Press.

Buber, M. (1970). *I and Thou*. New York: Scribner.

Burns, W. (1995). *Human rights*. Chicago: The New Encyclopedia Britannica.

Cammeli, M. (1982). Autogobierno. In N. Bobbio and N. Matteucci (eds), *Diccionario de política*. México: Siglo XXI.

Campbell, J. (1990). *Transformations of myth through time*. New York: Harper & Row.

Canetti, E. (1966). *Crowds and power*. New York: Viking Press.

Carrigan, A. (1995). *Chiapas: The first post-modern revolution*. Sais Review, Winter/Spring, 71–98.

Cayley, D. (1992). *Ivan Illich in conversation*. Concord, Ont.: House of Anansi Press.

Changeux, B., et al. (1985). *L'individu*. Paris: La Découverte/Le Monde.

Christie, N. (1981). *Limits to pain*. Oxford: Martin Robertson.

———— (1989). *Beyond loneliness and institutions: Communes for extraordinary people*. Oslo: Norwegian University Press.

———— (1994). *Crime control as industry: Towards gulags, western style*. London: Routledge.

Clastres, P. (1987). *Society against the state: Essays in political anthropology.* New York: Zone Books.

Cleaver, H. (1994). *The Chiapas uprising and the future of class struggle in the new world order.* Riff-raff. Padua, Italy, February.

——— (1996). *Pamphlets created by Acción Zapatista,* Austin, TX.

Cohen, J. L., and Arato, A. (1992). *Civil society and political theory.* Cambridge, MA: MIT Press.

Cougar, Y. (1973). Review of *Discovery of the Individual,* by Colin Morris. *Revue des Sciences Philosophiques et Theologiques,* 57, 305–7.

Cranston, M. (1973). *What are human rights?* New York: Tapinger Publishing Co.

Cronin, T.E. (1989). *Direct democracy: The politics of initiative, referendum and recall.* Cambridge, MA: Harvard University Press.

Dahl, R. A. (1961). *Who governs? Democracy and power in an American city.* New Haven, CT: Yale University Press.

Dewey, J. (1962). *Individualism old and new.* New York: Capricorn Books.

——— (1927). *The public and its problems.* Athens, OH: Swallow Press Books.

Dion-Buffalo, Y., and Mohawk, J. (1994). Thoughts from an autochthonous center: Postmodernism and cultural studies. *Cultural Survival Quarterly,* Winter, 33–5.

Dufresne, J. (1991). *Democracy in the world.* Document presented to the Assemblée nationale du Québec, October.

Dumont, L. (1977). *From Mandeville to Marx: Genesis and triumph of economic ideology.* Chicago: University of Chicago Press.

Dumouchel, P. and Dupuy, J.P. (1979). *L'enfer des choses.* Paris: Seuil.

Durning, A.B. (1989) Grass-roots groups are our best hope for global prosperity. *Utne Reader,* 40–9, July/August.

——— (1991). Asking how much is enough. In L. Brown (ed.), *The state of the world.* New York: W.W. Norton.

Duus, E. (1982). *Negotiating reciprocity: Food exchange in a rural community of the Dominican Republic.* Institute of Social Anthropology, University of Oslo. Typescript.

The Ecologist (1993). *Whose common future? Reclaiming the commons.* London: Earthscan.

Ellul, J. (1964). *The technological society.* New York: Alfred A. Knopf.

——— (1980). *The technological system.* New York: Continuum.

Esteva, G. (1980). *Economía y enajenación.* México: Universidad Veracruzana.

——— (1991). *Muerte y transfiguración de la ciudad de México.* México: Opción.

——— (1992a). *Fiesta – jenseits von Entwicklung, Hilfe und Politik.* Frankfurt: Brandes & Apsel/Sdwind.

——— (1992b). Development. In W. Sachs (ed.), *The development dictionary: A guide to knowledge as power.* London: Zed Books.

——— (1993). A new source of hope: the margins. *Interculture* XXVI(2), Issue 119, Spring, 2–62.

——— (1994a). Basta! Mexican Indians say "enough." *The Ecologist,* 24(3), May/June, 83–5.

——— (1994b). *Crónica del fin de una era.* México: Editorial Posada.

Esteva, G., Babones S., and Babcicky, P. (2013) *The future of development: A radical manifesto.* Bristol: Policy Press.

Esteva, G., and Prakash, M. (1992). Resistance to sustainable development: Lessons from the banks of the Narmada. *The Ecologist* 22(2), 45–51.

—————— (1996). Grassroots postmodernism. *Interculture*, XXIX(2), Issue 131, Summer/ Fall, 3–52.

Etzioni, A. (1993). *The spirit of community, rights, responsibilities, and the communitarian agenda*. New York: Crown Publishers.

Ferguson, A. (1969). *An essay on the history of civil society* (4th edition). Farnsborough: Gregg International Publishers.

Fernández, J. (1959). *La Coatlicue: Estética del arte indígena antiguo*. México: UNAM.

Foucault, M. (1977). *Power/knowledge*. New York: Pantheon Books.

Freire, P. (1993). *Pedagogy of the oppressed*. New York: Continuum.

Galeano, E. (2006) https://groups.google.com/forum/#!topic/red-tulips/cdsVGZi-ID9g (accessed 3 March 2014).

Galtung, J. (1986). Towards a new economics: On the theory and practice of self-reliance. In P. Ekins (ed.), *The living economy: A new economics in the making*. New York: Routledge & Kegan Paul.

Gandhi, M.K. (1946). *Hind Swaraj or Indian Home Rule*. Ahmedabad: Navajivan Press.

—————— (1953). *Towards new education*. Ahmedabad: Navajivan Press.

—————— (1970). *Essential writings* (selected and edited by V.V. Ramana Murti). New Delhi: Gandhi Peace Foundation.

García, P. (1994). *Temas didácticos de derechos humanas: Área sociológico militar*. El Salvador: Fuerza Armada de El Salvador.

Girard, R. (1978). *To double business bound: Essays on literature, mimesis and anthropology*. Baltimore, MD: Johns Hopkins University Press.

González Sainz, J.A., Lizcano, E., and Ibáñez, R. (1992). Editorial presentation of the dossier "La ilusión democrática." *Archipiélago*, 9.

Goodman, P. (1977). *Drawing the line: Political essays*. (edited by T. Stoehr). New York: Free Life Editions.

Goodman, P. , and Goodman, P. (1960). *Communitas: Means of livelihood and ways of life*. New York: Vintage Books.

Groeneveld, S., Hoinacki, L., Illich, I., and friends (1991). The earthy virtue of place. *New Perspectives Quarterly*, 8(1), 59.

Guéhenno, J. M. (1995). *The end of the nation-state*. Minneapolis: University of Minnesota Press.

Havel, V. (1985) *The power of the powerless*. Armonk, NY: M.E. Sharpe.

Hawken, P. (2007). *Blessed unrest: How the largest social movement in history is restoring grace, justice, and beauty to the world*. New York: Penguin.

Hobbes, T. (1914). *Leviathan*. London: J.M. Dent.

Hoinacki, L. (1995). *Friendship in the writings of Ivan Illich*. Pennsylvania State University, Science, Technology and Society Program. Typescript.

Ignatieff, M. (1985). *The needs of strangers*. New York: Viking.

Illich, I. (1970a). *Celebration of awareness*. New York: Doubleday.

—————— (1970b). *Deschooling society*. New York: Harper & Row.

—————— (1973). *Tools of conviviality*. New York: Harper & Row.

—————— (1977). *Toward a history of needs*. Berkeley, CA: Heyday Books.

—————— (1982). *Gender*. New York: Pantheon.

—————— (1985). *H2O and the waters of forgetfulness*. Berkeley, CA: Heyday Books.

—————— (1987a). La alfabetización de la mentalidad: Un llamamiento a investigarla. *Tecnopolítica*, 87(04), 1–9.

——— (1987b). *Hospitality and pain*. Pennsylvania State University, Science, Technology and Society Program. Typescript.

——— (1988). *Computer literacy and the cybernetic dream*. Pennsylvania State University, Science, Technology and Society Program. Typescript.

——— (1989). The shadow our future throws. *New Perspectives Quarterly*, 6(1), Spring, 20–4.

——— (1992). *In the mirror of the past*. London: Marion Boyars.

——— (1993). *In the vineyard of the text*. Chicago: University of Chicago Press.

——— (1994a). An address to Master Jacques. *Bulletin of Science and Technology*, 14(2), 65–8.

——— (1994b). *Guarding the eye in the age of show* (Science, Technology, and Society – Working Papers No. 4). Pennsylvania State University, Science, Technology and Society Program.

——— (1994c). *Blasphemy: A radical critique of technological culture*. Pennsylvania State University, Science, Technology and Society Program, April.

Illich, I. (1999) in *The Oxford dictionary of quotations*. Oxford: Oxford University Press.

Illich, I., and Rieger, M. (1996). *The wisdom of Leopold Kohr*. Typescript.

Illich, I., Zola, I.K., McKnight, J., Caplan, J. and Shaiken, H. (1977). *Disabling professions*. New York: Marion Boyars.

Interculture (1994). Philosophy and practices among the NGOs, XXVII(2) Spring.

Janeway, E. (1980). *Powers of the weak*. New York: Alfred A. Knopf.

Jeantet, T. (1979). *La révolution conviviale*. Paris: Entente.

——— (1983). *L'individu collectif*. Paris: Syros.

Kearney, M. (1996a). *Migration, the new indígena, and the formation of multi-ethnic autonomous regions in Oaxaca*. Paper presented at the annual meeting of the International Studies Association, San Diego, California, April.

——— (1996b). *Reconceptualizing the peasantry*. Boulder, CO: Westview Press.

Kohlberg, L., Levine, C., and Hewer, A. (1983). *Moral stages: A current formulation and a response to critics*. New York: Karger.

Kohr, L. (1986). The breakdown of nations. London and New York: Routledge & Kegan Paul.

——— (1992). Size cycles. *Fourth World Review*, 54, 10–11.

Korten, D.C. (1990). *Getting to the 21st century: Voluntary action and the global agenda*. West Hartford, CT: Kumarian Press.

——— (1996). *When corporations rule the world*. West Hartford, CT: Kumarian Press.

Kothari, R. (1974). *Footsteps into the future: Diagnosis of the present world and a design for an alternative*. New York: Free Press.

Kundera, M. (1984). The *unbearable lightness of being*. Boston: Faber & Faber.

——— (1991). *Immortality*. London: Faber & Faber.

Lafer, C. (1994). *La reconstrucción de los derechos humanos: Un diálogo con el pensamiento de Hannah Arendt*. México: Fondo de Cultura Económica.

Lappé, F. M. (1991). *Diet for a small planet*. New York: Ballantine Books.

Lauderdale, P. (1991). *Indigenous North American alternatives to modern law and punishment: Lessons of nature*. University of Innsbruck. Typescript.

Lefort, C. (1981). *L'invention démocratique: Les limites de la domination totalitaire*. Paris: Fayard.

Leroy, L.B. (1982). A concept of native title. *Native People and Justice in Canada*, 2–3, 71–99.

Linebaugh, P. (2008) *The Magna Carta manifesto: The struggle to reclaim liberties and commons for all*. Berkeley: University of California Press.

Linton, R. (1936). *The study of man: An introduction*. New York: Appleton-Century-Crofts.

Lipset, S.M. (1960). *Political man: The social bases of politics*. Garden City, NY: Anchor Books.

Luijf, R. (1989). *The sustainability of our common future*. Pennsylvania State University, Science, Technology, and Society Program. Typescript.

Lummis, D. (1996). *Radical democracy*. Ithaca, NY: Cornell University Press.

MacIntyre, A. (1981). *After virtue: A study in moral theory*. London: Duckworth.

——— (1988). *Whose justice? Which rationality?* Notre Dame, IN: University of Notre Dame Press.

McKnight, J. (1984). John Deere and the bereavement counselor. *Bulletin of Science and Technology*, 4, 597–604.

——— (1995). *The careless society: Community and its counterfeits*. New York: Basic Books.

McLuhan, M., and Powers, B. (1989). *The global village: Transformations in world life and media in the 21st century*. New York: Oxford University Press.

Macpherson, C.B. (1964). *The real world democracy*. Toronto: CBC.

——— (1977). *The life and times of liberal democracy*. Oxford: Oxford University Press.

Maldonado, B. (1988). *La escuela indígena como camino hacia la ignorancia*. Paper presented at the Second Reunion for the exchange of Educational Experiences in the Indigenous Environment, Oaxaca de Juárez, México, December.

Mandeville, B. de (1755). *The fable of the bees*. Edinburgh: Printed for W. Gray and W. Peter.

Marx, K. (1954). *Capital*, Vol. 1. London: Lawrence & Wishart.

——— (1975). *Contribution to the Critique of Hegel's Philosophy of Law*. In K. Marx and F. Engels, *Collected Works*, Vol. 3. New York: International Publishers.

Marx, K., and Lenin, V.I. (1968). *The civil war in France: The Paris Commune*. New York: International Publishers.

Menchú, R. (1984). *I, Rigoberta Menchú: An Indian woman in Guatemala*. London: Verso.

Merchant, C. (1989). *Ecological revolutions: Nature, gender, and science in New England*. Chapel Hill: University of North Carolina Press.

——— (1980). *The death of nature: Women, ecology, and the scientific revolution*. San Francisco: Harper & Row.

Mies, M. (1987). *Patriarchy and accumulation on a world scale. Women in the international division of labour*. London: Zed Books.

Mies, M., Bennholdt-Thomsen, V., and Werlhof, C. von (1988). *Women: The last colony*. London: Zed Books.

Mokos, J. (1996). *On a difficulty in discussing proportionality*. Typescript.

Moore, B. Jr. (1984). *Privacy*. Armonk, NY: M.E. Sharpe.

Morrison, R. (1995). *Ecological democracy*. Boston: South End Press.

Mumford, L. (1964). *The myth of the machine*. New York: Harcourt Brace Jovanovitch.

Nandy, A. (1983). *The intimate enemy*. New Delhi: Oxford University Press.

——— (1988). *Science, hegemony and violence: A requiem for modernity*. New Delhi: Oxford University Press.

——— (1992). State. In W. Sachs (ed.), *The development dictionary: A guide to knowledge as power*. London: Zed Books.

———— (1994). *Illegitimacy of nationalism*. New Delhi: Oxford University Press.

———— (1996). *Gandhi after Gandhi*. New Delhi: Centre for the Study of Developing Societies. Typescript.

Nicolau, A. (1993). Por la autonomia de la sociedad civil. *Opciones*, 6, March, 11–13.

Orr, D. (1992). *Ecological literacy: Education and the transition to a postmodern world*. Albany: SUNY Press.

Ostrom, E. (1990) *Governing the commons: The evolution of institutions for collective action*. Cambridge: Cambridge University Press.

Panikkar, R. (1978). *Myth, faith and hermeneutics*. New York: Paulist Press.

———— (1979). The myth of pluralism: The Tower of Babel – meditation on non-violence. *Cross Currents*, 29, 197–230.

———— (1990a). The pluralism of truth. *World Faiths Insight* (new series) 26, 1–16.

———— (1990b). The religion of the future. *Interculture*, LXXIII(2-3), Spring–Summer.

———— (1993). *La diversidad como presupuesto para la armonia entre los pueblos. Wisay Marka* (Barcelona), 20, 15–20.

———— (1995). *Invisible harmony: Essays on contemplation and responsibility* (edited by H.J. Cargas). Minneapolis, MN: Augsburg Fortress.

Papworth, J. (1995a). Editorial: The Bernard Levin question. *Fourth World Review*, 68, 3–6.

———— (1995b). Editorial: A strategy for change. *Fourth World* Review, 69, 3–7.

———— (1995c). *Small is powerful: The future as if people really mattered*. Westport, CO: Praeger.

———— (1996). The breakdown of the U.S. *Fourth World Review*, 73, 10–11.

Parsons, T. (1947). Weber's methodology of social science. In M. Weber (ed.), *The theory of social and economic organization*. New York: Free Press.

Pearse, A. (1980). *Seeds of plenty, seeds of want*. Oxford: Clarendon Press.

Polanyi, K. (1947). On belief in economic determinism. *Sociological Review*, XXXIX, 96–102.

———— (1975). *The great transformation*. New York: Octagon Books.

La Polémica Sobre los Derechos Humanos (1994). *Eslabones*, 8, July/Dec. Includes Sara Sefchovich, "Los derechos humanos: Teoría, práctica, filosofía, utopía"; interviews with Sergio Aguayo, Jorge Madrazo, Teresa Jardí, Miguel Concha, Isabel Molina, Luis de la Barreda.

Pörksen, U. (1995). *Plastic words: The tyranny of a modular language*. University Park: Penn State University Press.

P Poteete, A., R., Janssen, M.A. and Ostrom, E. (2010) *Working together*. Princeton NJ: Princeton University Press.

ound, R. (1972). *An introduction to the philosophy of law*. New Haven, CT, and London: Yale University Press.

Prakash, M.S. (1993). Gandhi's post-modern education: Ecology, peace, and multiculturalism relinked. *Holistic Education Review*, 6(3), Autumn, 8–17.

———— (1994). What are people for? Wendell Berry on education, ecology and culture. *Educational Theory*, 44(2), 135–57.

Prakash, M.S. and Esteva, G. (1997). *Escaping education: learning as living within grassroots cultures*. New York: Peter Lang.

Public Papers of the Presidents of the United States (1964). *Harry S. Truman. Containing the public messages, speeches, and statements of the President, January 1 to December 31, 1949*. Washington, DC: US Government Printing Office.

Radhakrishnan, S., and Raju, P.T. (eds.) (1966). *El concepto del hombre.* Mexico: Fondo de Cultura Económica.

Rahnema, J. (1986). Under the banner of development. *Development: Seeds of Change,* 1–2, 37–45.

Rahnema, M. (1988). A new variety of AIDS and its pathogens: Homo economicus, development and aid. *Alternatives,* 13, 117–36.

Rethinking Human Rights. (1994). International Conference organized by the Just World Trust, Kuala Lumpur, Malaysia, December 6–7.

Reyburn, W. (1971). *Flushed with pride: The story of Thomas Crapper.* Englewood Cliffs, NJ: Prentice-Hall.

Robert, J. (1996). *Trust people.* México: Habitat International Coalition.

Robertson, J. (1985a). *Future work: Jobs, self-employment and leisure after the industrial age.* London: Temple Smith/Gower.

———— (1985b). *Health, wealth and the new economics: An agenda for a healthier world.* London: TOES.

Robinson, J. (1995). Global participation. *The Ecologist,* 25(1), Jan./Feb., 38–9.

Rosenthal, P. (1984). *Words and values: Some leading words and where they lead us.* Oxford: Oxford University Press.

Rossant, M. J. (1989). Foreword. In T.E. Cronin, *Direct democracy: The politics of initiative, referendum and recall.* Cambridge, MA: Harvard University Press.

Rozat, G. (1993). *Indios imaginarios e indios reales en los relatos de la conquista de México.* México: Tava Editorial.

Sachs, A. (1995). *Eco-justice: Linking human rights and the environment.* Washington, DC: Worldwatch Institute.

Sachs, W. (1990) The archeology of the development idea. *Interculture,* XXIII, 4(109), 1–37.

———— (ed.) (1992). *The development dictionary: A guide to knowledge as power.* London: Zed Books.

———— (ed.). (1993). *Global ecology: A new arena of political conflict.* London: Zed Books.

———— (ed.) (2010) *The development dictionary: A guide to knowledge as power.* New Edition. London: Zed Books.

Sahlins, M.D. (1972). *Stone age economics.* Chicago: Aldine-Atherton.

Sale, K. (1995). *Rebels against the future: The Luddites and their war on the industrial revolution.* New York: Addison-Wesley.

Sardar, Z., Nandy, A., Davies, M., and Alvares, C. (1993). *The blinded eye.* New York: Apex Press.

Sbert, J.M. (1992). Progress. In W. Sachs (ed.), *The development dictionary: A guide to knowledge as power.* London: Zed Books.

Schumacher, E. F. (1973). *Small is beautiful.* New York: Harper & Row.

Schumpeter, J.A. (1975). *Capitalism, socialism and democracy.* New York: Harper.

Sen, A. (1981). *Poverty and famines: An essay on entitlement and deprivation.* Oxford: Oxford University Press.

Shanin, T. (1982). *Late Marx and the Russian road.* Berkeley, CA: University of California Press.

———— (1987). *Peasants and peasant studies.* Oxford: Basil Blackwell.

Shiva, V. (1988). *Staying alive: Women, ecology, and development.* London: Zed Books.

———— (1993a). The greening of global reach. In W. Sachs, (ed.), *Global ecology.* London: Zed Books.

——— (1993b). *Monocultures of the mind*. London: Zed Books.
——— (2010) Resources. In W. Sachs (ed.), *The development dictionary: A guide to knowledge as power*. London: Zed Books.
——— (2013) Freedom Starts with a Seed. *YES!* Winter.
Stavenhagen, R. (1988). *Derecho indígena y derechos humanos en América Latina*. México: El Colegio de México-Instituto Interamericano de Derechos Humanos.
Tagore, R. (1961). *The religion of man*. London: Unwin Books.
Taylor, C. (1989). *Sources of the self. The making of modern identity*. Cambridge, MA: Harvard University Press.
Tönnies, F. (1957). *Community and society = Gemeinschaft und Gesellschaft*. New York: Harper Torchbook.
Uexkull, J. von (1995). Global participation. *The Ecologist*, 25(1), Jan./Feb., 38.
Vachon, R. (1990). L'étude du pluralism juridique: Une approche diatopique et dialogale. *Journal of Legal Pluralism and Unofficial Law*, 29, 163–73.
——— (1991). *Human rights and dharma*. Intercultural Institute of Montreal.
——— (1991–3). The Mohawk nation and its communities. *Interculture*. Chapter 1: Some basic sociological facts. XXIV(4), Fall 1991, Issue 113, 1–35; Chapter 2: Western and Mohawk political cultures: A study in contrast. XXV(1), Winter 1992, Issue 114, 1–27; Part II: The Mohawk dynamics of peace. Chapter 3: The people of the Great Peace. XXVI(1), Winter 1993, Issue 118, 1–82; Chapter 4: The Mohawk nation: Its seven communities. A brief history. XXVI(4), Fall 1993, Issue 121, 1–49.
——— (1995a). Guswenta or the intercultural imperative: Towards a reenacted peace accord between the Mohawk nation and the North American nation-states (and their peoples). *Interculture*. XXVIII(2), Spring 1995, Issue 127, 1–73; XXVIII(3), Summer 1995, Issue 128, 98–111; XXVIII(4), Fall 1995, Issue 129, 146–71.
——— (1995b). From global perspective to an open horizon, an ever deepening synthesis. *Holistic Education Review*, 8(2), Summer, 54–6.
Valdés, L.M. (1996). El descubrimiento de la gran Manhattitlán. *Nexos*, 222, June, 27–9.
Villoro, L. (1995). ¿Crisis del estado-nación Mexicano? *Dialéctica*, 18–27, 16–23.
Van Gelder, S. (2013) The Many Joys of Food. *YES!* Winter.
——— et al. (2011) *This changes everything*. San Francisco: Berret-Koehler.
Vora, R. (1993). Gandhi's so-called inconsistencies: An analysis with reference to nonviolence, reason, and faith. *Gandhi Marg*, July-September, 137–53.
Winner, L. (1977). *Autonomous technology*. Cambridge, MA: MIT Press.
Zinn, Howard (1954) The art of revolution. Introduction to Herbert Read, *Anarchy and order: Essays on politics*. Boston, MA: Beacon Press.

INDEX

absolutism, denial of rights under, 121,
   156
Acción Zapatista, 35
   see also Zapatista movement
agriculture, local communities and, 25
aid projects, resistance against, 64–5
Ajanta, 206
alimento, use of term, 58, 59
alphabet, as tool, 68, 73, 74
Alvares, Claude and Norma, 14
Amnesty International, 134
An-Na'im, Abdullahi Ahmed, 145
   Human Rights in Cross-Cultural
      Perspectives, 143, 144
Ana María, Mayor, 174–7, 185
anthropologists, revelations of, 200
Aristotle, 154–5, 160
austerity, meaning of, 203–4
autonomy, 20, 21, 26, 36, 41–2

barrio, definition of, 106 n1
basic needs, defense of, 21
Berlin Wall, 37
Berry, Wendell, 15, 21, 22, 23, 24, 33,
   52–3, 95
Bill of Rights (1688), 140
Bishop, Jordan, 156
Boff, Leonardo, 24
bread labor, concept of, 145–6
breathing, as cultural act, 127
Burke, Edmund, 155

Canada, *see* Mohawk Nation
Canetti, Elias, 66
capitalism, 93–4, 152–3

Catholic Church, 31, 32, 74
Cervantes, Miguel de, 129
children, rights of, 141
Chipko movement, 13
Chonita, doña, 83
citizen, concept of, 170–1
civil society, concept of, 12–13
class *see* social class
Clastres, Pierre, 194
Clinton, Bill, 139
Coatlicue, 129–30
Coca Cola, 21, 25
Cold War, 152
colonialism, 29, 31–2, 89, 114, 115, 125,
   140, 200, 205
   see also recolonization
colonization, responses to, 45
comida, 55, 65–7, 95, 98
   use of term, 58–9, 63
Comité de la Unidad Tepozteca, 103
common sense, concept of, 159–60,
   203–4
commons
   concept of, 159, 195
   enclosure of, 38, 121
communal food, 52–4
   see also comida; impostura
communal identity, threats to, 130
communal memory, 69, 76
communal soil, 94
communal spaces, regeneration of, 81
communication, 75
communitarianism, as political option,
   161
Community Supported Agriculture

(CSAs), 25, 41
conmoverse, concept of, 142
consumer sovereignty, myth of, 51–2, 66
consumerism, concept of, 17 n3, 52
cultural autonomy, 115
Cultural Centre of Santo Domingo, 84,
    88
cultural imperialism, 117–19, 135, 137,
    145
cultural relativism, concept of, 202
cultures, incommensurability of, 128–9,
    137
customs
    concept of, 130–2
    translation of, into laws, 70

Dallas, 22
David, Comandante, 174
decentralism, use of term, 39
decentralization, control and, 38, 39
Declaration of the Rights of the Man
    and the Citizen of France (1789), 140
defecation, 95, 96, 99
democracy, 152–6, 158, 160–2 189 n1
    see also radical democracy
Dershovitz, Alan, 71
development, discourse of, 4, 197, 201
dharma, traditions of, 93, 115, 116, 118,
    120, 138, 145, 146
Dialogue of San Andrés, 45
Dion-Buffalo, Yvonne, 45
Domingo, 80
Dubos, René, 21
Duus, Erik, 60–2, 65

Earth Summit, 33, 34
Eco, Umberto, 153
eco-development, designs for, 23
Ecologist, The, 14, 26, 33, 34
economic development, history of, 32–3
economic rationality, creed of, 10, 123,
    194–5
education, 72, 124, 141, 207
Ejército Zapatista de Liberacieón
    Nacional (EZLN) *see* Zapatista
    movement
Ellora, 206
Enciso, Fernando Díaz, *A Thousand
    Stories of Santo Domingo de los Reyes*,
    82–3
environmental "problems," 22
    see also human waste; sewerage
    systems

environmentalism, 23
environmentalists, 196
equality, concept of, 122
    illusion of, 171
Esteva, Gustavo, 15
ethnos, 52
European Union, 27

family life, 58
Fernández, Justino, 129
food
    growth and consumption of, 52–3
    homogenization of, 59
    see also comida; communal food;
        impostura; industrial eating
Foucault, Michel, 167, 199

Fourth World Review, 14
France, workers on strike in, 9, 28, 29–30
Francisco, 81–2
free market, 40, 113
    see also capitalism; free trade
free trade, policy of, 19, 20
French Revolution, 140
Friedan, Betty, 42
frugality, meaning of, 203
Fuero Viejo de Castilla (1394), 140
fundamentalism, resistance to, 180

Gallo Ilustrado, El, 14
Gandhi, M.K., 23, 29, 30, 115, 116, 120,
    135, 144, 145, 164, 184, 202
    *The Collected Works of Mahatma
        Gandhi*, 116
Gates, Bill, 20
GATT (General Agreement on Tariffs
    and Trade), 28, 30, 31, 139
Gettysburg Address (1863) 159
global action, 21–2
global forces
    acquiescence to, 30–1
    local action of, 25
    oppression caused by, 20
    resistance to, 6, 24, 33, 178
Global Project 32
    democracy and, 152–3, 162
    economic plans for, 194
    fundamentalism of, 180
    human rights and, 114, 117, 119
    inhospitality and, 88
    population and, 94
    resistance to, 1, 9, 13, 27, 37, 41, 76,
        102–5, 166–7, 172–7, 186

use of term, 16 n1
see also globalization; human rights;
    social minorities
global thinking, 9–10, 14, 20, 21, 28, 32,
    33, 42, 193, 199
    see also local thinking
global tourism, 51
global village, 1, 15, 21, 22
    moral foundations of, 138–9
global warming, 22, 23
globalization 4, 20, 41, 88
grassroots movements, 3, 5
    democracy and, 153
    formal political discourse and, 166–7
    influence of, 6
    initiatives of, 192–3, 195
    organization of, 13, 171–2
    see also radical democracy
grassroots post-modernism, concept of, 3,
    63, 103, 105, 193–4, 197
Great Britain, 29
Green Party (British), 34
guerrilla warfare, 182

Havel, Václav, 163
Hegel, G.W.F., 161
Hind Swaraj, see India, Home Rule
Hindu morality, 118
Hobbes, Thomas, 114
Homo oeconomicus 10, 11, 63, 121–2
hospitality
    cultural practices of, 87–92, 100,
        101–2
    history of, 107 n7
    other cultures and, 129
housing industry, in Mexico, 85
human agency, 20
human nature, definition of, 122
human rights activists
    interference by, in indigenous
        communities, 113, 130, 133, 136
    morality of, 142
human rights, 14
    categories of violations of, 146–8 n1
    codification of, 124
    colonial intervention and, 125
    communal morality and, 116–17
    ideology of, 112, 115, 118, 119–23
    justice and, 113
    torture and violence, and 132–6
    universalizability of, 10–11, 114,
        131–2, 137–8, 143–6, 195
    violations of, in Mexico, 182

human waste, 96–7
    see also defecation; sewerage system;
        urination; Water Closet
humility, meaning of, 201–2

identity, construction of, 14, 51, 52, 95,
    106
Ignatieff, Michael, 89–91
Iliad, 16, 68, 91–2
Illich, Iván, 15, 23, 137
illiteracy, texts and, 73–5
impostura
    cultural practice of, 62, 65
    use of term, 60–2
India
    colonial government in, 29
    development projects in, 34
    Home Rule movement in, 115–16,
        164
    see also Gandhi, M.K.
Indian peoples
    struggles of, in Canada 39, 143
    struggles of, in Mexico 36–7, 38, 110,
        169, 177, 178–9
    see also Mohawk Nation; Triqui
        nation; Zapatista movement
individual self
    construction of, 54, 68, 73, 75, 91,
        113, 122
    consumption and the, 66
    food and, 52, 58, 63
    identity crisis of, 51
    personal identity of, 76–8
    resistance to becoming, 80
    see also social minorities
individualism, 54, 66, 114
industrial eating, 51–3, 55, 59,
    63
industrial memory, 67
Industrial Revolution, human rights
    abuses during, 139
Insider/Outsider dichotomy, 115–16
Intercontinental Encounter for
    Humanity and Against Neoliberalism
    (1996), 173–9, 185–7, 191 n11
Intercultural Institute of Montreal, 14,
    143
Interculture, 14, 144
International Group for Grassroots
    Initiatives, 14
International Network for Cultural
    Alternatives to Development, 14
International Women's Conference

(1995), 42
Islam, human rights and, 143

Jefferson, Thomas, 121, 156
Juppé, Alain, 29, 30
juridical procedures, function of, 169–70,
    172
jurisdiction, origin of term, 70
justice, system of, in Oaxaca, 111–12

Kearney, Michael, 65, 87
Kipling, Rudyard, 128
knowledge, forms of, 72
Kohr, Leopold, 23, 24, 26–7, 165
Korten, David C., 40
Kundera, Milan, 124
    The Unbearable Lightness of Being, 137

Langlais, Jacques, 143
language
    decline in number of spoken, 95
    as register of speech, 75
    use of, in struggle, 36
Lappé, Frances Moore, 26, 51
law, function of, 168–72
liberal pluralism 12
Lincoln, Abraham, 159
Linton, Ralph, The Study of Man: An
    Introduction, 78
local resistance, 33, 34, 35
local autonomy, meaning of term, 37,
    38
Local Government Act (1888), 38
local thinking, 21–2, 23, 32, 177
    see also global thinking
Lummis, Douglas, 12, 54, 159, 204

Magna Carta (1215), 140
Mahabharata, 16, 196
Manrique, Daniel, 84
Marcos, don, 55–6
Marcos, Subcomandante, 35, 36, 39, 178,
    179–80, 181, 182, 187
Marx, Karl, 160, 202
Maslow, Abraham, 125
mass media, use of, 155, 200
mass, origin of term, 66
matriarchy, oppression and, 66
McDonald's restaurants, 50, 51
McLuhan, Marshall, 22
memory, 68–70, 71, 72
    see also industrial memory; organic
        memory

men, social relations between, 60
Menchú, Rigoberta, 13, 133–4
Mexico
    autonomist struggles in, 36–7
    colonial administration in, 38
    economy of, 6, 66, 181–2
    see also Mexico City; Santo Domingo;
        Tepito; Zapatista movement
Mexico City, 66, 84, 166, 169
    earthquake in (1985) 64–5, 85, 96
    see also Santo Domingo; Tepito;
        Tepoztlán
migration, 65, 86–7
milpa, use of term, 58, 65
Miztecs, 86–7
modernity, 180, 192, 193, 203, 205
    democracy and, 153
    see also Global Project
modernization, impact of, on cultures, 2,
    85
Mohawk Nation, struggles of, 39, 144
    see also Canada; Indian peoples
Mohawk, John, 45
Monchanin Cross-cultural Centre see
    Intercultural Institute of Montreal
Monde, Le, 9
monoculturalism, 5, 28, 67, 124, 205
morality, state of "development" and,
    114–15
Mukherjee, Bharati, 96
multiculturalism, 11, 19, 28, 35
Municipal Corporations Act (1835), 38

Nader, Ralph, 51
Narmada project, 33
Narmada struggle, 13
nation-states, 21, 38, 114, 122, 130–2, 168,
    199
    centralism of, 168
    demise of, 164–5, 187
    democracy and, 157, 163
    rejection of, 39–41
National Assembly of Indian peoples, 70
national independence, cultural
    autonomy and, 115
National Indian Forum, 45
nationalism, 165
natural law, doctrine of, 121
neoliberalism, policy of, 19
    see also capitalism; global thinking;
        globalization
new leftists, poltical agenda of, 188
Nobel Prize, 13

noble savage, 196
norms, concept of, 131
North American Free Trade Agreement
(NAFTA), 27, 86, 182
nourishment, use of term, 59

Oaxaca, 111, 188
see also San Luis Beltrán
Opciones, 14
organic cycle, concept of, 95
organic memory, use of term, 67
Other India Book Store, 14
Other, the, cultural resistance to, 112, 202
otra bolsa de valores, La, 14
overpopulation, 4, 196
Oxford English Dictionary (OED), 72
ozone layer, 22, 23

Panikkar, Raimón, 15, 137, 144, 145
Paris Commune, 160, 189 n4
parochialism, 27, 42
patriarchy, oppression and, 66
Paz, Octavio, 35
PDP (Promocion del Desarolla Popular), 14
peasants, food production and, 58
people's power see radical democracy
people, the
construct of, 99
democracy and, 158–63
nation-state and, 165, 199
practices of, 166–8
public virtues of, 201–6
use of term, 2, 11–13, 15
Persian Gulf war, 72
personal identity, 76–8
Pesticides Action Network, 24
planetary consciousness, 23
Plato, 68, 74, 126
pluralism, concept of, 130
pluriverse, 36, 111
use of term, 41, 116, 125–6, 127, 130,
137
political party system, 155, 162
Poor Laws, reform of, 38
poorhouse, function of, 88
Popol Vuh, 16, 196
populism, concept of, 159–60
post-modernism, concepts of, 2–3, 8, 192
post-modernists, academic, 2, 3, 8, 9, 10,
11
postcolonial, era of, 194
power, communal control and, 161–3
Prakash, Madhu Suri, 15

PRATEC (Programa Andino de
Tecnologia Campesina), 14
privacy, ideals of, 96
progress, culture of, 2, 95, 100, 102, 115
public discourse, dominant style of,
69–70
Public Health Act (1848), 38
punishment, forms of, in Oaxaca, 111

radical democracy, 158–61, 163–7, 188
see also democracy
radical pluralism, 193
Ramayana, 68, 196
Reagan, Ronald, 59, 152
Realidad, La, First Declaration of (1996),
42–4
recolonization, 11, 105, 118, 136
resistance to, 30
education and, 133–4
see also Global Project
Red Intercultural de Acción Autónoma, 14
REDES, 14
Reebok International, 139
Refugio, doña, 55, 57–8, 66
representation, principle of, 170–1
Right Livelihood Award, 13
Rivera, Diego, 206
role, concept of, 78, 106 n2
role-models, 78

Sahlins, Marshall, 194
Sakharov, Andrei, 140
Salinas de Gortari, Carlos, 6, 182
Salt March, 29
see also M.K. Gandhi
San Andrés Chicahuaxtla, way of life in,
55–8
San Luis Beltrán, 98
Sandoval, Marcos, 111
Santiago, Rómulo, 112
Santo Domingo, 82–4
scarcity, laws of, 122–4, 194
Snyder, Gary, 96
Schumacher, Fritz, 23
Schumpeter, J.A., 154
self-determination, struggles for, 37, 125
self-government, meaning of term, 38–9
self-sufficiency, 26
Selva Lacandona, Fourth Declaration of,
(1996), 42
see also Zapatista movement
sentimentalism, 91, 129, 130
sewerage systems, 95, 96

alternatives to, 97–8
Simpson, O.J., trial of, 71, 72
social classes, 18 n7
  see also peasants
social majorities
  claims of, 198
  common sense of, 76
  cultural practices of, 197
  democracy and, 158, 164, 184
  education and, 141, 207
  food and, 53–4, 59
  grassroots initiatives of, 192–3
  hospitality of, 87–9, 92–3, 100
  as human surpluses, 93–4, 196
  illiteracy of, 73–4
  impact of modernization on, 4–5, 10, 139, 153
  individualism and, 51, 63, 80
  perceptions of, 79
  personal identities of, 77
  rejection of economism by, 194–5
  state laws and, 169–70
  symbols of progress offered to, 95
  use of term, 12, 16 n2
  see also the people; Global Project
social minorities
  consumption by, 108 n8
  democracy and, 161, 164, 188
  expectations of, 204
  globalization and, 10, 19
  human waste of, 96, 97, 99
  individual self and, 51
  industrial efficiency of, 100
  inhospitability of, 87–8
  state management and, 37
  use of term, 12, 16 n2
  welfare state and, 4, 204–5
social movements, new political forms of, 86
social order, the law and, 168
social rights *see* human rights
Somoza, Anastasio, 154
speech, as text, 69
standardization, growth of, 51
state control, strengthening of, 30

Tagore, Rabindranath, 92
Tepito, Mexico, 63–6, 84
Tepoztlán, 100–5
text
  dominance of, 73–5
  objectification of, 68, 69
  use of, in memory, 71

think tanks, 22
tolerance, concept of, 87, 89
Tolstoy, Leo, "What Men Live By," 92
Tocqueville, Alexis de, 54
torture, cultural conceptions of, 133–6, 142, 151 n12
tourism, resistance to, 102
transnational communities, organization of, 87
transnational corporations, 21, 24
Treaty of Westphalia (1648) 187
Triqui nation, 55–8, 111
  see also Oaxaca
Truman, Harry S., 154
Turner, John, 84
12–Point Platform, proposals of, 117, 119

United Nations, Charter of the, (1945), 140
United Nations Food and Agriculture Organization (FAO), 64, 65
United Nations Fourth World conference on Human/Women's Rights, 117
Universal Declaration of Human Rights (1948) 10, 112, 120–1, 138, 140, 193
  liberation from, 126
  morality decreed by, 142
urban squatters, housing of, 92
urination, 95
  see also human waste
Uruguay Round, 31

Vachon, Robert, 137, 143–4, 145
vecindad, 64, 65
  definition of, 106 n1
verdepinto, El, 14
violence, cultural conceptions of, 133–6
virtue, re-emergence of, 201–6
voters, manipulation of, 155–6, 160

Walters, Barbara, 69
Water Closet (WC), 95, 96, 97, 98, 99
welfare state, 188
  dismantling of, 4, 94
  function of, 139, 146
  see also nation-state
western project, the, concept of, 31
Whose Common Future?, 33
Williams, William, Carlos, 53
Wilson, Peter, 86
women
  social relations among, 60
  liberation movement, 141

human rights for, 117–19
World Bank, 21, 22, 25, 27, 31, 34
World Trade Organization (WTO), 19, 27, 31
World Watch Institute, 24
World Wide Web, 19, 197

xenophobia, 88

Zapatista movement, 6–7, 27, 35–7, 39–46, 103, 105, 172–87, 190 n9
communiqué of (1994), 182–4
see also Ana-Maria, Mayor; David, Comandante; Marcos, Subcomandante